THE TESTIMONY

OF

JUSTIN MARTYR

TO

EARLY CHRISTIANITY.

LECTURES

Delivered on the L. P. Stone Foundation at Princeton Theological Seminary, in March, 1888.

BY

GEORGE T. PURVES, D.D.,

PASTOR OF THE FIRST PRESBYTERIAN CHURCH OF PITTSBURGH, PA.

WIPF & STOCK · Eugene, Oregon

Wipf and Stock Publishers
199 W 8th Ave, Suite 3
Eugene, OR 97401

The Testimony of Justin Martyr to Early Christianity
Lectures Delivered to the L. P. Stone Foundation
at Princeton Theological Seminary, in March, 1888
By Purves, George T.
Softcover ISBN-13: 978-1-6667-6456-7
Hardcover ISBN-13: 978-1-6667-6457-4
eBook ISBN-13: 978-1-6667-6458-1
Publication date 11/10/2022
Previously published by Anson D. F. Randolph and Company, 1889

This edition is a scanned facsimile of the original edition
published in 1889.

PREFACE.

THE following lectures were delivered on the L. P. Stone Foundation at Princeton Theological Seminary, and are published at the request of the Faculty. The form in which they were originally delivered has been retained, and but few changes made in substance or language. They have been prepared in such leisure moments as could be found in a busy pastorate, and the author keenly realizes their many imperfections. He hopes, however, that they may stimulate more of our Presbyterian ministers to cultivate the field of early patristic literature. Its importance to Christian apologetics is very great. Its study will also contribute to clearer views of the nature and true unity of the Church. It should not be left, as it has so largely been, to Romanists and rationalists. While we firmly hold to the sole authority of the Scriptures for faith and practice, the history of the early ages of our religion and the careful examination of all the elements which, as time went on, entered into it will enable us to read the New Testament with fresh confidence and intelligence. Above all, in this age of historical criticism, when so many minds are honestly confused concerning the evidences for the faith of the Church, some acquaintance with the events and literature of the second century is demanded of those who would successfully guide the inquirer and help the doubter. The author may be allowed to add that, with the utmost desire to deal fairly with the evidence and to follow the facts, he has obtained, by his excursions into patristic literature, renewed assurance both of the divine origin of Christianity and of the correctness of the orthodox Protestant estimate of the New Testament.

ALLEGHENY, PA., 1888.

CONTENTS.

LECTURE I.

THE IMPORTANCE OF JUSTIN'S TESTIMONY TO EARLY CHRISTIANITY.

                                                                         PAGE

Importance of the Study of the Second Century. — Critical Theories of the Origin of Christianity. — The New Testament Canon. — The Christian Ministry. — The Union of Christianity and Philosophy. — The Unity of the Church. — The Life of Justin: his Birth; Philosophic Studies; Influence on Contemporaries; Death; Character; Conversion; Chronology of his Life; his Situation in Rome. — The Writings of Justin and their Date. — Analysis of the Apologies and the Dialogue. —The consequent Importance of Justin's Testimony. — Early and Modern Views concerning Justin. — Plan of the following Lectures .   1

LECTURE II.

THE TESTIMONY OF JUSTIN TO THE SOCIAL AND CIVIL RELATIONS OF EARLY CHRISTIANITY.

Justin as an Apologist. — The Diffusion of Christianity. — Organization of Christian Societies. — Popular Hostility. — Charges made. — Popular Impatience with the Christians. — Explanation of this Hostility. — Attitude of the Government. — Christianity illegal. — No formal Persecution. — Frequent Outrages. — Justin's Description confirmed by other Evidence. — Hadrian's Rescript. — Correspondence of Trajan and Pliny. — Sup-

vi CONTENTS.

PAGE

pression of Unauthorized Societies. — Membership in them a Crime. — Action of the Emperors with reference to Christianity. — Efforts to prevent Outrages. — The Sufferings of the Christians not so severe as often supposed. — Persecution but just beginning. — Justin's Defence. — He appeals substantially for the Legal Recognition of Christianity: (*a*) Because it was the true Philosophy — Strength and Weakness of this Plea; (*b*) Because of the Virtues of the Christians and Simplicity of their Customs. — His Description of Christian Life. — Power of this Argument — Its Value for us 50

LECTURE III.

THE TESTIMONY OF JUSTIN TO THE RELATIONS OF GENTILE AND JEWISH CHRISTIANITY.

Value of Justin's Testimony in this Particular. — The Tübingen Scheme and its Modifications. — Ritschl's View. — I. Estimate of the Old Testament by the Church. — Its Inspiration. — The Prophets. — Method of Interpretation. — The Old Testament a Christian Book. — Justin's Failure to appreciate the Hebrew Dispensation. — Total Rejection of Judaism. — Comparison of his Views with the New Testament. — The Church a Gentile Society. — Justin's Opinion of Jewish Christians. — Various Views in the Church. — Extremists on both Sides. — Justin's moderate but firmly anti-Jewish View that of the Majority. II. Had there been a silent Blending of Gentile and Jewish Christianity ? — Evidence alleged for this: (1) Abhorrence of "Idol-meat" — The Authenticity of "The Acts" — Justin's Position not due to Jewish Sympathies; (2) His Silence concerning Paul — The Facts in the Case — Use of Pauline Writings — References to "the Twelve" — Unity of the Apostles assumed; (3) Chiliasm — No Proof of Jewish Tendencies; (4) Legalism — Its Growth — Not necessarily due to Judaism. — Summary of Justin's Testimony, and Inferences from it 85

CONTENTS. vii

LECTURE IV.

THE TESTIMONY OF JUSTIN TO THE INFLUENCE OF PHILOSOPHY ON EARLY CHRISTIANITY.

PAGE

Contrast, as regards the Influence of Philosophy, between the Writings of Justin and the New Testament. — Progress of this Influence in the Early Church. — Character of the Philosophy of the Period: Eclectic; Theological. — Justin shows the Spirit of his Age. — His Criticism of the various Schools. — Relation to Stoicism; to Platonism. — The Influence of Philosophy on Justin's Theology, as shown in (I.) his Idea of God — Divine Transcendence unduly emphasized — Two Conceptions of God contending in his Mind; (II.) His Doctrine of the Logos in the sense of Reason — Relation of the Logos to the Father — Agent in Creation and Revelation — Relation to Man — The "Seminal Logos;" (III.) His Anthropology — Human Freedom and Ability — Power of the Demons — Idea of Sin; (IV.) His Soteriology — Christ primarily a Teacher — Nature of Salvation. — Inferences concerning the Influence of Philosophy on Christianity, and the Realization by the Latter of the best Aspirations of the Pagan World 128

LECTURE V.

THE TESTIMONY OF JUSTIN TO THE NEW TESTAMENT.

Its Importance. — Review of modern critical Opinion concerning Justin's Use of our Gospels. — I. Justin and the Synoptics. — The "Memoirs." — Justin's Account of Christ's Life remarkably full; agrees substantially with that of our Gospels. — The Differences trivial; Oral Tradition and Textual Corruption explain the most important of them; they do not destroy the Force of the Argument from the substantial Agreement. — The Variations in the Text of Justin's Quotations from that of our Gospels. — Extent of the Variation. — Examination of his Habits of Quotation, as shown by Quotations from the Classics and Old Testament. — Bearing of this on Quotations from the "Memoirs." — Comparison of Justin's Quotations and those of the Pseudo-Clementines. — Did Justin use a Harmony? — Bearing of the Evidence afforded by Justin of Corruption of Gospel Text on the Antiquity of our Gospels. — II. Justin and the Fourth Gospel. — Views of Thoma and Abbott. — Evidence for Justin's Use of the Fourth Gospel. — How did he use it? As historically True and presumably Apostolic, yet not with the same Fulness as Synoptics, and more as a Book of Doctrine. — Reasons for this. — Confirmation of Justin's Use of our Gospels afforded by Tatian's Diatessaron. — III. Justin and the New Testament Canon. — His Use of New Testament Books besides the Gospels. — Recognition of Authority of Apostles as Teachers. — Use of "Memoirs" as Sources for Belief and as "Scripture." — Yet "Memoirs" not called "Scripture" with same frequency as Old Testament. — No New Testament Book quoted, except Gospels and Apocalypse. — Mentions no public Use of the Epistles, and differs from their Teaching. — Considerations which balance these Items of Negative Evidence. — Conclusion 170

LECTURE VI.

THE TESTIMONY OF JUSTIN TO THE ORGANIZATION AND BELIEF OF THE POST-APOSTOLIC CHURCH.

Review. — Justin claimed to represent the true Christian Church. — His Opposition to Heresy. — Proves the Unity and Apostolicity of the Orthodox Churches. — His Testimony trustworthy. — I. The Organization of the Churches. — Description of Ceremonies and Worship. — One Church in each Locality. — A permanent President to each. — Deacons. — Why the Title of the President not given. — Absence of Sacerdotalism. — Justin accords with the known Facts of the Progress of Church Organization in the Second Century. — The Unity of the Churches spiritual. — II. The Faith of the Church: how to be obtained from Justin; (1) The Person of Christ; (2) The Trinity; (3) Redemption; (4) Privileges and Hopes of the Christians; The Sacraments; Eschatology. — Conclusion. — Post-Apostolic Christianity not created by Fusion; but modified by Paganism. — Inferences to be drawn from Justin's Testimony 251

THE TESTIMONY

OF

JUSTIN MARTYR

TO

EARLY CHRISTIANITY.

JUSTIN MARTYR.

LECTURE I.

THE IMPORTANCE OF JUSTIN'S TESTIMONY TO EARLY CHRISTIANITY.

THE first three quarters of the second Christian century form a period which demands the careful and repeated investigation of students both of the New Testament and of Church History. This is due, on the one hand, to the nearness of the period to the age of the Apostles, since the results of investigation in it will necessarily affect our views of their work and teaching; and, on the other hand, to the new influences which began during this period to affect the religion of Christ, and co-operated to form the Church and the theology of later times. *Importance of the second century.*

The period, however, is involved in much obscurity, owing to the scantiness of the literary remains from it. Of the apostolic age the New Testament enables us to form a fairly clear idea. Toward the close of the second century there begins, with the great work of Irenæus against heresies, a chain of witnesses, from whom we may obtain abundant testimony to the history of both the faith and order *Its obscurity.*

of the Church; but from the intermediate period our witnesses are few. Not that it was barren of literary productions; on the contrary, if all the works which issued from orthodox and heretic had been preserved, the Christian literature of the period would suffice probably to settle most of the now vexed questions concerning it. On the heretical side some of the Gnostics were voluminous writers.[1] On the orthodox side there appears to have been during the earlier part of the period less literary activity. A few letters and a brief manual (if the "Teaching of the Apostles" may be roughly classed in this period), and one or two religious romances,[2] are all that have been left to us, — though had only the work of Papias, entitled "Exposition of the Oracles of the Lord," been preserved, we should doubtless have been spared the necessity of much of the recent investigation into the origin and authority of the Gospels. Later in the century, however, the stream of apologetic literature began, directed either against assaults on Christianity by Jews or Pagans, or against heretical perversions of the faith. The earliest apologists, Quadratus and Aristides, are indeed assigned by Eusebius[3] to the reign of Hadrian; but it was under Antoninus Pius and Marcus Aurelius that the defences of the Christians became frequent and elaborate. Aristo and Justin defended Christianity against Judaism; while the latter, followed by Tatian, Athenagoras, Theophilus of Antioch, and Melito of Sardis,

---

[1] Cf. Iren. adv. Hær. iii. 12; Tert. de Præscr. 38.

[2] The Pastor of Hermas, and the Testaments of the XII. Patriarchs. The latter is now generally dated before the second Jewish war; cf. Sinker's Testamenta, XII. Patrr. The critical views are summarized in Dr. Warfield's article in Presb. Rev., January, 1880.

[3] H. E. iv. 3.

argued the truth of the new religion against polytheism and philosophy, and demanded its recognition by the State.[1] Meanwhile Hegesippus[2] had made the first attempt at an ecclesiastical chronicle, and the growth of heresy had begun to call forth defences of orthodoxy within the Church itself. But that many more Christian writings of this period have been lost than those which have been in whole or in part preserved, is evident from those mentioned by Eusebius in the fourth book of his History. The period, therefore, was far from being barren of literary productions. Only a few of these, however, have escaped the ravages of time, and we are left to feel our way in the darkness by the aid of the broken monuments and scattered fragments that yet remain.

But none the less, perhaps all the more, do the first three quarters of the second century call for repeated investigation by the student of Christianity; and this for several reasons. *Its study demanded:*

I. The scarcity of its literary remains has made possible in modern times a number of critical theories of the origin and early development of Christianity which are not only in conflict with the traditional view but often with each other. Without passing judgment on the truth or falsity of these theories, it is evident that but for the scantiness of the historical records such varieties of view would not be possible. Amid the scattered fragments of early Christian literature it is comparatively easy to find room in which to prolong the alleged *I. By modern critical theories of the origin of Christianity.*

[1] The anonymous Epistle to Diognetus, while certainly not by Justin, is probably to be referred to about the middle of the second century.

[2] Eus. H. E. iv. 8, 11, 21, 22.

process of the formation of Christianity. Those who assume that its rise must be conceived as a natural development have believed it possible to show that the final result was not attained till the middle of the second century. Starting with the assertion that original Christianity was divided into two hostile, or at least separate, parties, they have far more easily obtained the time necessary for the supposed fusion of these into the Catholic Church than would have been possible if more of the books of whose existence we know had been preserved. At least these books would in all probability have settled the question, pro or con, decisively. In their absence, the few letters of the apostolic fathers (written for local or personal objects), the lately recovered "Teaching of the Apostles," together with the so-called Epistle of Barnabas, the "Shepherd" of Hermas, and fragments of lost writings preserved by later authors, must be our only guides until the period of the Apologists, the middle of the century, has been reached. Yet these critical theories have claimed to be scientific reconstructions of primitive Christian history. Their truth or falsity involves the supernatural character of the Christian religion. Difficult as the task may be to refute what is claimed to be proved by criticism based on such scanty sources, the necessity of investigating these sources is imperative for all who would justly estimate the worth of either the theories themselves or their refutations. Finding, as we do when we enter upon these studies, how much is made to depend on the phraseology and incidental allusions of the early writers, we shall realize how slowly conclusions should be formed when supported by such delicate and easily misused methods of proof, and we shall re-examine the more closely such evidence as there is because of its very meagreness.

II. In connection also with these theories of the early history of Christianity, the history of the New Testament books and of their recognition by the Church is inseparably bound up with the study of the second century. At its close we find Irenæus,[1] for example, stoutly defending the apostolic authority of our four Gospels, and maintaining that there never had been and could not be more than these four of a sacred character. Tertullian likewise declares it to be the Christian doctrine that the four Gospels possess apostolic authority, and he knows none authoritative but these four.[2] The same fathers also recognized the authority of most of the other books now contained in our New Testament;[3] while their silence as to two or three cannot be used to prove that these were rejected, or, even if they were unknown or doubted by these particular fathers, that they are not entitled to recognition by us. It is certain that in the last quarter of the second century the Church fully accepted a collection of books, corresponding with our New Testament, as apostolic and therefore authoritative, and was, except in a few minor particulars, fully agreed as to the limits of that collection, appealing to these books as standards of doctrine, and maintaining their apostolic authority on the ground of the unbroken testimony of the principal churches. But the question has been raised whether Irenæus really expressed in this matter the traditional view of the churches, or a new opinion, reached by

II. By the question of the New Testament Canon.

[1] Adv. Hær. iii. 11. 8.
[2] Adv. Marc. iv. 2, 5.
[3] Cf. Reuss's Hist. of the Canon, pp. 103-116.

the Church of his own time as the result of its conflict with heresy and the consolidation of its originally separate parts. It is alleged by certain critics that our Gospels are in fact not authentic, but were composed, or at least thrown into their present form, in the second century itself, for the purpose of supporting one or other of the parties into which the early Church is said to have been divided, and that they thus represent the phases through which these parties passed. They are alleged to be only those which, out of a considerable number of early Gospels, the Church of the second century fixed upon as canonical because harmonious with the doctrinal views which had become established. It is said that the evidence of the earlier fathers shows that apostolic authority was but gradually recognized, while by the same gradual process the books of the New Testament were elevated to the position of inspired works which the Old Testament already occupied. These views involve of course the inference that, as Christianity was itself the result of a natural development, the New Testament also was the product, not of inspiration, but of the mind of the Church as in the process of her establishment she came to look upon her doctrines and to read her beliefs back into the life of Jesus and his Apostles. To all this it has been replied, that, while the Church's apprehension of the limits of the Canon was a result gradually reached, yet from the beginning the authority of the Apostles, as teachers of divine truth, as well as the authoritative character of their writings, was clearly recognized; that the authenticity of the several books of the New Testament can be satisfactorily proved; and that therefore the conception of the Canon which prevailed at the close of the second century was not a new idea, but only the

IMPORTANCE OF JUSTIN'S TESTIMONY.

more definite statement of that recognition of apostolic authority which existed from the days of Paul himself.

Between these opposing views the decision evidently rests with the testimony of the second century; and no student of the New Testament can afford to be without some personal acquaintance with the period which immediately followed that in which it was composed.

III. Apart, however, from these questions which concern the very foundations upon which Christianity rests, the period of which we are speaking offers other problems of particular interest both to the historian and to the practical Christian.

III. By the problem of the origin of the Christian ministry.

Prominent among these is that of the origin of the Christian ministry.

By comparing Irenæus, again, with the New Testament, it becomes evident that considerable change had taken place in the organization of the Christian communities during the intervening time. In the first century the local churches appear to have been governed by a body of officers called "bishops" or "elders,"[1] assisted by an order of "deacons."[2] The term "elder" appears, indeed, to have been also used in a wider as well as in its official sense;[3] so that a man could have been an "elder," but not a "bishop," though he could not have been a bishop unless an elder.[4] Still, this body of officers were of equal rank. *Ruling* was the original purpose of their office; but soon, as

---

[1] Cf. Acts xiv. 23; xx. 17, 28; Tit. i. 5, 7.
[2] Phil. i. 1; 1 Tim. iii. 8–13.
[3] 1 Tim. v. 1; 1 Pet. v. 1.
[4] I cannot accept Dr. Hatch's theory of the origin of the Episcopate. Cf. Lect. VI.

appears from the New Testament itself, the work of teaching was attached to it according as the spirit might qualify individual members of the official body.[1] Hardly, however, has the second century opened, when we find in at least some churches a single president, alone called the "bishop," surrounded by a college of "elders" as his advisers, and assisted in the active government and care of his church by the "deacons."[2] Thus the direction of the local churches seems to have been early appropriated by one presiding officer; a centre of unity was formed in the person and office of the "bishop;" until in Irenæus[3] all remembrance of the earlier arrangement seems to have been lost, and that writer speaks of the first presiding bishops of the principal churches of Christendom as having been appointed to office by the Apostles. Not yet, indeed, had the name "elder" ceased to be applied to the bishop,[4] nor were the two clearly regarded as distinct offices;[5] not yet had the Christian ministry been clothed with sacerdotal dignity; but the growth is very evident from the college of equal bishops portrayed by the New Testament to the influential chief officer of a century later, who had largely monopolized the functions of the original body, and who, in proportion to the prominence of the city of whose church he was the head, represented ecclesiastical tradition and exercised ecclesiastical power.

IV. Then, too, the period before us becomes of exceeding interest inasmuch as in its writers we may first

---

[1] 1 Tim. v. 12; 2 Tim. ii. 2.
[2] Cf. The Epistles of Ignatius.
[3] Cf. Adv. Hær. iii. 3.
[4] Cf. Iren. to Victor, Eus. H. E. v. 24.
[5] Iren. iii. 2. 2 and 3. 3.

recognize the mingling of philosophy with the doctrines of Christianity. There can scarcely be said to be a trace of the influence of current philosophy in creating the beliefs of the Apostles. They distinctly declare that the wisdom of this world is vain.[1] Already, indeed, was the young church imperilled by teachers who gave speculations under the guise of Christian phrases; but such teachers were condemned and denounced. "Beware," wrote Paul, "lest any man spoil you through philosophy and vain deceit."[2] Christianity was proclaimed as self-sufficient, as a revelation from God, dogmatic in its teaching, and needing no support from the conclusions of human reason; and though it really contained a philosophy of its own, and though it was in sympathy with not a few of the conclusions to which uninspired reason had attained,[3] it felt no need of the pagan philosophy of the day to form its doctrines. But as the new religion came into closer contact and conflict with pagan thought, it was inevitable that the latter should affect it in various ways. On the one hand, as the New Testament already shows, philosophical speculations began to be mingled with Christian ideas, or to be clothed in the new vestments of Christian language. For this tendency Jewish Alexandrianism and Cabalism had prepared the way; and the Gnostic systems, which reached their height in the middle of the second century, produced a total perversion of the simple Gospel of the Apostles. On the other hand, about the same time, pagan philosophy began to be aware of the existence and progress of the "new superstition," and to direct arguments against it; while orthodox Christianity in its turn began to attempt the

IV. Because of the union of philosophy and Christianity.

[1] 1 Cor. i. 19–21. [2] Col. ii. 8.
[3] Cf. Lect. IV.

solution of some of the great problems which its own existence and its relation to the former history of the world suggested to thoughtful minds. Claiming to be the only true religion, it was forced to say how it regarded other religions and other types of thought. Freed from connection with Judaism, it was forced to declare its attitude toward previous pagan ethics and philosophy. Some of the Christian writers, emphasizing the *newness* of their religion, sought to show the failure of all pagan philosophy to satisfy the mind and of all pagan religions to elevate life. Others, impressed with the *universality* of their religion and conceiving it as the revelation of eternal truth, sought to show the affiliation with it of whatever was noblest in pagan thought and ethics. Thus in various ways Christianity and philosophy came into contact. The contact affected, well or ill as we may judge, the definitions of doctrine; produced division in the Church, but caused that portion which clung to the apostolic teaching to realize more perfectly the unity and the significance of the faith; widened men's thoughts, yet often perverted the Gospel; in short, created the first phase of the long effort of reason to explain and of faith to apprehend the contents of revelation.

V. Finally, involved in all of these discussions there is presented the question of how far and by what means the Christian communities had become externally a unit. There can be no doubt that much progress had been made since the apostolic age in giving expression to the original moral and spiritual unity of believers, both by formulating their faith and by developing the conception of the Church. At the end of the second century there existed the idea of a Catholic (in the sense of orthodox)

V. By the problem of the unity of the Church.

Church,[1] membership with which was often regarded as essential to salvation, and the distinguishing features of which were fidelity to the apostolic doctrine and the regular succession of bishops from the Apostles. Evidently the progress and the conflicts of Christianity had united the scattered communities of believers into what was practically an external association. The pillars of this society were the churches of the principal cities, which had been founded by Apostles and which preserved, through a direct line of bishops and presbyters, the apostolic tradition. Of these the most conspicuous and influential was the Church of Rome. Not that these churches had been as yet formally welded into one external organization. They were only united by a common faith and order, a common dange and hope. But the idea of the universal Church as a visible society with a definite creed and a prescribed organization was predominating, and it is important to ask by what causes had this state of things been brought about. Was this Catholic Church the result, as some affirm, of a compromise, consciously or unconsciously made, between parties originally opposed to one another; or was it the result of the natural growth of Gentile Christianity, of the spirit and needs of the age and the conflicts with paganism and heresy? It would appear to be of great use, in view of present movements toward the unification of Christendom, to study carefully the original idea of the Church, the nature of its earliest unity, and the historical progress in ancient times toward the expression thereof in outward forms.

In view of these questions belonging to the first three quarters of the second century, I propose to examine

[1] Cf. e. g. Iren. iii. 4. 1.

afresh the testimony of one of the most important witnesses from that period whose writings are still accessible. This is Justin Martyr; and a brief sketch of the man and his works will enable us to perceive his great value as a witness to early Christianity.

Object of these lectures.

Our knowledge of the life of Justin is derived almost entirely from the notices scattered through his own writings; for Eusebius does little more than collect, as we may do, what Justin says about himself. He was a native of Flavia Neapolis,[1] a city founded not far from the ruins of ancient Sychem and named in honor of Vespasian. It was the same place which is now known as Nablûs. Justin was consequently a Samaritan by birth;[2] but his language makes it clear that his family was not of Samaritan but of purely Gentile descent.[3] Probably his immediate ancestors were colonists who had settled in the new city shortly after its establishment.

The life of Justin.

His birth can only be approximately placed in the closing years of the first or the beginning of the second century. Some older critics placed it as early as 89 A. D. Epiphanius[4] declares that Justin was martyred under Hadrian when only thirty years of age; but as the date thus given for his martyrdom is certainly wrong, so the age assigned the martyr is wholly improbable. We only know that Justin, as Eusebius

His birth.

---

[1] Ap. i. 1.
[2] Ap. ii. 15.
[3] Ap. i. 53; Dial. 41, 64, 120, 122, 130.
[4] Hær. xlvi. 1. Epiphanius states that Justin died under Rusticus the prefect, and when Hadrian was emperor; thus showing, since Rusticus was prefect A. D. 163–167, that his statement is confused and unreliable.

IMPORTANCE OF JUSTIN'S TESTIMONY. 13

relates,[1] "flourished" at Rome under Antoninus, and that he was probably martyred under Marcus Aurelius,[2] from which it is natural to infer that he was born about the beginning of the century, not far from the time when Saint John passed away. He thus belonged to the second generation after the Apostles, and lived at a period when the remembrance of their teaching was still strong and clear in the mind of the Church.

When Justin came to manhood, he gave himself with enthusiasm to the pursuit of truth. In the opening chapters of the Dialogue with Trypho, he gives a graphic account of his early efforts to find intellectual peace in the popular philosophic schools of the day. *His studies in philosophy.* From his very youth he seems to have been of an earnest and religious type of mind, — a type which was not uncommon in that age of transition from the old to the new, — and this occasioned his dissatisfaction with the teachings of philosophy. He found the Stoic instructor to whom he first joined himself unable to give him any knowledge of God. He found the Peripatetic, to whom next he went, more concerned about the fee than about the truth. He learned from the Pythagorean, whom next he sought, that a long course of discipline in music, astronomy, and geometry was necessary to enable the soul to apprehend spiritual and invisible realities. Finally, he became a disciple of Plato, and thought that he had indeed found "wings for his mind" in the "contemplation of ideas," and that he would soon attain the end of the Platonic philosophy, and "look upon God." It was while a Pla-

---

[1] H. E. iv. 11.
[2] Cf. Eus. H. E. iv. 16, with iv. 14 and 18. On the date of Justin's birth, cf. Barth. Aubé (Saint Justin, philosophe et martyr, p. 7), who places it in the first decade of the second century.

14   JUSTIN MARTYR.

tonist that he became a Christian; but he passed over to the new religion without any violent rupture with his previous love of philosophy. To him, as we shall see, Christianity was the true philosophy, the absolute truth, in the reception of which alone earnest minds could find peace. And therefore, after he became a Christian, he did not cease to be a philosopher. He always wore the philosophic mantle.[1] He appears, like other philosophic teachers of the day, to have moved from city to city to spread his doctrines. Like others, also, he gravitated to Rome, where he became actively engaged in teaching and defending Christianity to all whom he could reach. There is nothing to show that he ever held any ecclesiastical office. He was rather a philosophical evangelist. He gathered pupils about him, more after the style of the philosopher than of the Christian minister. But that he was highly influential in his own day, as well His influ- as honored by posterity, is attested by the references to him and to his works in writers so soon following as Irenæus[2] and Tertullian.[3] He distinguished himself in controversy with the powerful heretical teachers who had, like himself, drifted to Rome, and who were at that very time sowing the seeds of discord in the Christian Church. He engaged in public debate with the Cynic philosopher, Crescens, of whom he speaks with an acrimony which at least shows that the debate had been a sharp one,[4] and who, Tatian tells us,[5]

[1] Dial. 1.   [2] iv. 6. 2; v. 26. 2.
[3] Adv. Valent. 5.
[4] Ap. ii. 3.   Κρήσκεντος τοῦ φιλοψόφου καὶ φιλοκόμπου.
[5] Ad Græc. 19.   Eusebius (H. E. iv. 16) states that Crescens actually brought about Justin's death; but his statement is evidently an inference from Justin's own language (Ap. ii. 3), where he says that he expects Crescens to secure his death, and from Tatian's remark that Crescens "endeavored to inflict on Justin,

IMPORTANCE OF JUSTIN'S TESTIMONY.

plotted to secure the death of his Christian antagonist. Tatian himself, famous afterward as a heretic, and still more famous as the author of the first harmony of the Gospels, was a hearer[1] or disciple[2] of Justin's; and not till after the martyrdom of the master did the pupil venture to express his peculiar views. Thus we may imagine the meagre outline of Justin's life filled up with varied and courageous activities. With some intervals,[3] during one of which the dialogue with Trypho, if historical, occurred, he continued to reside in the capital until the early years of the reign of Marcus Aurelius, when, according to the testimony of antiquity, he suffered martyrdom under the prefect Junius Rusticus. Recent researches show that Rusticus held the prefecture of Rome A. D. 163-167.[4]

His death.

It is thus evident that Justin, even before his conversion, belonged to the class of sincere seekers after

---

and indeed on me, the punishment of death." Tatian's language, however, rather implies that Crescens had failed in his plots, and the Martyrology makes no mention of him. Cf. Von Engelhardt's Das Christenthum Justins des Märtyrers, p. 75 (who follows Daniel and Volkmar). Eusebius makes the same statement in the Chronicon, though he there places Justin's death in 152. Harnack (Die Überlieferung der Griechischen Apologeten, Leipzig, 1882, p. 142, note) supposes that Eusebius found in Julius Africanus a reference under 152 to the trouble caused Justin by Crescens and which partly led to the writing of the Apology, and that Eusebius understood it to mean that Crescens had then brought about Justin's death.

[1] Iren. i. 28. 1.   [2] Hippol. Refut. viii. 9.

[3] In the Martyrology, Justin is represented as saying, "I live above one Martinus at the Timiotinian Bath; and during the whole time (and I *am now living at Rome for the second time*) I am unaware of any other meeting than his." This at least shows the early tradition of Justin's travels.

[4] Cf. Borghesi (Œuvres Complètes), cited by Otto, Justini Opera, tom. ii. p. 268.

truth, and still more particularly to the number of seekers after God. It may be a question whether his later Platonism does not color his statement[1] of objections to the rival schools of philosophy. But the current philosophy of the day, so far as it was spiritual at all, was theological in its character;[2] and the best minds of even the pagan world felt that God, though abstractly conceived, was the supreme end of knowledge. Of this interesting and significant phase of philosophic thought, this conscious yearning after Deity, hampered by metaphysical limitations which made Deity appear as only the transcendent cause and source of all things, Justin was a type; and in his Christian writings we recognize the same sincerity and earnestness of which his earlier life afforded indications.

A seeker after truth.

He gives an account of his conversion in the introduction to the Dialogue with Trypho. He tells us that when deep in the study of Plato he one day went out to the seashore to meditate,[3] and there met a man, of venerable appearance, who engaged him in conversation. Their conversation fell into the subject dearest to both; namely, the search for truth. In reply to the stranger's question, Justin defined philosophy as "the knowledge of that which really exists, and a clear perception of the truth;" and happiness, as

His conversion.

---

[1] Dial. 3. [2] Cf. Lect. IV.

[3] The place of his conversion is quite uncertain. He calls it "our city." Some have supposed Ephesus; others Flavia Neapolis; but the latter was too far from the sea to answer the description. If we suppose that it was Ephesus, and that the dialogue with Trypho also took place there, we may infer that in early life Justin had made that city his home. The fact has some bearing on his acquaintance with the Fourth Gospel, and his familiarity with Alexandrian speculations. Cf. Lectt. IV. and V.

"the reward of such knowledge and wisdom;"[1] and God, as "that which always maintains the same nature, and in the same manner, and is the cause of all other things."[2] Thereupon the stranger, in quite a Socratic manner, forced the young Platonist to concede that the knowledge of God depends on the moral qualifications of the soul, rather than on either the nature of the soul itself, or its reminiscence of a previous existence; and argued that the soul is not naturally immortal, but dependent for continuance of life on the will of God. Having thus undermined Justin's confidence in his philosophical teachers, the stranger pointed him to the Hebrew prophets as more ancient than the philosophers, and more entitled to credence, since they "spake by the Divine Spirit, and foretold events which would take place, and which are now taking place." "Their writings," he said, "are still extant, and he who has read them is very much helped in his knowledge of the beginning and the end of things, and of those matters which the philosopher ought to know." Forthwith, says Justin, "a flame was kindled in my soul, and a love of the prophets and of those men who are the friends of Christ possessed me; and whilst revolving his [the old man's] words in my mind, I found this philosophy alone to be safe and profitable. Thus and for this reason I am a philosopher."[3] Now, it is ques-

---

[1] Dial. 3. φιλοσοφία μὲν ... ἐπιστήμη ἐστὶ τοῦ ὄντος καὶ τοῦ ἀληθοῦς ἐπίγνωσις, εὐδαιμονία δὲ ταύτης τῆς ἐπιστήμης καὶ τῆς σοφίας γέρας.

[2] τὸ κατὰ τὰ αὐτὰ καὶ ὡσαύτως ἀεὶ ἔχον καὶ τοῦ εἶναι πᾶσι τοῖς ἄλλοις αἴτιον, τοῦτο δή ἐστιν ὁ Θεός. In the preceding question, "Θεὸν δὲ σὺ τί καλεῖς;" Thirlby and Aubé read τὸ ὄν for Θεὸν. Otto, however, retains Θεὸν, and in either case the ultimate meaning of the question is the same.

[3] Dial. 3-8.

tionable if this narrative was meant by the author to be really historical. Its unusually careful composition, and its evident imitation of the Platonic Dialogues, as well as the character of the argument itself, suggest that it may have been intended to be a vivid portrayal of the course of thought by which Justin passed over, or would at least afterwards have passed over, from Platonism to Christianity.[1] Probably, however, there was a basis of fact in the story; but whether this were so or not, the narrative clearly exhibits not only Justin's continued fondness for Platonism, but also the fact, to which all his writings testify, that for him Christianity was the completion of philosophy, and the end to which all former systems, so far as they contained truth, naturally tended.

In the second Apology,[2] Justin declares that he was led to embrace Christianity by beholding the fearlessness of death which the Christians displayed. He could not believe that men who went cheerfully to such a doom could be the wicked people that they were represented to be. This account, however, is not inconsistent with the story given in the Dialogue. We may suppose that his interest having been aroused in "the prophets and those men who [were] the friends of Christ," he observed the Christians more closely, and was further convinced of their sincerity, and of the power of their religion.[3] At any rate, whatever was the order of events, the conduct of the Christians and the study of the prophets were the two means of Justin's conversion.

Here it is proper to remark that while the time of

[1] So Aubé, Saint Justin, p. 20.
[2] Chapter xii.
[3] So Von Engelhardt, Das Christenthum Justins, pp. 80–84.

IMPORTANCE OF JUSTIN'S TESTIMONY. 19

Justin's principal activity at Rome is undisputed, yet the details of the chronology of his life present many debated and difficult questions. It is probable that he did not become a Christian until early in the reign of Antoninus. The account which he himself gives of his previous search for truth implies that not until he had reached manhood did he find peace through believing in Christ. Moreover, according to Syncellus, the Chronicon of Eusebius had, under the year 140 A. D., the statement that then "Justin was called,"[1] — a statement which Eusebius probably took from the earlier Chronicle of Julius Africanus, and which, despite the fact that Eusebius in the same place erroneously assigns the Apology to that year, coincides with his evident belief, as expressed in his History,[2] that Justin was still a heathen in Hadrian's reign, and probably indicates the date of his conversion.[3] We may assume, then, that the Apologist was already in middle life at the time of his conversion; and if so, he must have immediately thrown himself

The chronology of his life.

[1] Ἰουστῖνος προσηγορεύθη, cited by Harnack, Die Überlieferung, etc., p. 143, note.

[2] H. E. iv. 8.

[3] So Harnack, Die Überlieferung, etc., p. 143, note. Aubé (Saint Justin, p. 24) thinks that the statement of Ap. i. 31, that "Barchochebas gave orders that Christians alone should be led to cruel punishments," implies that then (A. D. 132–136) Justin was a Christian. He admits, however, that Eusebius (H. E. iv. 8) understood that at the time of the apotheosis of Antinous (A. D. 131), Justin was still a heathen (cf. Ap. i. 29). Harnack thinks that both Eusebius and the Apology prove that Justin was a heathen in Hadrian's reign. To my mind, there is nothing in the Apology to show how long Justin had been a Christian; but the introduction to the Dialogue proves that his conversion was after he had reached manhood. Harnack well exposes the errors of Eusebius in his chronology of Justin's life; and his explanation of the Chronicon, as quoted by Syncellus, seems to me plausible.

into the thickest part of the battle in behalf of the cause which he had just espoused.

On the other hand, the traditional report that Justin was martyred under Marcus Aurelius may be accepted with reasonable confidence. It is not only given by Eusebius in his History,[1] but is also independently supported by the testimony of Epiphanius;[2] and the Martyrology, which relates the death of Justin and his companions, and which is an unusually trustworthy document for one of its kind, ascribes the martyrdom, as Epiphanius does, to the prefecture of Rusticus.[3] We may therefore assume that for about twenty-five years Justin continued to teach and defend Christianity; and that at some time in the period covered by the years A. D. 163-167 he sealed his testimony with his blood.

The time of Justin's arrival at Rome is determined by the date assigned to the great Apology. Fixing that,

[1] H. E. iv. 16.

[2] Hær. xlvi. 1. As already observed (cf. above, p. 12), Epiphanius erroneously places Justin's death under Hadrian. Nevertheless, his mention of Rusticus, and the absence of any reference to Crescens, show a tradition independent of Eusebius.

[3] For an account of the manuscript in which the Μαρτύριον is preserved, cf. Otto, Justini Opera, tom. ii. Proleg. See also, Harnack's Die Überlieferung, etc., p. 193. Eusebius, in the Chronicon, contradicts his History, and assigns Justin's death to 152. Harnack (Ibid., p. 142, note) supposes that Eusebius again misunderstood the language of his source (Julius Africanus). If so, his assignment in his History of the martyrdom to the reign of Marcus Aurelius would seem the more to confirm the antiquity of the tradition. Dr. Hort is quoted by Westcott (Hist. of Canon, p. 88, note 4) as assigning Justin's death to 148; but I have not been able to obtain his article (Journ. of Class. and Sacred Philology, iii. 139). The Martyrology states that Justin was beheaded; and the oldest church tradition assigned his death to the first of June. A later tradition made him die like Socrates.

IMPORTANCE OF JUSTIN'S TESTIMONY. 21

for reasons of which I will speak presently, in the year 147 (or 148), it is certain that the author had already dwelt several years in the capital, and had been actively engaged in theological controversy. He singles out Marcion as the most conspicuous living heretic.[1] He says of him that he "is even at this day alive and teaching ... and has caused many of every nation to speak blasphemies." He refers to a book of his own which he had already written against all the heresies that had existed,[2] and of which his book against Marcion in particular, which is quoted by Irenæus,[3] may have been a part.[4] Justin had thus become a vigorous champion of the orthodox faith, and had especially contended against that dangerous heresy which had recently been transferred from Pontus to Rome, and which threatened most seriously the peace and unity of the Church,[5] so much so that in the fol-

Time of his arrival at Rome.

---

[1] Ap. i. 26, 58.
[2] Ap. i. 26. σύνταγμα κατὰ πασῶν τῶν γεγενημένων αἱρέσεων.
[3] πρὸς Μαρκίωνα σύνταγμα. Adv. Hær. iv. 6. 2, and, perhaps, v. 26. 2.
[4] So Weizsäcker, "Die Theologie des Märtyrers Just.," Jahrb. für Deutsche Theol. 1867, p. 61, note 2. Harnack (Die Überlieferung, etc., p. 142) makes them separate works.
[5] Justin's Apology has been used to fix the date of Marcion's activity in Rome, and the latter in turn to fix the date of the former. Aubé (Saint Justin, p. 39) concludes from the notices in Eusebius (H. E. iv. 10) as to Marcion's appearance in Rome, that the Apology was at least written after 142, and probably about 150. Previously Volkmar ("Die Zeit Justins des Märtyrers," Theologische Jahrbücher, Tübingen, 1855) had also fixed the date of Justin's writings from Marcion's coming to Rome, assigning the Syntagma to 145 at the earliest, and the Apology to 147. Harnack, on the other hand (Zur Quellenkritik der Geschichte des Gnosticismus, p. 25), concludes that Justin only knew of Marcion's work in Asia, on the ground that his descriptions of Marcion's errors do not show the influence of

lowing generation he was as famous for being the opponent and historian of heresy as he was for being an Apologist.[1]

We may thus certainly affirm that early in the reign of Antoninus Justin fixed his residence at Rome. It was a time and a place which afforded large opportunity for his active mind and polemical spirit. The Roman Empire was at the height of its splendor, and after the conquests of Trajan had enlarged its limits until nothing more remained to be conquered, had enjoyed under Hadrian, and expected still more to enjoy under Antoninus, the blessings of peace. Intellectual activity was quickened. The restless curiosity of Hadrian and the philosophic culture of the Antonines stimulated the growth of intelligence and allowed the utmost liberty of thought. Into Rome there poured an increasing flood of teachers and scholars, even as into her also poured the commerce and the tribute of the world. It was the lull before the storm. It was the high noon of Imperial greatness preceding the decline of the long Roman day; and though the causes were already at work which shattered the splendid spectacle, though below the outward prosperity the people were impoverished by taxation, and though below the fair lives of the Antonines society was steeped in depravity, nevertheless the prospect was such as to seem to merit the epithet of "golden age."

The opportunities of Christian work afforded him at Rome.

Cerdo. Von Engelhardt (Das Christenthum Justins, p. 73) thinks that Marcion cannot be used to determine the date of the Apology, since it is not clear whether Justin referred to his activity in Asia or Rome. Justin's references to Marcion, however, seem certainly to imply an activity of the heretic and a spread of the heresy so considerable as to be scarcely applicable to the period before Marcion was separated from the Roman church.

[1] Cf. Irenæus, cited above. Tert. adv. Valent. 5.

The Christian Church at the capital was affected by these circumstances. We shall study hereafter the attitude of the Government toward her; but we may here remark that despite occasional persecution and local outrages and general contempt, she had not for a long time suffered severely. The Roman church had already become famous throughout the brotherhood for her charity, and hence, we may suppose, counted not a few wealthy people in her membership. Her influence, as the church of the metropolis, was already great. Into her poured the streams of Christian thought from all the churches of the Empire. She was the focus where the rays of Christian light converged. Already it was true, as Irenæus said a little later, that to her on account of her pre-eminence [1] — a pre-eminence which was due to her situation in the capital — did the faithful from everywhere resort; so that she was already becoming the mirror of Christendom, and her voice the clearest utterance of the universal faith. Thither came the leaders of speculation as well as the witnesses of apostolic tradition. Valentinus and Cerdo began to teach their heresies at Rome in the Episcopate of Hyginus. Marcion flourished under Pius and Anicetus. There were to be found representatives of nearly every type of professed Christianity. Even Ebionism could make itself heard in the church of the capital. Gentile Christians who would have no fellowship with observers of the law; Jewish Christians who would have no fellowship with those who did not observe the law; and between these two extremes, the greater number of both Gentile and Jewish believers who strove, with charity toward one another, to walk in the spirit and doctrine of the Apostles, caused the Christian community at Rome,

[1] "Propter potiorem principalitatem." — *Adv. Hær.* iii. 3. 2.

even at this early period, to offer an attractive field to the controversialist as well as to the earnest missionary. What place more likely to be sought by our philosophical evangelist? Where could he find a wider arena for the combat with error in which he was anxious to engage? From what portion of the ancient church is testimony more important than from this?

As might have been expected, Justin became an author; but of the many works which in various periods have passed under his name, only three remain which can certainly be considered his. Eusebius mentions [1] nine books by Justin of which he knew, and adds, "There are also many other works of his in the hands of many of our brethren." Of those named by him none are now extant except the Apologies and the Dialogue with Trypho. Other works, indeed, two of which [2] bear the same titles as works mentioned by Eusebius, are found in the manuscripts of Justin, but, on internal grounds, cannot be considered his. It is even probable that Eusebius himself was mistaken in several particulars of his life of Justin. He certainly had not read Justin's work against heresies, for he quotes it only through Irenæus.[3] He explicitly affirms that Justin wrote two Apologies, — one under Antoninus Pius, and the other under Marcus Aurelius. But not only were both the now extant Apologies certainly written under Antoninus, but Eusebius quotes from both of them as from *the first Apology*. It would thus appear that what are now known as the two Apologies of Justin were in Eusebius's time one; and that the second Apology, to which

The writings of Justin.

---

[1] H. E. iv. 18.
[2] περὶ μοναρχίας and πρὸς Ἕλληνας.
[3] Cf. H. E. iv. 18.

IMPORTANCE OF JUSTIN'S TESTIMONY.

he refers, but from which he does not quote, was either a genuine work of Justin's which has been lost, or else (and more probably) some other work of similar character which passed under Justin's name.[1] In fact, Justin was so prominent a character in the remembrance of the later Church, that many writings were purposely or by mistake attributed to him. During the Middle Ages he was not known by his genuine writings at all, but by a number of these spurious ones.[2] Our earliest manuscript of Justin's works dates from the fourteenth century, and contains twelve [3] works alleged to have

[1] In H. E. ii. 13, Eusebius quotes from Ap. i. 26, as from Justin's "first defence addressed to Antoninus." In iii. 26, he refers to the same passage as containing a notice of Menander. In iv. 8, he *quotes Ap. ii.* 12, as from "the Apology to Antoninus," after having quoted, as from the same work, Ap. i. 29 and 31. In iv. 11, 12, he says: "Justin, after having contended with great success against the Greeks, addressed also other works, containing a defence of our faith, to the Emperor Antoninus Pius and to the Senate of Rome. He also had his residence at Rome; but he shows who and whence he was in the following extracts in his Apology:" then follows Ap. i. 1. In iv. 16, he says that Justin, "having given a second defence of our doctrine to the above-mentioned rulers [viz., Aurelius and Lucius Verus]," was martyred. Then he quotes Ap. ii. 3, as "in the Apology already quoted (ἐν τῇ δεδηλωμένῃ ἀπολογίᾳ)," which seems to refer to his previous citations of the longer Apology. In iv. 17, he cites Ap. ii. 12, as from "the first Apology." In iv. 18, enumerating Justin's books, he says: "There is a discourse of his, addressed to Antoninus Pius and his sons and the Roman Senate, in defence of our doctrines; also another work, comprising a defence of our faith, which he addressed to the emperor of the same name, Antoninus Verus [i. e., Marcus Aurelius], the successor of the preceding." Harnack (Die Überlieferung, etc., pp. 172, etc.) argues with plausibility that the work now known as the Supplicatio of Athenagoras was mistakenly regarded by Eusebius as the second Apology of Justin.

[2] Cf. Harnack's Die Überlieferung, etc., pp. 148, etc.

[3] The work Adv. Gentiles is added in the manuscript as an

come from his pen; and it has been only modern criticism which has by careful examination separated from out of these those which may be reasonably considered genuine.[1] Most of the works contained in the manuscript are indeed easily condemned as spurious by their internal characteristics;[2] and none are now

appendix to the Confutatio Dogmatum Aristotelis, without any inscription.

[1] There exist only two complete manuscripts of Justin, — the Codex Regius Parisinus, 450, written in 1364; and the Codex Claromontanus (now Mediomontanus), which was taken in 1824 from Paris to England, and which was written in 1541. Either the latter, however, was copied from the former, or both were from a common exemplar. Cf. Otto's Justini Opera, tom. i. proleg. xx. etc. In both manuscripts the shorter Apology precedes the longer, and the latter is called δευτέρα. The text appears, by comparison with the quotations in Eusebius, to have been much corrupted (cf. Harnack's Die Überlieferung, p. 135, note). The works assigned to Justin by the Paris manuscript are, according to Otto: (1) Epistola ad Zenam et Serenam; (2) Cohortatio ad Gentiles; (3) Dialogus cum Tryphone; (4) Apologia Minor; (5) Apologia Major; (6) De Monarchia; (7) Expositio rectæ fidei; (8) Confutatio dogmatum, to which the tract Adv. Gentiles is appended; (9) Quæstiones Christianorum ad Gentiles; (10) Quæstiones et Responsiones ad Orthodoxos; (11) Quæstiones Gentilium ad Christianos.

[2] Cf. Harnack, ibid., pp. 154, etc. The question of the spuriousness of most of these works is so well settled that I have not thought it necessary to discuss it. The Cohortatio most closely resembles Justin's genuine writings; but the absence from it of the doctrine of the Logos is alone decisive the other way. Moreover, Schürer (Brieger's Zeitschrift für Kirchengesch., ii. 3, p. 319) has pointed out the apparent dependence of the Cohortatio on Julius Africanus, and assigned it, therefore, to the middle of the third century. Donaldson (Hist. of Christian Lit., ii. 96) had already taken the same view, following Ashton (Justini Ph. et M. Apologiæ, p. 294). More recently Völter (Zeitschr. für wissensch. Theol., 1883, pp. 180, etc.) has argued that the Cohortatio and Africanus drew from a common source (Justus of Tiberias), and that the Cohortatio is a work of the second cen-

considered Justinian except the Apologies and the Dialogue. The genuineness of these is undisputed, and to them alone can we appeal to learn the testimony of Justin. One cannot but express a passing regret that his work against heresies, from which Irenæus quoted and probably derived much of his own information upon the subject, and which would complete our knowledge of Justin's testimony to early Christianity by bringing out plainly his attitude as an orthodox Christian to the teaching of the Apostles, has not escaped the ravages of time.

The two extant Apologies of Justin form, then, perhaps the most notable monument of Christianity which has been preserved from the second century, at least from before the time of Irenæus. *The Apologies.* By Eusebius, as has been already stated, both were probably regarded as one work; and that they practically are such may be considered quite certain.[1] The shorter was in all probability a sort of postscript to the longer, added because of certain events which had just

tury, and probably the first part of the treatise $\pi\epsilon\rho\grave{\iota}$ $\grave{a}\lambda\eta\theta\epsilon\acute{\iota}as$ by Apollinaris of Hierapolis. As to the genuineness of the Dialogue, Prof. B. L. Gildersleeve (Introd. to his ed. of the Apologies of J. M., p. xxiii) writes: "Apart from the historical allusions to the second century, apart from the testimony of Eusebius, apart from the general agreement with the Apologies in doctrine and thought and want of method, the language is evidently the same; and though there are slight variations in vocabulary, as might be expected from the difference of theme, these have little weight in comparison with the remarkable coincidences in tricks of speech and irregularities of syntax."

[1] Boll (Zeitschr. für histor. Theol., 1842) is quoted by Von Engelhardt (p. 77) as holding that the shorter Apology was the original conclusion of the larger; but as Von Engelhardt says, the present conclusion of the larger Apology is complete, and no place for the insertion of the shorter can be found in it, or indeed elsewhere.

occurred. Like the longer, it betrays by its expressions that it was written in the reign of Antoninus,[1] and by its references to the longer conclusively indicates that it was written shortly after.[2] We regard it, therefore, as a supplement to the longer Apology ; and if so, it becomes of some assistance in fixing the date at which Their date. both were written.[3] Certainly this was not far from the middle of the century. The author speaks of the Jewish war as recent,[4] and of Christ's birth as having occurred one hundred and fifty years before.[5] Both these, however, are elastic expressions, and different critics have assigned the larger Apology to dates ranging from 138 to 150 A. D. But if the shorter Apology was written soon after the longer, a new element is introduced into the calculation, inasmuch as it states that at the time of its composition Urbicus was prefect of Rome. Now, Q. Lollius Urbicus was the legate of Antoninus in Britain when the famous wall of Antoninus was constructed. This was

[1] Cf. Ap. ii. 2 : "To thee, the Emperor." In the subsequent reign, Aurelius and Lucius Verus were co-emperors till the death of the latter in 169. So, also, " This judgment does not become *the pious Emperor* nor *the philosophic Cæsar*, his son," is conclusive for the reign of Antoninus. So c. 15 : " Would that you also would for your own sakes judge worthily of *piety* and *philosophy*."

[2] In Ap. ii. 4, "We have before stated that [God] takes pleasure in those who imitate his properties," etc., probably refers to i. 10. In ii. 6, " As we said before, he became man according to the counsel of God," etc., is a clear reference to Ap. i., for in Ap. ii nothing as yet has been said of the incarnation. In ii. 8, " We know Heracleitus, as we said before," seems to be a reference to i. 46.

[3] Most critics now take this view of the shorter Apology. Cf. Von Engelhardt, p. 77; Harnack (Die Überlieferung, etc.), p. 145. Aubé (Saint Justin, pp. 67, etc.) still holds that the shorter Apology was that mentioned by Eusebius as offered to Marcus Aurelius, and places its date late in the reign of Antoninus.

[4] Ap. i. 31 ; cf. also i. 47.   [5] Ap. i. 46.

in 140 A. D.; and several years may reasonably be supposed to have intervened before he became prefect of the capital.[1] Without presuming to be exact, we may safely say that between 145 and 150 A. D., and most probably in 147 or 148, the Apologies were written; and since the Dialogue refers[2] to the Apology, and yet still speaks[3] of the Jewish war as recent, it must have been composed shortly after.[4] Date of the Dialogue.
This agrees very well with what we have already learned of the time of Justin's conversion, and of his probable controversy with Marcion at Rome before the composition of the Apology.[5]

[1] Not necessarily, however, seven or nine years, as Aubé (p. 70) insists on the statement of Julius Capitolinus that Antoninus generally left his legates that length of time in the provinces. Even if it were so, however, Urbicus might have returned to Rome as early as 146, since he might have gone to Britain as early as 139.

[2] c. 120. [3] cc. 1, 9; cf. cc. 16, 108.

[4] For Urbicus, cf. Aubé's Saint Justin, pp. 68, etc. Aubé, however, introduces elements into the calculation which are unwarranted, and errs in saying that Antoninus took his third consulship in 145. Von Engelhardt (p. 78) follows Aubé, and is misled by him. See, also, the article in the Encycl. Britan., "Wall of Antoninus."

[5] All arguments on the date of the Apology, drawn from its opening address, are uncertain, because of the possibilities of textual corruption; yet as Aurelius was not fully associated in the government with Antoninus until 147, and as Lucius, who is described by Justin as a philosopher and lover of instruction, was born in 130, an earlier date for the Apology than 147 seems improbable. On it, in fact, all the probabilities converge. If, on the other hand, as Harnack supposes (Die Überlieferung, etc., p. 142, note), when Eusebius in the Chronicon assigned Justin's death to 152, he was misled by a statement of Julius Africanus, that in that year Crescens gave Justin trouble (meaning thereby that in that year the Apology was written as a result of the debate between Justin and Crescens), there would be reason for accepting that date for its composition, since Julius Africanus would be likely to have known the facts. To this date there is

These works, then, written at such a time and at such a place, demand our attention. Let us briefly observe their character and contents.

The longer Apology has, according to our present text, this introduction: "To the Emperor Titus Ælius Adrianus Antoninus Pius Augustus Cæsar, and to Verissimus,[1] his philosophic son, and to Lucius[2] the philosopher, by birth the son of Cæsar[3] and adopted son of Pius, a lover of instruction, and to the sacred Senate, and to all the Roman people, in behalf of the men of every race who are unjustly hated and abused, I, Justin, the son of Priscus and grandson of Bacchius, who are of Flavia Neapolis, a city of Syria, in Palestine, — being one of them, — have made this address and petition."[4] It

Analysis of the longer Apology.

no objection, except the references in the Apology and Dialogue to the Jewish war as recent, which make it undesirable to place the writings any later than possible; but Africanus may have referred to some subsequent action of Crescens against Justin, perhaps to the very plots of which Tatian speaks.

[1] M. Aurelius Antoninus. Hadrian called him Verissimus, his original name having been Marcus Annius Verus.

[2] L. Ceionius Commodus, afterwards L. Aurelius Verus.

[3] That is, son of L. Ælius Verus, who had been adopted by Hadrian, but died before the latter.

[4] Various parts of this address have been called in question by critics. Cf. Otto's note. Eusebius (H. E. iv. 12) quotes it as above, except reading Καίσαρι Σεβαστῷ for Σεβαστῷ Καίσαρι. Some (Ritter, Volkmar, Cave, Überweg) would read Ἀντωνίνῳ Εὐσεβεῖ Σεβαστῷ καὶ Καίσαρι Οὐηρισσίῳ. Volkmar would change Εὐσεβεῖ Σεβαστῷ to Σεβαστῷ Εὐσεβεῖ, after many inscriptions and coins; but Otto cites others like our text. Volkmar also thinks καὶ Λουκίῳ... παιδείας spurious; while others (Neander, Cave) read, instead of Λουκίῳ φιλοσόφῳ, Λουκίῳ φιλοσόφου Καίσαρος φύσει υἱῷ, on the ground that Lucius was only born in 130, and, while nominally Cæsar, was really a private citizen (cf. Von Engelhardt, p. 72). Otto, however, quotes Schnitzer to the effect that Justin could as well have called Lucius a philosopher as his

opens (c. 2) with a bold appeal for justice, evidently imitating Plato's Apology of Socrates. "Reason directs," says Justin, "those who are truly pious and philosophical to honor and love only what is true." He will not flatter, and he does not fear. He simply asks for justice. He demands, therefore (3, 4), that men should not be punished merely for a name, but only after examination of their lives and conduct, and alleges (5) that such unreasonable hatred as the Christians experience could only be due to the instigation of demons, who, as they slew Socrates, now war against the incarnate Word Himself. Justin then (6–12) enumerates three principal charges made against the Christians, — namely, atheism, immorality, and disloyalty, — and proceeds briefly to meet them. Christians are not atheists, for they worship the true God, the Father of righteousness and virtue, together with the Son who came forth from Him to teach us, and the host of angels who follow and are like Him, and the Spirit of prophecy. They are not immoral; or if any be convicted of crimes, they are willing that such should be punished. In fact, their refusal to lie in order to live should commend them to all thoughtful people. Their belief is innocent, however incredible it may be; while their rejection of the popular divinities and their spiritual worship and imitation of the Most High ought not to appear to philosophic rulers a crime. Finally, they are not disloyal, for the kingdom which they seek is a heavenly one. Hence they die the more willingly, that they may partake in it; and their doctrines would make

licentious father; and remarks that the title "philosopher" was used very loosely, and that the added clause, "a lover of instruction," indicates of itself that Lucius was not a philosopher as Verissimus was.

good citizens of all men. With this appeal for justice and refutation of slanders, Justin says that he might conclude; but in the hope of convincing some of the actual truth of Christianity, he undertakes to show its positive worth and credibility. He begins to do this by describing the reasonable worship which the Christians offer to God (13, 14), and by giving examples of the lofty ethical teaching of Christ (15–17), as well as by producing analogies between the Christian doctrines of immortality, resurrection and the end of the world and the teaching of nature and philosophy (18–20). He recites also some of the pagan fables about the sons of the gods and their marvellous exploits, to show how irrational was the honor bestowed on them, and how still more unreasonable it was for believers in these tales to persecute believers in the alleged facts of the life of Christ (21, 22). The object of this part of the Apology was to disarm unbelief and, by proving that Christianity was neither novel nor contemptible, to prepare for the positive argument in its favor. That argument will, he says, aim to establish three points: first, that the teaching of Christ and the prophets is alone true, and is older than all other writers; second, that Jesus Christ was alone and in the proper sense begotten as a Son to God, being His Logos and First-born and Power,[1] and having become by His will a man, taught us these things for the conversion and restoration of the human race; third, that before Christ came, some, influenced by the demons, related through the poets mythological tales intended to travesty the future revelation (23). These were Justin's main points in his defence of Christianity. The nature of Christ

---

[1] Ἰ. Χ. μόνος ἰδίως υἱὸς τῷ θεῷ γεγέννηται, λόγος αὐτοῦ ὑπάρχων καὶ πρωτότοκος καὶ δύναμις.

IMPORTANCE OF JUSTIN'S TESTIMONY. 33

as the incarnate divine Logos was the starting-point of his thought and the central truth by which Christianity was commended and its relations to previous thought and life explained. As contained in the Hebrew prophets, Christianity antedated all philosophy and all pagan religion. Whatever in them was true and good was derived from it, and whatever was evil was originated by the demons for the purpose of opposing it. To establish, therefore, the antiquity of the prophets and the nature of Christ, was the chief aim of his argument.

After descanting again on the unreasonableness of persecuting men who merely differ from others in religious opinion and yet live pure lives, while idols of lust are worshipped, religions of other kinds permitted, impostors like Simon Magus and Menander honored, and heretics like Marcion allowed (24–29), Justin at last takes up the argument. This consists of proof of Christianity from the fulfilment of prophecy, and includes a large portion of his book (30–53). He begins by giving an account of the prophets and of the preservation of their writings in the version of the Seventy, and relates that, centuries before Jesus lived, they predicted the main facts of his life and the mission of the Apostles to the world. Of these predictions he gives a number of examples,[1] following for the most

---

[1] He cites predictions of Christ's advent; His triumphal entry; His "cleansing by His blood those who believe on Him;" His birth from a virgin in Bethlehem; His crucifixion; the preaching of the Gospel to the Gentiles; the call of men to repentance; Christ's session in heaven; the hostility of the world to Christianity; the desolation of Judæa; Christ's miracles; His rejection by the Jews and acceptance by the Gentiles; His humiliation, ascension, majesty, and second advent; and the future resurrection and judgment, — the certainty of the last two of which may, he says, be inferred from the fulfilment already of the other predictions.

part in his explanations of them that ingenious and arbitrary method of interpretation for which the exegetes of the day and especially those of Alexandria were famous, — a method which regarded the Old Testament as either a prosaic writing beforehand of later history or else as oracular utterances of carefully concealed meaning. He explains also the different modes of prophecy, and defends belief in it against the charge of fatalism. He pauses to reply to the objection that since Christ came so late, those who lived before his coming were irresponsible, and does so by maintaining that the divine Logos was in the world from the beginning, and that men of every race who lived rationally[1] were really Christians, while those who lived irrationally[2] were enemies of Christ, and wicked. From all these fulfilled predictions he concludes (53) that the Christian's belief in Christ as the First-born of God and the universal Judge is completely justified.

Justin next (54-58) endeavors to show that mythology was a device of the demons to imitate the future Christ, of whom they had learned from the prophets; and he points out some of their attempts.[3] One thing, however (55), they failed to understand, namely, the predictions of the Cross, although this is the greatest symbol of Christ's power, as may be learned from its prevalence in nature and human life, as for instance in the shape of a ship's sail, a farmer's plough, the tools of the mechanic, and the features of the human body. To the same demoniacal source he refers also the rise of impostors, persecutions, and heretics in recent times

---

[1] μετὰ λόγου. [2] ἄνευ λόγου.
[3] Thus, e. g., Bacchus, the son of Jupiter and discoverer of the vine, was a travesty of Gen. xlix. 10: "He shall be the desire of the Gentiles, binding his foal to the vine." Æsculapius was an imitation of the coming Healer, etc.

(56–58). He then tries to show that Plato himself (59, 60) was directly dependent on Moses for his account of the origin of the world and of the second and third powers in the universe.[1] Then follows the closing part of the Apology (61–67), in which Justin describes Christian baptism, the celebration of the Eucharist and the proceedings at the weekly assemblies of the Christians, for the purpose of removing the false impressions which were current among the populace. With a final appeal for at least liberty of opinion and a solemn reminder of God's judgment of all men, Justin concludes his Apology by appending Hadrian's letter to Minucius Fundanus, a proconsul of Asia, in which that emperor directed that Christians should only be punished after a legal trial. The Apologist adds, however, that he depended not so much on Hadrian's letter as on the justice of his cause.

Thus the proof on which Justin relied in his argument for Christianity was its fulfilment of prophecy. It should be carefully noticed that this was not the ground on which he pleaded for the toleration of Christianity. *Its argument.* For that he pleaded on the ground of justice, and for reasons which will appear in our next lecture. Nor was his argument intended to exhibit the only authority on which Christians themselves rested their belief. The assertion that it was has been a fruitful cause of error in the understanding of

[1] What Plato says in the Timæus of the World-soul, "He placed it like a χ in the universe," Justin thinks he took from the account of the brazen serpent, identifying Plato's World-soul with his own personal Logos. In the Ps-Platonic Ep. ii. occurs an obscure phrase, "τὰ δὲ τρίτα περὶ τὸν τρίτον," which Justin considers a reminiscence of the Spirit brooding over chaos. Athenagoras (Supplic. 23) sees also in the same phrase a reference to the Spirit.

Justin and his age. His argument was simply an apologetic one. It outlined the course of thought along which his own mind travelled in assuring itself of the credibility of the new faith, and the course along which he believed others would be led to the same conclusion. The simplicity of the Christian ceremonies, the nobility of Christian ethics, the analogies with paganism, were meant to remove obstacles from the minds of his readers, in order that the marvellous fact of prophecy and its fulfilment might lead to the conviction that Christianity was the absolute and eternal truth.

The shorter Apology was called out by Justin's indignation at a new outrage which had just occurred. Analysis of the shorter Apology. It opens abruptly and vehemently. It is addressed to the Roman people, though it appeals also to the emperor and the Cæsar as the highest representatives of the people. It declares that Christianity was being used as a charge to cover private malice. Of this a most outrageous instance had just taken place. A dissolute man, angry at his Christian wife for having rebuked his vices and finally left him, had charged her teacher, Ptolemæus, with being a Christian; and the prefect Urbicus had sentenced to death Ptolemæus and two others, simply because they confessed their religion (1, 21). Justin adds that he himself expects to fall a victim to the malice of Crescens, whom he had publicly shown to be an ignorant demagogue (3). He then briefly discusses two more popular objections brought against the Christians. They were asked why, if they were so willing to die, they did not kill themselves. Justin replies (4), that God made the world for man, and is pleased with those who do the things which are like Himself. To kill themselves would be, so far as they were concerned, to end the race and prevent the spread of the divine doctrines. At the same time, when examined, they confess because it is wicked not to tell the truth. They were asked, also, why their God did not protect them. To this Justin replies (5) by declaring that God placed the world in charge of angels, but that some of these fell, and that to them and their offspring, the demons, are the evils endured by good men due. In contrast to these demons whom the wicked serve, he sets forth the one ineffable God whom the Christians worship, and His begotten Logos who became man to deliver men from the demons (6). Having determined to save men through Christ, God spares the world for the sake of the Christians (7). Men, too, are responsible for their treatment of the truth, and hence God allows opportunity for repentance before the final judgment comes. In all ages those who followed Reason have been persecuted by the demons (8). What wonder, then, if Christians are? But the time of judgment will come (9). Justin therefore repeats his favorite idea (10), that Christianity is superior to all other teaching, because it reveals the whole Logos (or Reason) of God. Others have known Him in part, but now He is completely manifested, and with such power over men as to demonstrate His claims. People should remember (11) that vice may easily simulate the appearance of virtue, but that on really obeying and suffering for virtue does the future reward depend. In fact (12), the way Christians regard death is a crowning proof of the truth of their religion and of the falsity of the slanders reported about them. "I am a Christian," he concludes (13); "and I find in Christianity nothing hostile to Plato, but only the completion of that which Plato and other philosophers taught." Justin then (14) prays that his book may be authorized. He distinguishes himself from the Simonians, with whom he was afraid that he as a Samaritan might be confused, and remarks with no little sarcasm that his writings were at least not so injurious to the public morals as some others which were authorized and popular.

It is clear that this supplement to Justin's Apology was called out by a special occasion. It attempts no
Its character. elaborate proof of Christianity, but deals with two popular sneers cast at the Christians. It is far more passionate than the longer Apology. It breathes a pathetic and indignant sense of injustice, and utters a conviction of the truth so intense as to be willing to face popular hatred without flinching and even death with indifference.

When now we turn to the Dialogue with Trypho, we find ourselves in a quite different atmosphere from that
Analysis of the Dialogue with Trypho. of the Apologies. The book is a recital, addressed to a certain Marcus Pompeius,[1] of a debate which Justin says he had had with the Jew Trypho and some of Trypho's friends. He met them while walking in the xystus [2] of a certain city which Eusebius says was Ephesus.[3] Saluted by Trypho as a philosopher, and asked for his opinions, Justin refers the Jew to the prophets of his own nation, and is led to relate, as we have already described, the story of his conversion to Christianity, and his subsequent delight in the prophets as inspired teachers of truth. He declares that Christianity is the true philosophy, and points Trypho to Jesus as the Messiah whom the proph-

[1] Cf. cc. 8, 141.
[2] Or covered colonnade in a gymnasium.
[3] H. E. iv. 18. Weizsäcker (Jahrb. für deutsche Theol., xii. 1, pp. 60–119) thinks it was Corinth.

ets foretold. This leads to the discussion, which is conducted on the part of Justin with great elaboration, with many repetitions and quotations from and explanations of the Old Testament, and on the part of Trypho at first with amusement, sometimes with earnestness, but generally with a rather too docile spirit to increase our confidence in the historical character of the narrative. The work is much longer than even the large Apology; and yet, in the judgment of some scholars, portions of it have been lost.[1] The debate appears to have lasted at least two days.[2] How far the dialogue actually occurred, is a difficult question to answer. Perhaps it did take place, but the recital of it was afterwards elaborated by Justin. Fortunately, however, this is a matter of small consequence, since our interest in the work consists entirely in the view of Christianity and its circumstances expressed by the author.

While the progress of the argument is often interrupted, while tedious repetitions occur and no careful plan is laid down for the debate, it is yet possible to recognize in the Dialogue three principal topics.

The first (9–31) concerns the Mosaic ordinances, which Trypho represents as perpetually and universally binding. The Jew does not indeed credit the infamous reports about the Christians, and has read and admired the "precepts in the so-called Gospel," but thinks nevertheless that Justin might better have remained a disciple of Plato than have believed in Jesus, and urges him to obey the ritual law. Thereupon Justin declares that the prophets themselves predicted a new law and covenant which have been revealed in Jesus. He contends that the Old Testament itself required men to

[1] Cf. Otto's note 7 on c. 74, and note 9 on c. 105.
[2] Cf. c. 85.

keep the eternal, moral decrees rather than the ceremonial. The latter, he says, were given to the Jews because of that nation's persistent disposition to sin. God thus sought to remind them of Himself, or else, as in the case of circumcision, to mark them out for punishment. Justin appeals to the example of the patriarchs for proof that righteousness does not consist in these observances. The true fast is abstinence from evil (15); the true circumcision is that of the heart (24); the true Sabbath is repentance and obedience (12). Such rites are useless to those who have been witnessed to by God and have been baptized with the Holy Ghost. Christians have learned the true righteousness from Christ (28), who has power now to deliver them from the evil demons (30), and of whose greater power at his second advent Daniel the prophet spake (31).

The last remark turns the discussion to the nature of Christ as taught by the Hebrew prophets, and to the proofs of the Messiahship of Jesus; and this subject, with several digressions, occupies the larger part of the Dialogue (32–129). When Trypho objects to the humble lot of Jesus, Justin shows that the prophets foretold two advents, — one of humiliation and the other of glory (32–34). He shows also that Christ is called by the prophets God and Lord as well as Jacob (36–38). He points out various types of Christ and Christianity (40–42),[1] and infers from them that the law was to have

[1] He mentions as types the paschal lamb; the goats of the day of atonement; the offering of fine flour, which, he says, prefigured the Eucharist; circumcision, which typified spiritual circumcision wrought in believers by Him who rose from the dead on *the eighth day;* the bells on the high-priest's robe, which, he says (incorrectly, cf. Exod. xxviii. 33), were twelve in number, and typified the Apostles.

IMPORTANCE OF JUSTIN'S TESTIMONY. 41

an end in Christ, who was, in accordance with prophecy, born of a virgin (43), and whom all must believe and obey in order to be saved (44). After a digression (45–47) in which the salvability of those who lived in pre-Mosaic times and of Jewish Christians is maintained, Trypho declares it absurd to believe that one who existed as God should be born a man, and contends also that Elias was to precede the Christ. Thereupon Justin — having put in the caution that even if the divine pre-existence of Jesus be not proved, still his Messiahship may be held — explains the mission of John the Baptist, adding, however, that before the second advent Elias will appear in person (48-51). He adduces also Jacob's prediction (Gen. xlix. 10–12) in proof of the two advents of Christ, and of the fact that Jesus is indeed the promised one (52–54). When, however, Trypho insists that he prove plainly from the Scriptures that the Christ is God, Justin undertakes to do so (55–62) by arguing that the Old Testament theophanies explain themselves, not as appearances of the divine Father, but of another person, called Angel and Lord and God and Beginning and Wisdom, who was subject to the Father and Maker of all things.[1]

The debate then turns to the Incarnation, which, including the birth from a virgin, was specially offensive to Trypho. Justin proves it (63–88) from the Psalms,[2] and still more particularly from Isaiah.[3] In doing so, he also defends the doctrine from the allegation of the Jew that it was on a par with the tales of mythology (67–70); maintains that the Jews had cut out certain

---

[1] He appeals also to the eighth chapter of Proverbs, and to the words of Gen. i. 26, "Let *us* make man."
[2] Ps. cx. 3, 4; xlv. 6–11; xcix. 1–7; lxxii.; xix. 1–6.
[3] Explaining Isa. xlii. 8; vii. 10–17; and viii. 4.

42   JUSTIN MARTYR.

important passages from the Scriptures which bore on the subject,[1] and adduces other passages to prove the

[1] Dial. 71–74. Justin says the following passages had been cut out: (1) "Esdras said to the people: This passover is our Saviour and our Refuge. And if ye have understood, and your heart has taken it in, that we are about to humble Him on a standard, then this place [Jerusalem] shall not be forsaken forever, said the God of Hosts. But if ye will not believe Him nor listen to His preaching, ye shall be a laughing-stock to the nations" (καὶ εἶπεν Ἔσδρας τῷ λαῷ· Τοῦτο τὸ πάσχα ὁ σωτὴρ ἡμῶν καὶ ἡ καταφυγὴ ἡμῶν. καὶ ἐὰν διανοηθῆτε καὶ ἀνεβῇ ὑμῶν ἐπὶ τὴν καρδίαν, ὅτι μέλλομεν αὐτὸν ταπεινοῦν ἐν σημείῳ καὶ μετὰ ταῦτα ἐλπίσωμεν ἐπ' αὐτόν, οὐ μὴ ἐρημωθῇ ὁ τόπος οὗτος εἰς τὸν ἅπαντα χρόνον, λέγει ὁ θεὸς τῶν δυνάμεων· ἐὰν δὲ μὴ πιστεύσητε αὐτῷ μηδὲ εἰσακούσητε τοῦ κηρύγματος αὐτοῦ, ἔσεσθε ἐπίχαρμα τοῖς ἔθνεσι). This passage is also quoted, with slight verbal differences, by Lactantius (Instt. Div. iv. 18). Its source is not known, but it reads like a Christian interpolation attributed to Ezra. (2) "And from the things spoken by Jeremiah, they cut out the following: I [was] as a [harmless] lamb led to be slaughtered. They devised a device against me, saying, Come, let us lay wood to [for] his bread, and let us blot him out from the land of the living, and his name shall be remembered no more (Δεῦτε, ἐμβάλωμεν ξύλον εἰς τὸν ἄρτον αὐτοῦ καὶ ἐκτρίψωμεν αὐτὸν ἐκ γῆς ζώντων καὶ τὸ ὄνομα αὐτοῦ οὐ μὴ μνησθῇ οὐκέτι). And since this passage from the words of Jeremiah is still written in some copies in the synagogues of the Jews (for it is only a short time since they were cut out), and since from these words it is shown that the Jews deliberated concerning the Christ Himself, plotting to crucify and slay Him, He is himself declared to be, as was also prophesied by Isaiah, led as a sheep to the slaughter, and is here represented as a harmless lamb; and so, being in a difficulty about it, they [the Jews] gave themselves to blasphemy [i. e., by cutting the passage out]." This passage, however, is still found in all our manuscripts of Jeremiah xi. 19. (3) "And from the words of the same Jeremiah, they likewise cut out the following: The holy [so Otto, reading ἅγιος for the ἀπὸ of the manuscripts] Lord God of Israel remembered His dead who lay asleep in the grave, and descended to them to preach to them His salvation." This passage is quoted by Irenæus (adv. Hær. iii. 20. 4) as from Isaiah, and again (iv. 22. 1) as from Jeremiah, and elsewhere (iv.

divinity of Christ as well as His incarnation.[1] He then brings forward predictions and types of the crucifixion and its attendant events (89–105), of the resurrection, the call of the Gentiles, and the conversion of the world (106–118). In fact, the Christians, not the Jews, are, according to the Old Testament itself, the holy people promised to the patriarchs (119, 120); and the conversion of the Gentiles is a crowning proof, by its fulfilment of prophecy, that Jesus is the Christ (121, 122). It was Christ and the Christians of whom the prophets spake as Israel and sons of God (123–125); and the many names under which Christ is set forth in the Old Testament show his double nature. It was He who appeared to the patriarchs (127), — a second divine person begotten by the Father's will from His own substance (128) before all creation (129).

In the remainder of the Dialogue (130–142) Justin shows that other prophecies foretold the conversion of the Gentiles, and maintains that they are more faithful to God than the Jews ever were (131–133). The synagogue was typified in Leah, but the church in Rachel (134). The Christians, he repeats, are the true Israel,

---

33. 1, 12; v. 31. 1) without mention of the writer's name. It is found, however, in no ancient version of the prophets. (4) He states that the words "from the wood" (ἀπὸ τοῦ ξύλου) were taken away from Ps. xcv. (xcvi.) 10, which should therefore read, "Say among the heathen, The Lord reigned from the wood." So Justin quotes it in Ap. i. 41. The words which he claims were cut out are not found in any manuscript of the Psalm. They are quoted by Tertullian (adv. Marc. iii. 19, and adv. Jud. 10) and by later Fathers. These passages, at least, show the uncritical use of manuscripts of Scripture by the early writers, and the ease with which textual corruptions could be introduced. They show, also, the fact of textual variations in the manuscripts of the LXX. as well as of the New Testament.

[1] Cf. Dial. 75, 76, 83, 85–88.

while the Jews have rejected in Christ both God and the prophets (135, 136). He therefore exhorts his hearers to be converted, that they may be saved, like Noah, " by water, faith, and wood," and may inherit the promised possession ; for God will receive, as the prophets and Christ declared, all of any race who seek Him, while he that perishes does so through his own fault (137–140). Finally, that it might not be said that the crucifixion of Christ, having been thus predicted, was necessary, and that they who crucified Him were unable to act otherwise, he declares that God created men and angels free, and that repentance is open to all (141). With this the discussion closes. The Jews express their gratification with what they have heard, and Justin parts from them with the remark, " I can wish nothing better for you than that you, perceiving that by this way it is given to every man to be happy, may yourselves also in all respects agree with us that Jesus is the Christ of God."[1]

Such is a rapid survey of the course of thought in Justin's books. It should be added that in the Dialogue three important digressions occur, of which particular mention will be made in the following lectures. One of these (35) pertains to Christians who ate meat which had been offered to idols, — a practice which Justin strenuously repudiates as heretical and impious. The second pertains to the salvation of the ancient Jews and of Jewish Christians (45–47), — the latter of whom Justin admits will be saved if they do not compel Gentiles also to observe the law. Some, however, he adds, will not fellowship with them ; but he takes a more charitable view. The third digression (80, 81) pertains to the millennium. Justin expects a visible

---

[1] We have followed Otto's text, which happily emends the manuscript.

reign of Christ in Jerusalem for a thousand years, and quotes for it Rev. xx. 4, 5; but he admits that many good Christians believe otherwise. But without dwelling at present upon these points, it is sufficient to observe that as Justin himself lived in the very centre of the turmoil and conflict, the perils and the progress of early Christianity, so his writings, whatever we may think of the worth of his arguments, bear evidence to an earnest, thoughtful, and brave spirit that gives additional value to the testimony which he offers in them.

The importance of Justin's testimony to early Christianity we shall now be able to perceive. The external features of his life do of themselves make him a witness of the highest value. Travelling, as he seems to have done, to the great cities of the Empire; residing, as he certainly did during many years, in the capital itself, and thus at the principal focus of the literary and religious as well as of the social and political activity of his day, he was likely to know Christianity, not in its local peculiarities, but in its universal and essential features. His inquiring mind, his love of truth, his acquaintance with philosophy, — though, as we shall see, they affected injuriously his theology, — made him a trustworthy witness to the broader relations which Christianity was beginning to acquire; while his sturdy honesty and his hearty devotion to his religion assure us that his testimony is sincere, and that the power of the Gospel of which he wrote was a living reality to him. *The importance of Justin's testimony, because of his life and character,*

But besides this, the books of whose substance we have given an account evidently bear most directly upon the questions of special interest to us in the second century. As an Apologist, *and the nature of his writings.*

Justin throws light upon the civil and social relations of early Christianity. As the author of the Dialogue, he throws light on the mutual relations of Gentile and Jewish Christianity. As a philosopher, he illustrates the relation of Christianity to pagan thought, the influence of older systems upon the rising theology of the Church, and the dawning sense in the Church herself of the problems with which, as a world religion, Christianity would have to grapple. In the course of his writings, moreover, he quotes frequently from what he calls "the memoirs of the Apostles," or "Gospels," and thus becomes an important factor in the discussion of the canonicity and authenticity of our evangelical narratives. He describes, also, the ceremonies of the Christians, and thus testifies to the institutions of the early Church. Finally, his attitude toward the Apostles; his agreements with and differences from the teaching of the New Testament epistles; his claim to represent, not a section, but the majority of the Christian community, taken in connection with what has already been mentioned, make Justin a witness of the very first importance to the origin and character of early Catholic Christianity.

And such a witness has Justin been considered by all classes of critics. Not only do we find him referred to with honor, or quoted with approval, in the generations immediately succeeding his own;[1]

Estimate of Justin by the Church,

[1] Cf. Tatian ad Græc. 18 ("ὁ θαυμασιώτατος 'Ιουστῖνος") and 19 ("Crescens endeavored to inflict on Justin and, indeed, on me the punishment of death, . . . because, by proclaiming the truth, he [Justin] convicted the philosophers of being gluttons and cheats"). Tertullian (adv. Valent. 5), speaking of those who, being contemporary with the Gnostic heresiarchs, had refuted them, mentions, first, "Justin, philosopher and martyr." Irenæus (adv. Hær. iv. 6. 2) quotes from Justin's book against Marcion and (v.

IMPORTANCE OF JUSTIN'S TESTIMONY. 47

not only do we find Eusebius at a later date giving a careful account of the man and of his writings;[1] not only do we find his statements repeated, and his arguments used by his contemporaries and successors,[2] and his reputation as an orthodox father and a holy martyr cherished by all the later Church;[3] but modern criticism has, in a different spirit, found him a prominent factor in the solution of the problems of early Christianity. *and modern criticism.* Protestant writers were the first to assail the reputation of Justin, for the purpose of destroying the authority of the Church Fathers generally. They pointed out his errors, and declared his theology more Platonic than Christian, while the Roman Catholics defended him.[4] The Protestant attack acquired new vigor with the appearance of Semler's writings[5] in 1762; but it still followed the old lines of debate until Eichhorn[6] and Credner[7] brought the crit-

---

26. 2) from a writing of Justin's, the title of which is not given. Hippolytus (Refut. viii. 9) mentions Tatian as a disciple of Justin the Martyr.

[1] Cf. H. E. ii. 13; iii. 26; iv. 8, 9, 11, 12, 16–18; v. 28.

[2] Cf. Otto's Justini Opera, tom. i. pars ii. index iv. Also Harnack's Die Überleiferung, etc., pp. 130, etc.

[3] The post-Eusebian notices of Justin are scanty, and mostly taken from Eusebius or Irenæus, and show little or no acquaintance with Justin's writings. Photius depends on Eusebius in his account of Justin, except that he mentions three (spurious) writings of the Martyr which alone, of the so-called Justinian books named by him, he seems to have read. Cf. Harnack's Die Überlieferung, etc., p. 150.

[4] Cf. Von Engelhardt's Das Christenthum Justins, pp. 9, etc.

[5] Geschichte der Christlichen Glaubenslehren, in the Introduction to S. J. Baumgarten's Untersuchung theologischer Streitigkeiten.

[6] 1752–1827. His Einleitung in das N. T. called out, in America, Norton's Genuineness of the Gospels.

[7] Beiträge zur Einleit. in d. bibl. Schriften, 1832.

ical question of Justin's relation to our Gospels into the foreground. A little later, the Tübingen school of critics undertook to reconstruct early Christian history on a naturalistic basis, and forthwith the study of Justin took a wider range among scholars of all schools, and his entire relation to both the formation of the Canon and the development of the early Church came into consideration. For the present, it is sufficient to remark that the most opposite opinions about him have been held by modern critics. He has been called Ebionite,[1] and Pauline;[2] an Ebionite at bottom, overlaid with Paulinism;[3] a degenerate Paulinist;[4] a representative of a so-called free Petrine party,[5] or, as Hilgenfeld puts it,[6] of a Jewish-Christian or original-apostolic heathen Christianity; while Baur declared that Justin cannot be positively assigned to any of the early parties, but marks the transition from them to Catholicism.[7] While Credner considered Justin essentially Jewish-Christian, Von Engelhardt, his latest critic, considers him so essentially Gentile that his thought is declared to have been substantially pagan, though his language was colored and his heart won by Christianity. If the Tübingen school and their followers have labored to assign him to his proper place in their various schemes, others[8] have labored to show that he grew substantially

[1] Credner.   [2] Neander, Semisch, Weizsäcker.
[3] Schwegler.   [4] Ritschl, Overbeck.
[5] Credner, Geschichte des N. T. Can. 1860.
[6] Zeitschr. für wissensch. Theol., 1872. Most of the above classification has been taken from Von Engelhardt.
[7] Christianity of the First Three Centuries, Eng. trans., vol. i. p. 146.
[8] As Semisch, Dorner, Otto, and, more recently, Stählin, in reply to Von Engelhardt (Justin Martyr und sein neuester Vorurtheiler, Leipzig, 1880).

on the soil of the orthodox apostolic tradition. But, whatever the estimate of the man and his position, all agree that he is one of the most important witnesses for the times in which he lived, and the problems connected with them. "For the historical understanding of the second Christian century, he first of all forms the key;"[1] and the very diversity of opinion concerning him shows him to be still a fit subject for renewed examination.

Of course, in taking the testimony of one witness, we shall be careful not to consider him as representing more than we have reason to believe he really does represent. In confining ourselves to the testimony of Justin, we shall not expect to learn the whole story of his age. It is possible, however, to discover from him the chief forces which were operating in post-apostolic Christianity. His witness is a typical one. We shall not neglect, indeed, other testimony related to his; but with him as a guide, to glance at the external and internal conditions of the Christianity of the first half of the second century, at the dangers which threatened it, the influences which affected it, the foundation on which it claimed to rest, and the living power which it possessed, will be the object of the following lectures.

Plan of these lectures.

[1] Von Engelhardt's Das Christenthum Justins, p. 490.

LECTURE II.

THE TESTIMONY OF JUSTIN TO THE SOCIAL AND CIVIL RELATIONS OF EARLY CHRISTIANITY.

JUSTIN is best known, as we learned in the last lecture, as an apologist for Christianity to the Government and people of the Roman Empire in the reign *Justin as an* of Antoninus Pius. He may be regarded as *apologist.* in most particulars a representative apologist. Not only was he the first whose writings are extant, but he paved the way for those who followed him. While the defenders of Christianity in the second century often differed from one another in the positive exposition of their religion; while some fiercely denounced paganism in its philosophical no less than in its practical forms, and others, like Justin, took a kindlier view of previous human thought, — they were perfectly agreed in their defence of Christianity and in the exhibition and refutation of the charges brought against it.[1] From Justin, therefore, we may accurately learn the social and civil relations of the Christianity of his time. With great boldness of speech, with evidently deep conviction and trustworthy information, he pleaded the cause of the despised religion, met the slanders which were circulated against it, and demanded its toleration by the State. He addressed himself to both the magistrates and the people. He pleaded for Christianity both before the law and before

[1] Cf. Aubé's Saint Justin, pp. 276, etc.

the tribunal of popular opinion. His Apologies, therefore, exhibit both the civil and the social relations of Christianity in the middle of the second century; the attitude toward it of the Government and of the populace, and its attitude in turn toward both.

In the first place, Justin speaks of the diffusion of Christianity in strong though general terms. Christians were "men of every race."[1] They comprised representatives of both the educated and the ignorant classes.[2] They were "from all nations;"[3] and "all the earth," says our author, "has been filled with the glory and grace of God and of His Christ."[4] The sacrifice of thanksgiving was offered in the Eucharist "in all places throughout the world;" for, he adds, "there is not one single race of men, whether barbarians or Greeks, or whatever they may be called,— nomads or wanderers or herdsmen living in tents,[5]— among whom prayers and giving of thanks are not made to the Father and Maker of the universe through the name of the crucified Jesus." Such language of course tells nothing as to the actual numerical strength of the Christians, and is not perhaps to be taken too literally.[6] Even in much earlier

The diffusion of Christianity.

---

[1] Ap. i. 1, 25, 32, 40, 53, 56.   [2] Ap. ii. 10.
[3] Dial. 52, 91, 121.   [4] Dial. 42.

[5] Dial. 117. ἢ ἁμαξοβίων ἢ ἀοίκων καλουμένων ἢ ἐν σκηναῖς κτηνοτρόφων οἰκούντων. Otto, in his note, says that Scythians are called ἁμαξόβιοι in Horat. Od. iii. 24. 10; Plin. H. N. iv. 12. 25; Justin. Hist. ii. 2; that nomads, such as lived in India (Plin. vi. 17. 20), Ethiopia (vi. 30. 35), and Numidia (v. 3), are called ἄοικοι; and that ἐν σκηναῖς κτηνοτρόφοι οἰκοῦντες are especially the tent-using tribes of Arabia (Plin. v. 24. 21; Jul. Solin. Polyhistor. 33; Genesis iv. 20). The terms thus show how broadly Justin meant to speak.

[6] Yet cf. the Epitaph of Abercius, quoted in Lightfoot's Ignatius, i. 480.

times similar expressions had occasionally been used.[1] But the frequent employment of such language by Justin does indicate in the Christians of his time the sense of growing strength, the consciousness of being an aggressive power which had already diffused itself through all classes of society and had representatives in all known nations. Such language could not have been used, if Christianity were not proving its adaptation generally to the various races within and beyond the Empire. It is impossible to express the result by figures; but the fact of a diffusion, at even this early period, wide enough to demonstrate the universal fitness and to promise the universal triumph of Christianity, may certainly be assumed.

Not only, however, does Justin represent Christianity as widely diffused, but he also represents the Christian communities as forming a collection of close associations, the members of which were bound together by what seemed to them the strongest bonds. It is true that Justin does not testify to any organization of these separate communities into provincial or imperial leagues. He says nothing of the relation of one "church" to another; and we shall hereafter[2] infer from his language that the Christian communities were bound together only by their common faith and mutual sympathy. We do not find in him any allusion to a universal church externally organized into one association, but only to a now universal faith professed by separate communities in all parts of the known world. Negative evidence is of course less weighty than positive; but inasmuch as in this particular Justin coincides with other writers of his day, it may be so far considered trustworthy. The moral

The Christian societies.

[1] Col. i. 6, 23; Ign. ad Eph. 3.   [2] Lect. VI.

and spiritual unity of Christendom was to our Apologist very real, but he gives no indication that it was expressed in external organization.[1]

But at the same time Justin distinguishes sharply between heretical Christians and those who, as he claims, held to the true and apostolic doctrine. To him the heretics were not Christians at all,[2] though popularly so called; and the division between them and the local communities which in Justin's view were orthodox[3] was evidently severely drawn. These latter are represented by our Apologist as associations the members of which were very closely united. They practically held their possessions in common;[4] were "always together;"[5] assembled weekly for stated worship[5] and assisted one another in time of need.[5] So far, indeed, as dress and outward manners were concerned, they lived like other people;[6] but they had their officers and meeting-places and ceremonies,[7] and thus formed in the strictest sense a brotherhood. Thus Christianity was not merely the diffusion of new truth or the progress of a new idea, but was also the spread of a new society. It was the establishment of churches which gave to the new faith local habitation and organized power; and as such, its relations to the law and to popular sentiment were necessarily different from what they would have been if it had only spread as a new opinion from one individual to another.

Now, Christianity, thus locally organized and widely diffused, is represented as encountering the intense enmity of the Roman world; and the principal causes

---

[1] Cf. Lect. VI.
[2] Ap. i. 4, 26; Dial. 35, 82.
[3] Ὀρθογνώμονες. Dial. 80.
[4] Ap. i. 14, 67.
[5] Ap. i. 67.
[6] Dial. 10.
[7] Ap. i. 61–67.

of this enmity are explicitly stated by Justin. He complains that the Christians were "unjustly hated and abused,"[1] and that report charged them with the utmost "impiety and wickedness."[2] It was alleged that in their secret assemblies hideous crimes were committed, — that human victims were sacrificed and their blood drunk by the worshippers, and that this impious banquet was followed by indulgence in hideous and lustful orgies.[3] Such charges were manifestly born of the impure heart of paganism itself. They indicate, however, the suspicion and hatred with which the Christians were regarded. Justin complains[4] that the charge of being a Christian was often used as a means of gratifying private malice; and these infamous reports were evidently invented by an enmity which itself rested on deeper reasons, and found in such slanders an easy means of increasing the popular prejudice.

Hostility toward the Christians.

He mentions, however, three charges in particular which were commonly made against the Christians.[5] The first was that of atheism,[6] — a charge which was made from the beginning and so long as paganism remained the ruling power of the State. It sounds strangely enough in an age when the gods were denied by philosophers, ridiculed by popular writers and neglected by the people; and it was probably little more than a battle-cry against the hated sect. It meant, of course, that the Christians denied the gods of the State, and thus it involved a charge of want of patriotism as well as want of piety. It was an effective cry by which occasionally

Particular charges made against them: (1) Atheism.

---

[1] Ap. i. 1.　　　　　　　[2] Ap. i. 2, 3.
[3] Ap. ii. 12; i. 26; Dial. 10.　[4] Ap. ii. 1, 2.
[5] Ap. i. 6–12.　　　　　[6] Ap. i. 6.

to kindle the fury of the mob or excuse oppression; and the Christians could only meet it by showing the folly of worshipping gods who were made by men and in which few of their professed votaries really believed, and by declaring the deeper sense in which they were anything but atheists.[1] The second charge was, as Justin puts it, that "some Christians have been arrested and convicted as evildoers."[2] (2) Wickedness. To this the Apologist replies, that as there are various kinds of philosophers, so are there various nominal Christians, and that all should not be condemned because of the wrongs committed by some who bear the name. He demands that every accused person be examined, not as to the name he bears, but as to the life he has led, being apparently confident that no orthodox Christian will be found guilty of wrong-doing. The third charge was that of disloyalty to the Government.[3] (3) Disloyalty. It was apparently justified by what the Christians said of their King and his future kingdom; but it was doubtless confirmed in popular opinion by their refusal to worship the emperor, and their denial of the gods with whose recognition political duties were often involved in the ancient world, as well as by the appearance of Christianity as a widely diffused secret society. In vain did the Christians reply that they obeyed the laws, prayed for the emperor, paid their taxes, and often fought in the army.[4] In vain did Justin argue[5] that the principles of Christianity would make good citizens of all men. The suspicion of the growing society remained; and when to the charges of atheism and licentiousness that of disloyalty was added, it is evident that the popular

[1] Ap. i. 6, 9, 10.   [2] Ap. i. 7.   [3] Ap. i. 11.
[4] Ap. i. 17; cf. Tert. Apol. 42, etc.   [5] Ap. i. 12.

prejudice against Christianity was such as to be ever liable to break out into acts of open violence.

And quite as significant as these formal charges against Christianity was the popular impatience with it to which Justin likewise bears witness. It was felt by individuals who knew its real purity to be a rebuke to society.[1] The willingness of its confessors to die rather than deny it was in the eyes of even a Stoic like Marcus Aurelius a piece of senseless obstinacy with which neither the rabble nor the philosophers had any sympathy.[2] Neither could paganism understand why the Almighty God whom the Christians confessed did not protect His worshippers.[3] Their very sufferings seemed to disprove their religion. The ability to punish them seemed to their enemies a quick and decisive settlement of the whole question in debate. With such demented people society in general had little patience; while, as we have seen, the Christian communities appeared in several ways dangerous to the public welfare. The Jews in particular led the Gentiles in hatred and ridicule of the new sect,[4] and spread abroad the worst misrepresentations of it.[5] Despite the progress which Christianity was making; despite the fear with which the name of Christ, as the name of a mighty spirit, was sometimes invoked by the superstitious;[6] despite the recognition, given here and there even by unbelievers, of the moral grandeur of Christ's teaching and

[1] Ap. ii. 2.
[2] Ap. ii. 4. Marcus Aurelius (Med. xi. 3) called it $\psi\iota\lambda\dot{\eta}\nu$ $\pi\alpha\rho\alpha\tau\acute{\alpha}\xi\iota\nu$, — mere ambition.
[3] Ap. ii. 5.
[4] Dial. 6, 117, etc.; cf. Lucian's De morte Perigrini.
[5] Dial. 17.
[6] Dial. 121, 131.

the moral enthusiasm of his followers,[1] — the Christians were looked upon in Justin's time by the mass of their fellow-citizens with either haughty contempt or blind, impatient hatred.

Such was the disposition of pagan society toward Christianity; and we may remark that Justin's description is precisely that which from the testimony of the preceding and following periods we should expect to hear. Even in the New Testament, though the sentiment of the pagan world toward Christianity there comes but little into notice, we can recognize the substance of the charges which Justin mentions already beginning to appear. The Jews in Thessalonica accused the Christians before the magistrates of "doing contrary to the decrees of Cæsar, saying that there is another King, one Jesus;"[2] the rabble at Ephesus cried out against the injury done by Paul and his companions to their patron goddess Diana;[3] and Peter warned his readers[4] of the reproach and suffering which was impending over them as Christians at the hands of the Gentile world. When, then, Christianity, at last distinct from Judaism, appears on the pages of secular or ecclesiastical history, the hostility against it is found to have followed the same lines, though with increasing force. Nero made the Christians the scapegoats of his crime because they were, as Tacitus informs us,[5] "convicted of hatred of the human race" and "detested for their crimes;" while Suetonius,[6] speaking of the same period, calls their religion a "new and mischievous superstition." Domitian put to death Flavius Clemens

Justin's description confirmed by other evidence.

[1] Dial. 10; cf. Ep. to Diog. 1.
[2] Acts xvii. 7.
[3] Acts xix. 23, 39.
[4] 1 Pet. iv. 12–17.
[5] Ann. xv. 44.
[6] Nero, 16.

and banished Domitilla, the wife of Clemens, on the charge of "atheism;"[1] and Clement of Rome, about the same time,[2] testifies that he and his fellow-Christians were "hated wrongfully," while in his prayer for rulers[3] he proves how law-abiding and loyal they really were. Pliny in his letter to Trajan, though inclined to judge the Christians leniently, nevertheless betrays the temper of the age when he affirms that whatever their character, they deserved punishment on account of their obstinacy;[4] while the silence concerning Christianity on the part of such writers as Plutarch and Dio Chrysostom, who had so much in common with it and who could scarcely have been ignorant of it, shows with what contempt it must have been regarded by the cultured as well as by the popular paganism of their day. And when, on the other hand, we turn to the writers subsequent to Justin, we find the same hatred which he describes and the same charges which he refutes described and refuted with even more elaboration, as for example in the Supplicatio of Athenagoras, the Apology of Tertullian, and the Octavius of Minucius Felix. His description of the popular enmity toward the Christians is, therefore, the common testimony of the whole century to which he belonged. Society was suspicious of the political aims of the Christians. The dying embers of religious zeal were kindled into fresh outbursts of flame by the Christian's practical contempt for the old gods, — a flame which the sceptical philosophy had been too theoretical to kindle. Individual hatred of goodness, the traditional enmity of the Jews, the love of the rabble

---

[1] Dion. Cass. lxvii. 44; Sueton. Domit. 15. That Flavius Clemens and Domitilla were Christians, cf. Lightfoot's Commentary on Philippians, pp. 22, 23, and on Clement, of Rome, pp. 257, etc.
[2] Ad Cor. i. 60.   [3] Ibid., 60, 61.   [4] Cf. below.

for cruelty, the ill-will or fanaticism of magistrates, the terror caused by national calamities, combined in various proportions to impute infamous deeds to these quiet, isolated people, and to make them the objects of unreasonable hatred to the mass of their fellow-men.

As we consider this social prejudice of the Roman world against the followers of Christ, two observations may be made in explanation of it. Manifestly the main charge against them, the charge which caught most quickly the ear of the populace, was a political one. The charge of "atheism" was itself a political charge. Religion and politics were formally united in the pagan world. Religion was chiefly supported by political considerations, and this not only because of the deliberate policy of statesmen, but because of the political fears and superstitions of the people. The habits of the Christians lent plausibility to the charge. Their refusal to sacrifice was naturally interpreted as disloyalty. Their necessary separation from much of the daily life and from many of the pleasures of their fellow-citizens, because these involved in countless little ways a recognition of the gods, added to the charge of disloyalty the impression that they were at war with society itself. They were thus inevitably objects of dislike. The slanders invented against them were but the expression of the feeling that whatever was unhuman belonged to the Christians, and in any popular outbreak they were the natural victims selected to gratify the anger or satisfy the terror of the mob. And hence it is equally manifest that this political and social antipathy was ultimately due to the radical difference in character between pagan and Christian life. The former could not understand the latter.

Explanation of this popular hostility.

The Christians unpatriotic.

Immorality could not but hate morality; and there was a profound truth expressed by Justin in a crude way, when he attributed persecution to the rage of the demons. Besides this, a society to which this world was the only real place of happiness, and force the only real divinity, and religion only a political safeguard, and ethics only a public law founded on expediency, could not understand the Christian's sense of immediate responsibility to God and practical hope of a future life. Pride of race and the spirit of conquest could not understand universal love and the spirit of self-sacrifice. Even pagan culture had been too much accustomed to regard itself as the privilege of a select few to understand a philosophy of artisans and slaves, of women and children; and had too often bowed in the temples of the gods whom it denied to understand the firm refusal of the Christians to live at the cost of a lie. We see, therefore, in the antagonism of pagan society toward Christianity, the clash of natural foes, the inevitable repulsion of fundamentally opposed moral forces; and the vulgar hatred and slanders, the outbursts of violence, the vengeance of private malice, as well as the contempt of the cultured classes, were but the results, as Justin himself felt and said, of an hostility too deep and radical to be due to any causes save those which determined the very foundations of character. To the historian, no less than to the theologian, must the explanation lie in the necessary antipathy of the ideals, standards, and principles of the old world to those of the new.

The enmity of the new and the old ideas inevitable.

All this popular prejudice, however, might have availed little, if it had not been for the fact that in the eyes of Roman law Christianity was, almost of necessity, illegal. The attitude

Attitude of the Roman Government.

toward the new religion of the Roman Government in general, and particularly that of Trajan, Hadrian, and the Antonines, has long been a matter of dispute. Let us first examine on this point the testimony of Justin, and compare it with other known facts of history.

Justin complains that the Christians were condemned merely for a name,[1] and that no investigation was held as to their moral character or conduct.[2] The simple denial of Christianity was sufficient to secure the release of the accused.[3] He relates[4] that the prefect Urbicus put to death three persons on this ground alone, and shows that in the enforcement of the law much depended on the caprice of the magistrate. Finally, he appends to his larger Apology a letter written about twenty-five years before[5] by Hadrian to Minucius Fundanus, a proconsul of Asia, which Justin seems to have considered favorable to at least fair treatment of the Christians. Of this letter I shall speak in a moment. For the present it should be observed that, according to Justin's own testimony, Christianity was illegal. It was itself a crime in the eyes of the law. While individual magistrates may have acted arbitrarily in their proceedings, such action as Justin describes could not have occurred, if at least the letter of the law had not proscribed the professors of the new religion. *Christianity illegal.*

At the same time Justin does not complain of any formal, governmental persecution. To the fact of outrages he bears explicit testimony, but not to a systematic war against the Christians, directed from headquarters. He rather complains that the Imperial rulers did not ac- *No formal persecution, but frequent outrages practised.*

[1] Ap. i. 4.   [2] Ap. i. 2, 7.
[3] Ap. i. 8.   [4] Ap. ii. 2.
[5] Cf. Lightfoot's Ignatius, i. 460.

tively interfere to prevent such outrages.¹ He certainly writes as if these latter were not infrequent;² but the example of them which he adduces in his smaller Apology³ illustrates merely the way in which private malice was sometimes the cause of persecution, while he lays the blame more on magistrates like Urbicus⁴ than on the Imperial rulers themselves. He declares, indeed,⁵ that "children or weak women" had been tortured to procure evidence against the Christians; but this may have been no more than the work of occasional fanaticism; nor does Justin speak as if such cruelties had recently occurred,⁶ and he intimates in one place⁷ that the Government prevented the hatred of the Jews from venting itself as it would otherwise do. The scope of his testimony, in short, is to represent persecutions as outbursts of popular or individual anger, permitted or abetted by magistrates, and rendered possible by the existing laws. Of any organized or systematic persecution he does not speak.

How far Justin's complaint justified by other evidence.
The question therefore arises, how far this representation of the state of the case is confirmed by other evidence.

Hadrian's letter.
If we examine the letter of Hadrian which Justin appended to his Apology, and which in the Latin form preserved by Rufinus in his translation of Eusebius⁸ may reasonably be considered genuine,⁹ we find that it was directed merely against

---

¹ Ap. i. 2.

² Ap. i. 4, 57. He speaks of "unutterable cruelties, death and torments" (Dial. 18; cf. too 110).

³ Ap. ii. 2.   ⁴ Ap. ii. 1.   ⁵ Ap. ii. 12.

⁶ Pliny (Letter to Trajan) says that he tortured two women to learn from them the truth about the Christians.

⁷ Dial. 16.   ⁸ H. E. iv. 10.

⁹ Cf. Lightfoot's Ignatius, i. 460, etc., where the history of opin-

assaults upon the Christians made without observance of the forms of law. Hadrian allows process against them, if there be a regular prosecutor. He prohibits his officers from yielding to the cries of the mob, and further directs that false accusers shall be themselves severely punished; but he assumes that Christianity may be itself a punishable offence. The letter was, in a certain measure, favorable to the Christians. It protected them from mob-violence and brutal assault, and it evinced a disposition on the part of the emperor not to encourage persecution, but rather to restrain it. Still, the sentence, "If any one make an accusation, and prove that the said men do anything contrary to the laws, you shall adjudge punishments in proportion to the desert of the offences," left the existing laws unchanged, and shows that the emperor intended to follow the already established usage.

Light is thrown on that usage by the earlier correspondence of Trajan and Pliny. Pliny the Younger was proprætor of Pontus and Bithynia, and wrote his famous letter to Trajan in A. D. 112.[1] In it he expresses his ignorance of how far it was customary for the Government to punish or seek out the Christians. He had hesitated as to whether the age of the accused should affect his sentence; whether the name of Christian was to be itself punished, or only the offences that might be added to the name. As it was, he had asked the accused if they were Christians. When they confessed, he had asked a second and a

Correspondence of Trajan and Pliny.

ion concerning the letter, and the argument for its genuineness, is briefly but satisfactorily given.

[1] Cf. Lightfoot's Ignatius, i. 532, note, where an account is given of Mommsen's investigations, based on the recent discovery of an inscription, by which the date of the correspondence is accurately fixed.

third time, threatening them with punishment. When they persisted, he had ordered them to execution, not doubting that, whatever their belief might be, their obstinacy deserved punishment. Those of them, however, who were Roman citizens he had ordered to be sent to the capital. But this treatment of the matter had only shown him the difficulties of his position. Various classes of accused persons came before him. Many were anonymously accused. Those who denied Christianity, and called on the gods, and adored the image of the emperor, and cursed Christ,— which, Pliny adds, he had been told no true Christian would do,— he had dismissed. Others confessed that they had been Christians, but had ceased to be so; yet these assured the governor of the innocuous character of the Christian doctrines and habits, and that the Christians had even abandoned their practice of celebrating an evening meal[1] together, in obedience to the emperor's prohibition of clubs. Pliny, in short, found Christianity to be merely a "perverse, extravagant superstition."[2] He therefore, especially in view of the large number of Christians in his province, consulted the emperor as to what course he should pursue. It seemed to him possible to correct this superstition, if severity were tempered with mildness. Already, he declares, had his action revived the worship in the temples. In reply, Trajan commended Pliny's action. He directed that Christians should not be sought after, but that, when accused, they should be punished unless they denied Christianity and adored the gods; in which case, even although suspected of having formerly been Christians, they should be set free. No anonymous accusations, however, should be received.

[1] The ἀγάπη.
[2] "Superstitionem pravam immodicam."

JUSTIN AND EARLY CHRISTIANITY. 65

It is evident from these letters that neither Trajan nor Pliny cared anything for Christianity in its religious aspects, and did not consider it as more than a transient phase of superstition. They had no wish to be religious persecutors. But they were determined to insist on the loyalty of all subjects of the Roman Empire. To them the first of all duties was obedience to the State; and it was wholly as a political matter that they viewed religion in general, and Christianity in particular. Trajan, moreover, had strongly enforced the earlier laws directed against secret associations or clubs. Only such associations as had been specifically authorized were permitted. Such was the law passed as early as the times of Julius Cæsar,[1] to check the political influence of the clubs, which had been injurious to the State in the later days of the Republic; and the emperors found it necessary to watch the formation of such associations with jealous eyes. In a previous letter to Pliny, Trajan had refused to sanction even a small association which it was proposed to form in Nicomedia for the purpose of putting out fires. Under this prohibition of "hetæriæ" the Christian communities came as soon as Christianity was clearly separated from Judaism. As a religion, Christianity, unlike Judaism, was not recognized. It could not be, since it had no national or local habitation. It could only be viewed as a secret association; and De Rossi[2] has shown that at a later period the church was first recognized by the law as an authorized burial-club.

Determination of the Government to suppress unauthorized societies.

The Christian societies therefore illegal, and Christianity a crime.

[1] Cf. Mommsen's Hist. of Rome, iv. 601.

[2] Roma Sotterranea, i. 10, etc., cited by Lightfoot, Ignatius, i. 20, note 2.

Hence, to Trajan and Pliny the Christian societies were illegal, and membership in them a crime. To the emperor and his propraetor there was but one test of loyalty to be applied to all subjects of the Empire. The latter must sacrifice to the gods of Rome, and adore the emperor's image. This requirement, it should be remembered, was simply a political one. The worship of the emperors was the one cult in which the Roman world was united, and was the universal symbol of political fealty. Refusal to render such homage was, to Pliny's mind, madness and invincible obstinacy. Whatever else they might believe, in this all loyal citizens would concur. In vain might the Christians protest that they were law-abiding citizens, that they prayed for the emperor, and discharged their civil duties. The worship of the emperor was part of the oath of allegiance; and these men, who were joined together in a secret, unauthorized association, and who refused to render the required homage to the majesty of the Empire, were of necessity proscribed and amenable to punishment, and all the more so in the eyes of those magistrates who were zealous for what they deemed the public welfare.

Trajan, therefore, is not to be considered, as has often been done, as having issued an edict against Christianity, or as having first legalized persecution.[1] There is nothing to show that such an edict was ever issued till the beginning of the third century.[2] He simply enforced already existing laws, under which Christianity was illegal, and had been treated as such. Nor was either he or Pliny solicitous to destroy Christianity

Position taken by Trajan.

---

[1] Cf. this subject discussed in Lightfoot's Ignatius, i. 7, etc.

[2] Cf. Gibbon's Decline and Fall, ch. xvi.; Aubé's Saint Justin, ch. i. of Introduction, p. 44.

as a religion. Both show a disposition to as much mildness as was, in their view, consistent with the peace and loyalty of the community; while at the same time both assume that the Christian societies were illegal, and that membership in them was a heinous offence.

With this, then, corresponds the letter of Hadrian to Minucius Fundanus. It is written in the same spirit as Trajan's to Pliny, and was clearly intended to continue the same policy. Consequently Justin could not properly plead Hadrian's letter as granting toleration to Christianity. *Force of Justin's appeal to Hadrian's letter.*

He could plead it against all acts of popular or private violence. He could plead also the spirit of mildness and conciliation which is manifest in it. It would seem, indeed, from his language,[1] that he thought it granted the very thing which he demanded; namely, the trial of Christians only for what was generally esteemed criminal. So he seems to have interpreted the direction of the letter that accusers should show that the Christians had done something *contrary to the laws*.[2] But since, as we have seen, the laws forbade membership in unauthorized societies, Justin's interpretation, if such were really meant by him, would not stand, and the law still left it possible for Christians to be punished "merely for a name." The Apologist could only appeal from the mild and just spirit of Hadrian to the still milder and juster spirit of Antoninus.

[1] Ap. i. 68. "Though from the letter of Hadrian we could demand that you order the judgment to be given as we have asked."

[2] Gieseler (Ch. Hist. i. 126, note 4) sees this interpretation of Hadrian's letter, imputed by the Christians to Antoninus in the spurious letter of the latter to the Commune of Asia, where Hadrian is quoted as forbidding molestation of the Christians, unless φαίνοιντό τι ἐπὶ τὴν ἡγεμονίαν Ῥωμαίων ἐγχειροῦντες.

But the condition of things described by Justin is precisely that which from these Imperial letters we should have expected to find. It is easy to see that being thus under the ban of the law without being specifically proscribed, Christians were likely to be variously treated in different places and at different times. The enforcement of the general law would naturally vary with the temper of officials and communities.

His description confirmed.

The evidence [1] goes to show that neither Trajan, Hadrian, nor Antoninus took any active part in the persecution of Christians, but sought rather to restrain all violent outbreaks, and acted consistently upon the lines laid down in the letter to Pliny which we have discussed. This had not been the case in the previous period. The two Roman persecutions of the first century of which we have any clear account were directed by Nero and Domitian themselves.[2] But with the accession of Trajan, and indeed of Nerva before him, a new class of princes occupied the throne of the Cæsars, — princes who were neither jealous nor tyrannical nor serious enough to persecute religion as such, and who were too just to countenance popular violence. While, therefore, during their reigns the Christian societies were unlawful, these emperors appear to have been more and more inclined to deal gently with the offenders, and to have insisted that their officers should only condemn such as were convicted by legal process. We are told by Melito [3]

The Government not a persecutor.

---

[1] See this collected by Lightfoot, Ignatius, i. 1–69, 460–529.

[2] For Nero's persecution, cf. Tac. Ann. xv. 44; Eus. H. E. ii. 25. For Domitian's, cf. Dio Cass. lxvii. 14, and Eus. H. E. iii. 17, 19, 20, who quotes Hegesippus and Tertullian. Cf. also Cl. Rom. ad Cor. i. 1.

[3] Eus. H. E. iv. 26.

that Antoninus "wrote to the cities forbidding any strange movements against us." "Among these," he adds, "were the ordinances to the Larissæans, to the Thessalonians and Athenians and all the Greeks."[1] By "strange movements" we are doubtless again to understand popular or irregular assaults. It would thus appear that the mild policy of the emperors continued. If Trajan, resolved though he was to put down illegal associations, and clearly though he recognized membership in a Christian society to be a crime, yet directed that Christians should only be condemned when accused by a responsible party and convicted in legal form, Hadrian still more emphatically laid down the same rule, even directing that false accusers should be severely punished; and Antoninus, who possessed a more amiable temper than either of his predecessors, rebuked, apparently on several occasions, the spirit of lawless persecution. We are certainly not to suppose that Christianity was regarded with any more respect for not being officially persecuted. We are to attribute the Imperial policy as much to indifference toward and contempt for the Christians as to the humanity of the reigning princes. If the letter of Hadrian to the Consul Servianus be genuine,[2] that emperor looked on at least the Christians of Egypt as merely one of the many varieties of fanatics which Alexandria contained,

[1] The letter to the Commune of Asia, one form of which is given by Eus. H. E. iv. 13, and another form appended in the manuscripts, together with the pretended letter of Marcus Aurelius to the Senate, to the larger Apology of Justin, is obviously spurious, whether it be attributed to Antoninus or to Aurelius. It is a eulogy of the Christians. Cf. Lightfoot's Ignatius, i. 465–469; Gieseler's Ch. Hist. i. 126, note 4; Neander's Ch. Hist. i. 104.

[2] Lightfoot (Ignatius, i. 464) seems inclined to accept its genuineness.

and as being as insincere as the rest. They all, he says, have one God; namely, money.[1] But whatever the cause, such was the policy of these emperors; and it is not till the reign of Marcus Aurelius that direct opposition to Christianity can be laid at the Imperial door. It is he, the most serious of all the emperors and the one most devoted to the Roman ideal of obedience to the State, to whom responsibility for active persecution of the Christians can first, after Domitian, be plausibly attached. Not only were the sufferings of the Christians in his reign greatly increased, but he himself, while still nominally acting on the principles of his predecessors, seems to have favored the active search for offenders which his officials instituted in Gaul and Asia;[2] while his expressions concerning the Christians,[3] and his decrees against what he considered "superstitions" and "new religions,"[4] plainly indicate the positive hatred which he must have felt toward the rising sect. His son Commodus, on the contrary, more than returned to the mild policy of his father's predecessors.

If, moreover, the evidence shows that under Trajan, Hadrian, and Antoninus the Imperial Government, while

---

[1] "Unus illis deus nummus est." Some read "nullus" for "nummus" (cf. Weiseler's Die Christenverfolgung der Cäsaren, p. 33); but the emperor's contempt is none the less plain. "Nummus," however, is generally accepted.

[2] For the persecution at Lyons and Vienne, cf. Eus. H. E. v. 1, 2. That new violence in persecution was begun in Asia by the Roman officials is attested by Melito (Eus. H. E. iv. 26), which Neander (Ch. Hist. i. 105) thinks could not have happened without the emperor's permission. Cf. also Lightfoot's Ignatius, i. 500, 510. The so-called letter of Aurelius to the Senate is a Christian fable (cf. Lightfoot's Ignatius, i. 469, etc.; Gieseler's Ch. Hist. i. 127, note 10).

[3] Meditat. xi. 3, quoted above.

[4] These are quoted in Lightfoot's Ignatius, i. 486.

JUSTIN AND EARLY CHRISTIANITY. 71

regarding Christianity as illegal, sought to restrain popular outbreaks, it also seems to show that under these emperors the actual sufferings of the Christians were, after all, not very severe. In conceiving of these, we should not take too literally the statements of later Christian writers, nor accept without critical examination the martyrologies, nor reckon to this early period the slaughters of the succeeding century. By the side of the evidence for persecution, we may place other facts which show that oftentimes the presence and activity of the Christians were practically tolerated. Thus Ignatius, on his journey to Rome, though a prisoner under guard, received deputations from the churches of Asia, and had apparently free intercourse with them. Lucian also, at a period but little later than the time of Justin's writings, describes the attentions paid by the Christians to their brethren in prison;[1] and Justin himself[2] speaks, as do other writers, of those in bonds as regular objects of the charity of the church. These facts certainly imply no great rigor of persecution, and quite accord with the spirit of the Imperial rescripts. Bishop Lightfoot[3] concludes, after a careful examination, that only one known martyrdom can be confidently ascribed to the reign of Hadrian, and, besides the Bithynian sufferers of whom Pliny informs us, we know of only two in the reign of Trajan.[4] Under Antoninus the number of

The sufferings of the Christians not as severe as at a later time.

---

[1] De morte Perigrini, 12. [2] Ap. i. 67.

[3] Ignatius and Polycarp, i. 486, etc. Under Hadrian, Telesphorus, Bishop of Rome, suffered; probably in A. D. 137 or 138. Iren. adv. Hær. iii. 3, 4.

[4] Symeon of Jerusalem (according to Hegesippus, in Eus. H. E. iii. 32) and Ignatius. This statement, however, is not to be understood as affirming that no other martyrdoms occurred, but only that they were fewer than has been supposed.

martyrs was larger. The letters of the emperor to the Greeks, to which Melito refers, imply that assaults upon the Christians had been renewed in violent forms; and from Dionysius of Corinth,[1] we hear of persecutions occurring about this time at Athens, in which Publius the bishop had been martyred. The death of Polycarp, of Smyrna, is also to be placed in 155 or 156, and therefore in the reign of Antoninus.[2]

With all this the testimony of Justin, as we have presented it, coincides; but it is not to be so interpreted as to hide the fact that the era of real persecution was but just beginning. Such, indeed, was Justin's own opinion. He expected persecution to wax worse and worse until Christ should return.[3] As things then were, the Christians had truly reason enough to complain. Suspected and hated by their fellow-men, they were liable to be made at any moment the victims of popular fury. Their societies being illegal, private malice could always procure their imprisonment or death. Proscribed by the law, the possibility of suffering "for a name" was always impending over them. Enough had already suffered to justify the Apologist's complaint and appeal. But the great conflict was only beginning. As at first Christians had been protected through being identified in Roman eyes with the Jews, so were they afterwards in some measure protected by the Providence which placed on the Imperial throne rulers too tolerant and just to permit popular hatred to express itself without the forms of law. Thus measurably shielded while suffi-

Persecution but just beginning.

[1] Eus. H. E. iv. 23.

[2] Cf. Lightfoot's Ignatius and Polycarp, i. 629, where Waddington's researches are given.

[3] Dial. 39, 110.

ciently disciplined by suffering, Christianity was enabled to prepare for the later struggle. In Justin's time the omens of the coming battle were beginning to appear. But it was not till the following century that the hand-to-hand conflict of Christianity and paganism — the former now strong in numbers and widely pervading society, and the latter upheld avowedly by emperors and Government — was in reality fought.

With, then, this view of the social and civil relations of early Christianity, we are ready to appreciate the defence of his religion which Justin offered to the rulers and people of the Empire. Let us observe his plea, estimate its force, and consider its implications. *Justin's defence of Christianity.*

Justin's Apology was manifestly in substance an appeal against that policy of the Government which, as we have seen, classed Christianity in the number of illicit societies. It is true that Justin did not say this formally, but it is implied in what he did say. He complained against the injustice of condemning men merely for a name. He insisted that each man should be tried on the ground of his moral character and conduct. He indignantly appealed to the equity of the rulers, and asked how they could permit such manifest tyranny. He interpreted Hadrian's letter as opposed to such treatment of guiltless men. In short, he appealed for liberty of opinion and worship, for the toleration of Christianity and its protection from violence. He demanded that it be placed on a level with other worships and beliefs which were allowed by the authorities. If it be asked why he did not couch his demand in legal terms, the reply may be made that Justin was not a lawyer, and that he was going to offer a deeper reason *He appealed substantially for legal recognition of the Christian societies.*

for the toleration of Christianity than could be given by any merely legal argument.

On what grounds, then, did Justin base his demand for toleration? He could not show that Christianity was entitled to recognition as a national form of worship; for such it was not, least of all in Justin's mind. It knew no locality for its home, no nation for its special possessor. On what ground, then, could its apologist plead for toleration, and the Christian societies for liberty of worship? Justin was led by the bent of his own mind, and perhaps by a shrewd appreciation of the real force of the plea, to appeal for toleration on what, under the circumstances, were the strongest grounds which he could have taken. He presented Christianity as a philosophy, and joined therewith a description of the moral purity of the Christians and the innocence and simplicity of their worship. The first of these pleas constituted his real, positive argument for toleration. The second was meant to remove suspicion and give force to the first. Christianity was a philosophy. Why, then, should it be persecuted? Why should liberty of thought be curtailed?

On the ground that Christianity was philosophy.

That such was actually Justin's plea will appear from his language. Though it is in the Dialogue that he formally declares Christianity to be the true philosophy,[1] yet this idea moulds the Apologies and forms their fundamental thought. He appeals to the rulers, as philosophers, to be governed by reason rather than custom in their treatment of the Christians.[2] He declares that Christ is the incarnate Reason of God, who had formerly enlightened Socrates and others, and whom the evil demons had always opposed.[3] He

---

[1] Dial. 8. [2] Ap. i. 2, 3. [3] Ap. i. 5.

JUSTIN AND EARLY CHRISTIANITY. 75

compares the differences among Christians to those among philosophers, who, however, are not indiscriminately condemned.[1] He dwells on the reasonableness of the Christian worship of God[2] in contrast to the follies of idol-worship, and explains the non-political character of his aims and hopes.[3] He exhibits the ethical teaching of Christ,[4] frequently shows that the Christian doctrines were such as in whole or in part had been taught by honored philosophic teachers or schools,[5] and even points out resemblances between the facts of Christ's life and the fables of mythology.[6] He reminds his readers of the varieties of heathenism itself,[7] and endeavors to give a rational explanation of the world's hatred of the Christians by attributing it to the hostility which in all ages the evil spirits had aroused against truth and goodness.[8] For the same purpose he enters at length upon the proof of Christianity from prophecy.[9] This may seem a method of proof little likely to have affected his pagan readers, yet it was not so ineffective as we would suppose. It would at least impress them as convincing, if true. We know that the Stoics attributed great value to prophecy;[10] while the frequent use of this method of proof by the early Apologists generally certainly implies that it appealed strongly not only to their own minds but to the mind of their age. In fine, Justin represents Christianity[11] as the complete manifestation of Reason, accredited as such by its fulfilment of prophecy. He

[1] Ap. i. 7.
[2] Ap. i. 10, 13.
[3] Ap. i. 11.
[4] Ap. i. 15–17.
[5] Ap. i. 6, 8, 18, 20, 59; ii. 8.
[6] Ap. i. 21, 22.
[7] Ap. i. 24.
[8] Ap. i. 14, 26; ii. 8.
[9] Ap. i. 31–53.
[10] Cf. Zeller's Outlines of Greek Philosophy, p. 254.
[11] Ap. ii. 13.

exhibits it as the perfect philosophy, of which other systems had been partial gleams; as the final truth which had made God known, and duty plain, and future retribution certain, — the truth, therefore, against which error and evil had always waged war, and which must always expect to receive the blows and the sneers of a misguided world.

It is not my purpose here to indicate the place which these views took in Justin's theology,[1] but simply to point out their bearing on his defence of Christianity. If a philosophy, why should it be proscribed? Were not philosophers of all kinds free to teach their peculiar doctrines? Were they not to be met in every city? Did they not found schools? Why should this particular set of opinions, which contained so many elements with which the most illustrious philosophers agreed, be alone condemned merely for its name? Such, if I mistake not, was the real substance of Justin's plea, and it is not hard to perceive both its force and its weakness.

Plausibility of his plea.

It was a plausible plea. If Christianity had really been nothing but a philosophy, it would probably never have been persecuted. Justin may well have felt that his presentation of the case would commend his cause to cultured readers. For such he chiefly wrote. He spoke as a philosopher as well as a Christian, and to the philosophic as well as to the popular ear he addressed his words. He ever had in mind the "philosophic Cæsar" as well as the "pious Emperor," and he may have not unreasonably expected that the just and gentle Antoninus would agree with the young philosopher who shared his throne in granting freedom of opinion and of speech to every school of thought. In

[1] Cf. Lect. IV.

view of the universal respect paid to philosophy, why should not Christian philosophy be tolerated? In view of the prevailingly theological character of nearly all philosophy at that period, why should not the Christian doctrine of God be also permitted? In view of the manifest affinity of many of Justin's ideas with those of the honored master of the Academy, in view of the Apologist's sympathy with philosophical doctrines and use of philosophical language, why should he and his fellow-believers be classed with the superstitious, and punished as enemies of the State? Justin seems to have honestly felt that no reasonable prince, who knew the real character of the Christian doctrine and life, could fail to admit that such teaching ought not to be proscribed. This was a new way of defending Christianity. Never before, unless in the lost Apologies of Aristides and Quadratus, had it been boldly claimed by an orthodox Christian writer that his doctrine was the superior on their own ground of those of the Academy and the Porch. By some of Justin's successors the affinity of Christianity and philosophy was openly repudiated.[1] But his position was more likely to win for his cause a hearing; and if his Apology ever reached those for whom it was intended, if it was ever seriously read by any cultivated heathen, the reader must have felt that, however incredible Christianity might be, it was assuming a new and more intelligible form, and that its prayer for liberty was not wholly unreasonable.

Its novelty.

And yet, plausible and novel as Justin's plea was, it was hopeless, if for no other reason than because it was in fact only a one-sided presentation of the case. For Christianity was more

Its hopelessness, because a one-sided presentation of facts.

---

[1] So Tatian, Hermias, and, later, Tertullian.

than a philosophy. It was an association. It was a society which met in secret, was rapidly spreading over the Empire, and was firm in its refusal to adore the emperor. The worship of the emperors was assiduously fostered by the Antonines. Their humanity and their philosophy did not prevent their insistence on it. Their desire to strengthen the unity of the Empire led them to encourage it. It was vain, therefore, to say that the Christian societies, with their unauthorized meetings and their refusal to take in the usual form the oath of allegiance, were but a collection of philosophers. The facts were against Justin's plea. Christianity was more than a philosophy. Without meaning to be disloyal, by its war with heathenism it was undermining the foundations of the State, which rested upon heathenism. It was by its very nature a social revolution. Neither friend nor foe could then perceive what was involved in the progress of the new religion. But while the reports circulated against it were false, it was not the politically harmless thing which Justin innocently sought to represent it; and while philosophers greeted with scorn his claim to be a philosopher, the magistrates and the people were as little likely to regard him and his co-religionists as aught but a disloyal faction.

But if Justin's presentation of Christianity as a philosophy was not likely to obtain for it the toleration he sought, his description of the moral teaching and living of the Christians was more likely to impress his readers. As we have said, his exhibition of Christianity as a philosophy seems to have been his real, positive argument in its defence. Yet, on the purity of its teaching, on the morality of its followers, on the simplicity of its ceremonies, he laid no little stress. It was necessary for

<small>His argument from the virtues of the Christians,</small>

him to do this, in order to meet the sneers and slanders of its foes. In order to refute the popular reports, in order to remove the prejudices of higher circles, in order to appeal to the conscience of the better part of the community, in order to dispel the prevalent idea that Christians were dangerous to society, he set forth the habits of his fellow-believers, — their moral ideals and hopes, their lofty aspirations and pure practices. Thus he cleared the way for the positive presentation of the reasonableness of Christianity and its truly philosophical character.

Justin's description of Christian morals is well worthy of attention. Of his particular replies to the charges of atheism and disloyalty, we have already spoken. Of his description of the Christian ceremonies it is sufficient here to say that he represents them as very simple and entirely innocent. *and the simplicity of their customs.* The rite of initiation [1] was but washing with water "in the name of God, the Father and Lord of the universe, and of our Saviour Jesus Christ, and of the Holy Spirit." This was to the convert a self-dedication to God, an assumption of Christian duty, a new birth into purity and knowledge. He describes in like manner the simple ceremony of the Eucharist;[2] and while he evidently regarded both baptism and the Eucharist as rites which conveyed some mystical benefit,[3] yet he was careful to show their perfect purity. At the weekly assemblies of the Christians,[4] naught was done except to read "the memoirs of the Apostles or the writings of the Prophets," to listen to an exhortation from the presiding officer, to pray, to celebrate the Eucharist, and to make offerings for the needy. Yet it is not so much in these

[1] Ap. i. 61.   [2] Ap. i. 65.
[3] Cf. Lect. VI.   [4] Ap. i. 67.

formal descriptions that Justin exhibits the moral character of the Christians as in phrases and facts which are scattered through the Apology. He shows us men and women who were absolutely without fear of death,[1] who loved truth more than life,[2] and yet who, while willing to depart from the scene of trouble, deemed it a duty to preserve life so long as God, the giver, delayed to take it.[3] Here were persons who lived in the earnest desire for fellowship with God,[4] who were resting their hope of the future upon God's promises alone, who felt the duty of faithful obedience to Him and ever remembered that to Him they were to render their account.[5] Here, says Justin,[6] are "we who formerly delighted in fornication, but now embrace chastity alone; we who formerly used magical arts, now dedicate ourselves to the good and unbegotten God; we who valued above all things the acquisition of wealth and possessions, now bring what we have into a common stock and communicate to every one in need; we who hated and destroyed one another and on account of different customs would not even use the same fireplace with men of another race, now, since the appearance of Christ, live familiarly with them, and pray for our enemies, and try to persuade those who unjustly hate us to live according to the good precepts of Christ, to the end that they may become partakers with us of the same joyful hope of a reward from God, the Ruler of all." He then cites examples of Christ's teaching, taken mostly from the Sermon on the Mount, — directions to be pure, temperate, and generous.[7] He boldly[8] sets the Christian morals in

His testimony to their noble living.

---

[1] Ap. i. 2, 11, 45; ii. 2; Dial. 30.   [2] Ap. i. 2; ii. 4.
[3] Ap. ii. 4.   [4] Ap. i. 8, 14, 25, 49.   [5] Ap. ii. 8.
[6] Ap. i. 14.   [7] Ap. i. 15, etc.   [8] Ap. i. 27.

contrast with the horrible vices of pagan society, and speaks of the Christians' care for children,[1] their solemn estimate of the value of human life,[2] their peaceableness,[3] their pity for their enemies and desire to save them,[4] their patience and prayerfulness even when persecuted,[5] their wide philanthropy.[6] He evinces in himself, and he describes in others, a quickened sense of the inherent difference between right and wrong[7] and of man's responsibility for his moral choice.[8] Through all these virtues there also shines a strong, bright hope[9] of personal immortality, of divine reward, and of the final destruction of the devil and his works. Christianity is thus shown to have been a real change of life, a practical communism, a universal brotherhood.[10] Justin, in common with later Apologists, does not hesitate to assail fiercely the follies and immoralities of paganism. He declares it to have been the work of demons;[11] he scorns and ridicules its idolatry;[12] he points out its contradictions,[13] and denounces its impure stories[14] and shameless rites.[15] He could safely do so, for pagan writers themselves had already done the same. But he even dares to denounce the more recent deification of Antinous,[16] in order to exhibit in still more glaring contrast the lofty ideal of purity which the Christians displayed. He writes not as the satirist, but as the intense moralist. He was himself filled with enthusiasm for morality, and in this he claimed to represent all true

[1] Ap. i. 27.
[2] Ap. i. 29.
[3] Ap. i. 39.
[4] Ap. i. 57; Dial. 133.
[5] Dial. 18.
[6] Dial. 93, 110.
[7] Ap. ii. 7, etc.
[8] Ap. i. 10; Dial. 124, 140.
[9] Ap. i. 14; ii. 8.
[10] Ap. i. 14, 67.
[11] Ap. i. 5, 23, 54, 64; ii. 5.
[12] Ap. i. 9.
[13] Ap. i. 24.
[14] Ap. i. 25.
[15] Ap. ii. 12.
[16] Ap. i. 29.

Christians. These men, therefore, were wholly different from what slander reported. They had totally repudiated the vices of pagan religion and life. Holiness was their aim. Universal love was their motive. Fidelity in all human relations was practised by them because of the fidelity due to God. Truth, purity, generosity, humility with fearlessness, patience with courage, were their characteristic traits. They had broken down the barriers of class and nation. They sought to love even their enemies. They had risen above the fear of death. They lived as in the presence of the Almighty, and expected their reward from Him. They might be slain, but they could not be injured,[1] since they believed death for Christ's sake to be only a deliverance.

It is evident that such a lofty morality would do more to commend Christianity than volumes of learned Apologies. Justin declares that his observation in former years of the Christian character had much to do with his own conversion,[2] and that many others also had been converted by the same practical demonstration.[3] This we can well believe. While philosophers disproved Christianity, while the magistrates oppressed and the populace assaulted the followers of Christ, while Apologists vainly argued for their faith, the actual moral power of the new religion was quietly impressing thousands of men and women, and slowly but surely pervading society. Such is the picture which Justin gives. "No one," he says, "was persuaded by Socrates to die for this doctrine; but in Christ, who was partially known even by Socrates, not only philosophers and scholars believed, but also artisans and people entirely uneducated, despising both

Power of this argument.

[1] Ap. i. 2.   [2] Ap. ii. 12.   [3] Ap. i. 16.

glory and fear and death, since He is a power of the ineffable Father, and not the mere instrument of human reason."[1]

It was in vain that Justin pleaded for toleration. It was in vain that he proclaimed the true philosophy, and furnished proofs of the truth of Christ's claims, and described the pure ideal of Christian life. But as we consider the picture which he gives of the progress of this moral enthusiasm and godly life in the face of hatred and persecution, we are led to ask what explanation can be drawn from him of so singular a phenomenon in the Roman Empire. *Whence arose this new morality?* How came it that men were thus not only suddenly possessed of such lofty ideals, but were able to follow such unselfish and holy practices? How arose this vivid sense of an almighty but personal God, this quickening of conscience, this confident hope not only of immortality but of eternal happiness, this universal love, this new valuation of human rights and human life, this intense yet practical, this holy yet pitiful religion, with its bold defiance of suffering and death, its pure and patient life? The answer, at least of Justin, is very clear. All was due, he says, to the actual incarnation of the Son of God.[2] The divine Logos had always indeed been in the world,[3] but the suggestions of reason had been overcome by the power of the demons. It was by His actually becoming man that Christianity arose. We shall find occasion hereafter to point out what we think to have been errors in Justin's conception of God and of the Logos.[4] We shall observe, also, an incompleteness in his idea of the way in which Christ saves, at least as viewed by the standard of

[1] Ap. ii. 10. [2] Ap. i. 5, 13, 14; ii. 13, etc.
[3] Ap. i. 5, 46; ii. 13. [4] Cf. Lect. IV.

New Testament teaching. But there is no doubt that Justin's faith and philosophy, his doctrine and life, turned on the fact of the Incarnation; and he declares the same great fact to be the foundation of all Christianity. It was the teaching of Christ which had given men their new ideal. It was the life, words, death, and resurrection of Christ which had created their hope, had brought life and immortality to light, had made them fearless and pure. It was the historical Christ, as they had heard of and believed in Him, who had made God once more real to men, and had united them to God in reverent love and to one another in brotherly fellowship. Such, at least, was the foundation of Christianity in the mind of Justin. The actual appearance on earth of the Divine Son had given the new doctrines which men were believing and the new rules which they were following. This was the force to which these early Christians were conscious of yielding, and which moulded their religious experience. It was the historical Christ who in their thoughts had created Christianity. In Him they believed, and Him they loved and served; and in view of the deep gulf which lay between their practical morality and that of the society about them, and in view of the proved inability of even the best philosophy to produce on such a large scale a similar moral life, is it possible to believe that they were regenerated by a fiction?

LECTURE III.

THE TESTIMONY OF JUSTIN TO THE RELATIONS OF GENTILE AND JEWISH CHRISTIANITY.

WHILE Justin is best known as an Apologist, more interest has attached in modern times to the evidence which he affords of the mutual relations of Gentile and Jewish Christianity in the post-apostolic age. In his larger Apology he describes and quotes from the Old Testament, and expresses his valuation of the prophets, thus exhibiting his attitude to the Hebrew revelation; while other expressions show incidentally his position toward not only Judaism but Jewish Christianity. This appears still more clearly, as we would expect, in the Dialogue with Trypho. There he formally combats Judaism. He thus states explicitly the way in which he looked upon the old dispensation. In the course of the Dialogue, also, he openly expresses his opinion about Jewish Christians. If we add to this his testimony as to the origin and character of the majority of Christians in his day, his expressions concerning the authority of the Apostles, his treatment of those doctrines which would naturally come into debate between Jew and Gentile, and finally his claim to speak for the majority of the Christian community, we shall perceive that he is an important witness to what were the actual relations of these two sides of early Christianity.

Value of Justin's testimony to the relations of Gentile and Jewish Christianity.

The value of this part of Justin's testimony is, of course, greatly increased by the modern critical theories of the apostolic and post-apostolic ages. Rationalistic criticism seeks to explain the rise of the Catholic Christianity which was confessedly established by the time of Irenæus on the supposition that it was from beginning to end a natural process. It alleges that so far from Christianity having been taught and the Church founded in the way set forth by our New Testament, these were a growth which gathered around the simple moral teaching of Jesus, through the addition thereto of ideas which were already germinating in Gentile and Jewish thought, and which combined to form the Christian beliefs and societies of the first and second centuries. The corner-stone of these rationalistic theories is the alleged opposition between Paul and the original Apostles, which is claimed to be proved from those epistles of Paul which are admitted by the critics as genuine. Original Christianity was, they tell us, entirely Jewish. Paul, realizing the universality of the Gospel, proclaimed that all men might be saved through faith alone, and hence that, Christ being the end of the law to every one that believeth, the Jewish economy was abolished. This, it is said, the original Apostles denied; and thus there arose two types of Christianity, — the Pauline or Gentile, and the apostolic or Jewish, — which were antagonistic to each other. When the apostolic age drew to a close, however, these two divisions began to come together. The spread of Pauline Christianity and the political calamities which befell the Jews led the Jewish Christians to make concessions. The death of Paul was followed by a less determined hostility to Judaism among his followers. Concessions became

Marginal notes: Modern rationalistic theories. The Tübingen scheme.

mutual. The need of unity in the face of the world's opposition was more deeply felt. Church organization became more fixed and ecclesiastical power centralized, and thus the truth held in common was exalted above the points in which men differed. The extreme views of some aided the coalition of the more moderate of both sides. Practical necessities dulled the edge of theological rancor and personal animosities. Finally, the union became complete. The extreme views of Paul were toned down. The spirit of the Jewish law and hierarchy united with Paul's doctrine of the universalism of the new religion; but Paul himself, as the special object of Jewish dislike, was relegated to the background, and Peter came to be reckoned as the true founder of the Church. Catholic Christianity, a confused medley of the originally opposing views, was the result; and the union of the two parties was so perfect that by the end of the second century all remembrance of the division of the Apostles had been blotted out.

Along the lines, then, of these two periods of conflict and reconciliation, the books of the New Testament and the remains of post-apostolic literature are placed by the critics, and the development of early Christian thought and life is correspondingly described. Of course it is admitted that the facts should determine our theories; but amid the scanty testimony which survives from this period, the internal evidence of the books themselves has been chiefly relied upon to determine their dates according to the requirements of the theories. Consequently the traditional origin of many of the New Testament books has been denied. By their supposed doctrinal or ecclesiastical or even personal "tendencies," they have been assigned to this or that phase of the formation of Christianity. The value of the New Testament histories has thus been undermined. The phases of New Testament doctrine have been attributed to the natural development of thought, to reaction from opposing views, and to contact with outside philosophy and life. The resulting Christianity is represented not as a revelation, but as the expression by the human mind of certain religious and moral truths in dogmatic forms and historical narratives which were but the accidents of their birth.

Such is, in brief, the famous Tübingen reconstruction of early Christian history, of which F. C. Baur's "The Christianity and the Christian Church of the First Three Centuries," published in 1853, is still the completest representative. Baur was joined by other scholars whose industry pursued the subject into the minutest details; and it is but fair to admit that the investigations to which the Tübingen theory led both friend and foe have resulted in a clearer conception of the historical relations of early Christian literature than Biblical scholarship had ever before possessed. Nevertheless, the earlier forms of this theory have now been generally abandoned. Its extreme positions have in many cases been retracted by rationalistic scholars themselves.[1] The evidence for an earlier date of the principal New Testament books than it would allow has been freshly exhibited. It has been shown that other forces besides those originally sup-

Modifications of the Tübingen scheme.

[1] Cf. e. g. Hilgenfeld's Review of "Supernatural Religion" in Zeitschr. für wissensch. Theol. xviii. 582, where he admits that Barnabas used ὡς γέγραπται of Matt. xxii. 14; that the to him pseudo-Ignatius used our Gospels; that Papias's Matthew, though not ours, was not a mere collection of Christ's words, and that we can hardly distinguish his Mark from ours; that Justin used our Gospels with one or more others; and that Marcion's Gospel was not independent of Luke's.

posed must be admitted to have co-operated to produce the result. Especially has the Alexandrian philosophy been made to play a larger part in the modification of Paul's teaching;[1] and the period of the reconciliation of the antagonistic parties has been pushed back from the second to the first half of the second century, and its beginnings assigned even to the apostolic age itself.[2] I am speaking now from the standpoint of the rationalistic critics. But, in fact, I should go further. The Johannean authorship of the Fourth Gospel, the composition of the Synoptic Gospels in the first century, the authenticity of the later Pauline epistles, and the genuineness of the seven short Greek epistles of Ignatius have, we believe, been firmly re-established, and thereby the whole Tübingen scheme overthrown. Still its essential spirit remains, and by some writers is carried to extreme lengths.[3] The antagonism between Paul and the original Apostles is now indeed represented as less violent than was at first maintained, and is said to have only originated *after* the events at Antioch described in Galatians ii.[4] A moderate party, also, is now recognized as having existed from the first among the Jewish Christians;[5] while among the Gentile Christians, on the other

[1] Cf. e. g. Pfleiderer's Paulinism, vol. ii. chap. ix.
[2] Cf. Ibid., ii. 38, etc. (on the Epistle to the Romans).
[3] Cf. Pfleiderer's Paulinism, and the same author's "Influence of the Apostle Paul on the Development of Christianity," Hibbert Lectures, 1885. Volkmar's Jesus Nazarenus, 1882. See also Weiss's Einleitung, 1886, pp. 9–18, for a brief review of the Tübingen and more recent schools.
[4] Cf. e. g. Holtzmann's "Der Apostelconvent," Zeitschr. für wissensch. Theol., 1883, pp. 129, etc.; and Holsten, quoted by Weiss, Einleitung, p. 14; and Pfleiderer's Paulinism, ii. 8, etc., Hibbert Lectures, ch. ii.
[5] Cf. Pfleiderer, Hibbert Lectures.

hand, Hilgenfeld[1] distinguishes from the Paulinists a party which was Jewish-Christian in spirit and claimed to follow the original Apostles. But in spite of these important modifications of the theory, in spite of the additional parties into which the early Church has had to be divided and the admission of which gives the impression that the theory itself is in a stage of dissolution, the fundamental thesis of the division of the Apostles and of the apostolic Church into two hostile or at least independent parties is still assumed; the narrative of the Acts is still held to represent the principles of compromise or fusion which in the second century were established; and therefore whatever will throw light upon the relations of primitive Gentile and Jewish Christianity becomes of the highest service.

Its spirit remains.

Another view of the second century was adopted by Ritschl,[2] who was himself reared in the Tübingen school, and has been widely followed by critics of various tendencies. He denied that Catholic Christianity was the result of the union of the Jewish and Pauline types, and insisted that the former ceased to grow, but that the latter degenerated from the views of its founder, and, by reason of forces acting wholly from within itself, descended to a more legalistic conception of religion. Ritschl maintained, therefore, that Catholic Christianity was wholly Gentile in its origin; and he thus took a position quite different from that of his master Baur. Already Neander[3] had declared that besides the influence of Judaism on Christianity, it is possible to detect in the development of Gentile Christianity in the second century a tendency similar to

Ritschl's view.

---

[1] Cf. Zeitschr. für wissensch. Theol., 1872, pp. 495, etc.
[2] Die Entstehung der altkath. Kirche, 3d ed. 1857.
[3] Cf. his Ch. Hist., Amer. ed. i. 365.

GENTILE AND JEWISH CHRISTIANITY. 91

Judaism but born of paganism itself; and the theory of Ritschl served at least to show that there was not nearly so much need of assuming a compromise with Jewish principles in explaining the phenomena of the early Church as had been supposed. Ritschl's view not only influenced rationalistic scholars,[1] but has also been followed in modified forms by scholars who wholly deny the alleged division of the Apostles. The most recent critic on Justin, Von Engelhardt,[2] carries the Ritschlian view so far as to make Justin essentially pagan in his modes of thought, and the Christianity of his day wholly unaffected by later Judaism. Thus Justin again appears as one of the most important witnesses in the question at issue. We find in him a witness whose testimony is specially valuable for the simple reason that the date of his writings is generally admitted. *Importance of examining Justin's statements.* We strenuously object to the habit of determining the dates of early Christian books by the places which they are made to fill in the various schemes of early Christianity. We hold at least that this is often done in such wise as to be practically a begging of the question, and we turn, therefore, with more confidence to Justin, about whose date there is no serious doubt. His testimony should go far toward determining our opinion of the condition of affairs in the generation preceding him as well as in his own.

Before examining his testimony, however, it is proper to repeat the caution that we should not expect too much from it. The criticism of the New Testament

[1] Cf. Overbeck's "Das Verhältniss Justins des Märtyrers zur Apostelgeschichte," Zeitschr. für wissensch. Theol., 1872, p. 305; and Weizsäcker's "Die Theologie des Märtyrers Justinus," Jahrb. für deutsche Theol., 1867 (vol. xii.), p. 60.

[2] Das Christenthum Justins des Märtyrers, Erlangen, 1878.

books themselves must furnish the main source for our knowledge of the apostolic age. If it be not true that the Pauline Epistles contradict the Acts of the Apostles, if it be not true that the Synoptists and the Fourth Evangelist contradict one another, if it can be shown that the evidence for the Pastoral Epistles and First Peter and the Hebrews points to a date agreeable to the traditional view, then the foundation of the rationalistic criticism melts away and leaves it a castle in the air. But the condition of affairs in the second century is important, though subsidiary, testimony. It forms part of the historical evidence for the literature and history of the first. It may be reasonably expected to exhibit the effects of causes alleged to have operated in the first, as well as to reveal additional causes which modified those of an earlier time. From it we may logically look back; so that the testimony of Justin to the relations of Jewish and Gentile Christianity, or of Christianity and Judaism, may contribute to our understanding of original Christianity itself.

Let us begin, then, with Justin's use and valuation of the Old Testament. He quoted it copiously, not only in the Dialogue with Trypho, but also in the larger Apology. He used the Septuagint translation, and after having described[1] how Ptolemy procured its translation from the Hebrew, refers the readers of the Apology, not to the Jews, but to the Egyptians, as preservers of the sacred volume. If it be thought that he did this in order to increase the confidence of his pagan readers in the prophets, it is yet to be observed that he entirely distrusted the Jews'

<small>Estimate placed on the Old Testament.</small>

---

[1] Ap. i. 31. Justin makes the astonishing mistake of saying that Ptolemy procured the Hebrew Scriptures from *Herod*.

copies of their own Scriptures, alleging that these had been altered through hostility to the Christians.[1] At any rate, the Septuagint was for him the correct expression of the language of the prophets.

This collection, then, Justin considered infallibly inspired. He calls it "the Scripture,"[2] or "the Scriptures,"[3] or simply "Scriptures,"[4] and again "the holy Scriptures."[5] He calls it "the Word of God,"[6] "the Word from God,"[7] and again simply "the Word."[8] More particularly, the writers were "prophets of God," through whom "the prophetic Spirit" spake.[9] Elsewhere he says that "God" spake through them,[10] and again that the divine Logos did.[11] They were therefore "inspired"[12] and "inhabited by the Spirit,"[13] or "filled with the Holy Spirit."[14] Their writings do not contradict one another,[15] nor can any fault be found with them, if their meaning be understood.[16] The collection of Hebrew Scripture, in fine, was

Its inspiration.

[1] Ap. i. 41; Dial. 71-73, 124. Cf. also Dial. 68, 131, 137. Cf. also Lect. I. Justin, however, was not ignorant of the Hebrew text (Dial. 124, 131), nor of the interpretations adopted by the Palestinian Jews (Dial. 68), though certainly his explanation of the etymology of Σατανᾶς ("apostate serpent," Dial. 103, Otto's note) and Ἰσραὴλ ("man conquering strength," Dial. 125) do not indicate thorough acquaintance with the Hebrew language. Cf. Kaye's Justin Martyr, p. 19.

[2] ἡ γραφή. Dial. 37, 56, 60, 84.
[3] αἱ γραφαί. Dial. 39, 56, 86, 119.
[4] γραφαί. Dial. 75.   [5] Dial. 55.
[6] ὁ τοῦ θεοῦ λόγος. Dial. 38, 58, 62, 63, 141.
[7] παρὰ τοῦ θεοῦ. Ap. i. 53.
[8] Dial. 56, 92, 102, 103, 117, 129, 137.
[9] Ap. i. 31, 32, 35, 38, 39, etc.; Dial. 7, 34.
[10] Cf. e. g. Ap. i. 40; Dial. 15.   [11] Ap. i. 33, 36.
[12] θεοφοροῦνται. Ap. i. 33, 34.
[13] ἐμπεπνευσμένοι. Ap. i. 36. τὸ ἐν τοῖς προφήταις πνεῦμα. Dial. 52.
[14] Dial. 7.   [15] Dial. 65.   [16] Dial. 112.

regarded by Justin as in the highest sense an inspired volume, a series of infallible communications of truth from God by His Logos through the Spirit.

Looking still more closely, we find that Justin's high valuation of the Old Testament rested on his high valuation of the prophets themselves. He approached the subject in the spirit of an inquirer seeking reasons for belief in Christianity; and he found these in the marvellous predictions and anticipations of the latter which were contained in the prophetical writings. The Old Testament, therefore, was to Justin the "writings of the prophets."[1] Through them, either when in trance or otherwise,[2] the divine Word, or Spirit, preached the eternal truth which was afterwards to be taught by Christ,[3] and predicted, explicitly or in figure, the events of Christ's life and of apostolic history.[4] Justin, as we shall see, regarded the divine Logos as the only medium of revelation, and as having always been in the world making the truth known to those able to receive it. But through the prophets the Logos particularly spoke. By the prediction of what had subsequently occurred as well as by the miracles which they wrought,[5] were they authenticated as messengers from God. From them, in fact, Justin, like other Christian writers of his day, maintained that the Greek philosophers had learned much of their wisdom, and even the demons had learned against what to direct their wicked efforts.[6] The prophets appealed to his

The prophets.

---

[1] Ap. i. 23, 31, etc.; Dial. 7, 52, 136.

[2] Dial. 115, where the special mention of Zechariah's ἔκστασις shows that Justin did *not* consider inspiration as always a state in which the ordinary faculties were suspended. The contrary view is expressed in the Cohortatio, viii., which is not Justinian.

[3] Ap. i. 44; Dial. 136.   [4] Ap. i. 31, etc.; Dial. passim.
[5] Ap. i. 31; Dial. 7.   [6] Ap. i. 23, 31, 44, 54, 59, 60.

GENTILE AND JEWISH CHRISTIANITY. 95

mind as the most convincing proof of Christianity; and while their prominence in his writings was no doubt partly due to the nature of the latter as addressed to pagans and Jews, yet it is clear that the miraculous testimony borne by the prophets to Christianity underlay the high estimate which Justin placed upon the Hebrew Scriptures as a whole.

This is confirmed by his use and interpretations of the prophecies. He finds in them, as suits his purpose, either a writing beforehand of Christian history, or a plain declaration of Christian doctrine, or else mystical utterances and actions intended to both conceal and exhibit later teaching or facts.[1] His method of interpretation combined excessive literalism with a speculative search in the letter of Scripture for hidden meanings. He speaks of the intentional obscurity of Scripture;[2] finds Christ and Christianity typified or openly taught on every page; sees the cross predicted no less in the shape in

Method of interpretation.

[1] Thus, to take one illustration, he quotes (Ap. i. 32; cf. also Dial. 54) Gen. xlix. 10: "The sceptre shall not depart from Judah, nor a lawgiver from between his feet, until He come for whom it is reserved; and He shall be the desire of the nations, binding His foal to the vine, washing His robe in the blood of the grape." This, he says, predicted, first, the continuance of Jewish civil power until the time of Christ, after whom the Romans took possession of the land. Then, "He shall be the desire of the nations" predicted the present expectation among the Gentiles of the second advent. "Binding His foal to the vine" predicted Christ's triumphant entry into Jerusalem; while the sentence "washing His robe in the blood of the grape" was prophetic of His "cleansing by His blood those who believe on Him," for believers are "His robe," since the Logos dwells in them; and the "blood of the grape" was a symbol of His own blood, and so called, because He came not of human generation, but, like the grape, of divine power.

[2] Dial. 68.

which the paschal lamb was dressed for roasting [1] than in the fifty-third chapter of Isaiah itself;[2] finds in Malachi's word about the "pure offering" a prediction of the Eucharist,[3] in "the twelve bells on the high-priest's robe" a symbol of the Apostles, and in the Nineteenth Psalm a description of the spread of Christianity.[4] These are but a few samples of his method of interpretation. We must judge it by the habits of his day. It rested on the same principle as the exegesis of the Jews themselves, as Justin himself points out.[5] It was evidently the same method of which the Alexandrian Jews made use to discover their philosophy in the writings of Moses.[6] Nay, it was the common way of interpreting prophecies among the Gentiles as well as among the Jews, as may be implied in the fact that Justin places the Sibyl and Hystaspes[7] side by side with the prophets.

But the important point is that to Justin the Old Testament was purely a Christian book. He says[8] to Trypho, "Your Scriptures are not yours, but ours." "The law of the Lord," which in the Nineteenth Psalm is called "perfect," is not the Mosaic, but the Christian law.[9] The prophets taught just what Christ taught,[10] but in parts and by figures. True, the Old Testament contains [11] some injunctions intended only for the Jews; but in his own estimation

The Old Testament a Christian book.

---

[1] Dial. 40.   [2] Ap. i. 50.
[3] Dial. 117, etc. So the "Didache," 14.
[4] Ap. i. 11.   [5] Dial. 112.
[6] Cf. Zeller's Outlines of Greek Philosophy, p. 320.
[7] Ap. i. 20, 44.   [8] Dial. 29.
[9] Dial. 34. So, speaking of Zechariah's vision of Joshua, the high-priest, Justin says (Dial. 116): "I assert that even that revelation was made for us who believe on Christ the High-Priest."
[10] Ap. i. 23, 44; ii. 8.   [11] Dial. 44.

GENTILE AND JEWISH CHRISTIANITY. 97

and use of it, Justin passes over these to represent it as a book of Christian doctrine directing what Christians are to believe and do.

In the next place, the question arises, How did Justin regard the Hebrew dispensation? It must be admitted by all, we think, that at least in the Apology he gives no indication that he looked upon the relation of the Hebrews to God as having differed in any respect from that of other nations. He mentions Socrates and Heraclitus before Abraham, Elias, and other Hebrews, as examples of men who lived conformably to truth before Christ came.[1] He quotes Isaiah as declaring the constant unbelief of the Jews but the readiness of the Gentiles to accept the Gospel.[2] He does not say, in describing the origin of the Old Testament, that the prophets were Hebrews because of any special relation of the Hebrew people to God, but on the contrary does say that the Jews did not understand the prophets.[3] In quoting Micah v. 2, as it is quoted in Matt. ii. 6, he significantly omits from the clause "who shall rule my people Israel" the word "Israel."[4] He classes the Jews and the Samaritans together in distinction from the Gentiles.[5] Certainly, the drift of these passages is to show that Justin looked upon the Hebrews as merely one of the nations. The fact that the prophets were of that people indicated to him no special superiority of the Hebrew race, while the latter's inability to understand the prophets was a symptom of their extraordinary blindness of heart. If distinguished

The Hebrew dispensation.

[1] Ap. i. 46.
[2] Ap. i. 53. The words cited by Justin are not found in Isaiah, but in Jer. ix. 26. This is an example of his numerous slips of memory.
[3] Ap. i. 31.   [4] Ap. i. 34. So also Dial. 78.
[5] Ap. i. 53.

at all, it was for their unbelief. To this it may be added that in the smaller Apology [1] Justin explains that the Divine Son is called Christ "on account of his having been anointed and *because God arranged all things through Him*," — a sentence which is remarkable for deriving the title of Messiah from the cosmical and universal work of the Logos, and which shows that the influence of Alexandrian philosophy had united with other forces in leading our Apologist far from the original Jewish view.

It may be said, however, that we should not expect to find in the Apologies a presentation of the peculiar vocation of the Hebrews. What, then, is the testimony of the Dialogue? We must reply that here also Justin shows himself far from able to appreciate the full relation of the Hebrew and Christian dispensations. He knew, indeed, that God had specially favored the Hebrews by choosing them for Himself, by delivering them from Egypt, by protecting them in the wilderness, and by pointing them to the coming Saviour.[2] He knew that God had given them a national law and covenant.[3] But he declares that the Mosaic ceremonial was given them solely because of their sins.[4] Meats were forbidden or allowed solely to keep God before their eyes.[5] The Sabbath, likewise, was instituted that they might not forget God, as they were specially prone to do.[6] Sacrifices were enjoined on them simply to keep them from joining in the idolatry of their neighbors.[7] Circumcision was instituted actually to mark them out beforehand for punishment when they should

---

[1] Ap. ii. 6. κατὰ τὸ κεχρῖσθαι καὶ κοσμῆσαι τὰ πάντα δι' αὐτοῦ τὸν θεόν
[2] Dial. 130, 131.   [3] Dial. 11.   [4] Dial. 132.
[5] Dial. 20.   [6] Dial. 21.   [7] Dial. 22.

have filled up the measure of their wickedness by crucifying Christ.[1] These rites never had any inherent value, as may be proved from the fact that the pious patriarchs did not observe them.[2] In fact, God called the Hebrews "to conversion and repentance while in a sinful condition and laboring under spiritual disease,"[3] and their ceremonial was intended only for themselves, partly as a restraint and partly as a punishment. Justin, however, recognizes two elements in the Mosaic law, — the religious and moral element and the ritual.[4] Both were incumbent on the Hebrews; but the ritual was designed to bring to their minds the religious and moral element,[5] and of this purpose its prefiguration of Christ was a part. Salvation, therefore, did not consist in performing the ritual, but in the doing "that which is universally, natturally, and eternally good."[6] The prophets, indeed, repeated the ritual commands of Moses,[7] but taught salvation through repentance for sin and doing righteousness;[8] and as now "the true, spiritual Israel are we who have been led to God through this crucified Christ," so in old time God's people were not the Jews as such, but only those who, like Abraham, Isaac, and Jacob, were well pleasing to Him. Hence, finally, the Mosaic law came to an end when Christ appeared and established the everlasting law and covenant.[9] The Jews have been signally condemned for their wickedness.[10] Only those can now be saved who "become acquainted with Christ, are washed in the fountain spoken of by Isaiah for the remission of sins, and for the rest live sinless lives."[11]

[1] Dial. 16.   [2] Dial. 19.   [3] Dial. 30.
[4] Dial. 44.   [5] Dial. 27.   [6] Dial. 45.
[7] Dial. 27.   [8] Dial. 12-15. [9] Dial. 43.
[10] Dial. 16, 74. [11] Dial. 44.

From this it appears that Justin recognized that the Hebrews had been, at the beginning of their history, selected by God as objects of His favor, but that from the beginning and with increasing wilfulness they had as a nation rejected the divine teaching. Their ordinances had been meant for themselves alone; and while these contained a typical Christian element,[1] the rebelliousness of the people is made to have been the chief reason for their enactment. On the other hand, prophecy had always taught just what Christianity teaches, and had predicted the latter. Jews, as such, were not Israel, but only the righteous among them; and the way of salvation had always lain in following those moral and religious duties of which all men had some knowledge, which the prophets had preached, and which at last Christ had fully made known.

Total rejection of Judaism.

Justin's view of the Hebrew dispensation differs, therefore, in certain notable respects from those expressed in the New Testament. He does not say, as Paul did, that the law was a schoolmaster to bring men to Christ, but rather a schoolmaster of the Jews to remind them of God and righteousness. The latter statement differs from the former in looking at the matter, not from the standpoint of a progressively revealed redemption of which the Mosaic law was a positive factor, but from the standpoint of an always revealed duty with reference to which the Mosaic law was a reminder and a warning. Nor does he say that the Hebrew saints were saved through faith but through obedience, though he mentions Abraham's faith.[2] Nor does he, like the

Differences between Justin's view and that of the New Testament.

---

[1] Dial. 44, Otto's text; cf. Dial. 40–42, 111.
[2] Dial. 23.

Epistle to the Hebrews, see in the ritual an harmonious system intended to typify the priestly work of Christ; for his selection of types is arbitrary, and he does not bring into sufficient prominence the idea of Christ's sacrifice. Yet to each of these New Testament ideas is Justin's akin. Even the points of apparent difference are found in subordinate and disconnected places in his writings. With the Pauline rejection of Judaism he is, on the other hand, in perfect accord. Stephen's speech [1] arraigns the Jews for persistent rebellion very much as Justin does. With Paul, Justin declares the total abolition of Jewish ceremonies since the advent of Christ. With the Epistle to the Hebrews he teaches the identity of Christian life with that of the patriarchs and saints of past time. Thus he is like and unlike the New Testament writers in his estimate of the Hebrew system. The cause of his differences we shall observe hereafter.

But for our present purpose it is significant that the point which Justin failed to appreciate was the positive, educational side of Judaism. Of development in revelation he had no idea; for he represents Christianity as having been taught as completely though not as clearly or persuasively in the Old Testament as by Christ. *His failure to appreciate the positive worth of Judaism.* That God through the ritual had been educating men for Christianity, was a thought quite foreign to his mind. Judaism was to him a now abolished law, which had only been called out by the follies of the Jews; an adaptation to their sinfulness; an exclusively national law; and a system, therefore, with which the Christian had nothing to do save as it might here and there typify Christ, or covertly reveal some truth which He had

[1] Acts vii.

taught and which it was of interest for Christians to observe.

It must already begin to appear that Justin was far from sympathizing with Judaism. His high valuation of the Old Testament did not in the least imply such sympathy, and his failure to grasp the positive value of the Mosaic ordinances indicates that he himself stood strongly on Gentile ground. We shall not be surprised, therefore, to find him representing the Christian Church as a distinctively Gentile society. Christ has been accepted, he says, among the Gentiles rather than among the Jews.[1] Prophecy, in fact, foretold the conversion of the Gentiles in such a way as to make it the characteristic mark of the Messianic kingdom,[2] and so did Christ Himself predict.[3] Not only was Justin an uncircumcised man himself,[4] but he speaks of Christians generally as uncircumcised.[5] Christ is the priest of the uncircumcised, though He will receive those of the circumcision who approach Him.[6] Some Jews, indeed, believe in Him,[7] and others are daily leaving the paths of error and becoming His disciples.[8] Yet they are but a few, if compared with the body of their nation,[9] — a mere "remnant left by the grace of the Lord of Sabaoth unto the eternal salvation."[10] The Church was distinctively Gentile. So Trypho regarded it,[11] and so Justin describes it. "We, out of all nations;"[12] "Christ and His proselytes, namely, us Gentiles;"[13] — such are his expressions. Christians in general do not observe the Mosaic ordi-

The Church therefore a Gentile society.

---

[1] Ap. i. 31, 40.
[2] Ap. i. 31, 49; Dial. 13, 28, 69, 109, 117, 122.
[3] Dial. 76.   [4] Dial. 28.   [5] Dial. 10, 15, 16, 29, 33.
[6] Dial. 33.   [7] Dial. 120.   [8] Dial. 39.
[9] Dial. 120.   [10] Dial. 32.   [11] Dial. 10, 64.
[12] Dial. 120.   [13] Dial. 122.

nances.¹ The Gentiles are to receive the inheritance "along with the patriarchs and prophets and the just men who have descended from Jacob." ² In the ass and the colt, which were brought to Jesus for his triumphal entry, were symbolized the fact that "you of the synagogue, along with the Gentiles, would believe in Him;"³ but He is now the expectation of all nations,⁴ Jews must become proselytes to Him or to Christianity,⁵ and the distinctive mission of the Apostles was to the whole world.⁶ Finally, Justin says expressly that "the Christians from the Gentiles are both more numerous and truer than those from the Jews and the Samaritans." ⁷

Thus the Christianity which Justin knew was clearly not regarded by him as the development of Judaism. It was a Gentile religion. The great bulk of its adherents were Gentiles. With them, indeed, Jews were welcome to unite, and many did so. But Christianity was the establishment of a universal faith. It was characteristically a non-national religion. Though Jesus and the prophets were Hebrews, yet the truth they taught was for all mankind, and even in ancient times was known by some out of all nations; and the prophets predicted and Christ instituted a religion into which Jews must come on precisely the same basis as Gentiles. So far, indeed, was Justin beyond the idea, which the apostolic Church maintained, that the Gentiles were fellow-heirs with the Jews, that he rather felt called upon to admit that the Jews were fellow-heirs with the Gentiles. Again we must observe, that Justin did not in this matter reproduce the ideas

Christianity not the development of Judaism.

Differences from Pauline view.

---

¹ Dial. 10–29. ² Dial. 26. ³ Dial. 53.
⁴ Dial. 32. ⁵ Dial. 28. ⁶ Ap. i. 39.
⁷ Ap. i. 53. πλείονάς τε καὶ ἀληθεστέρους.

of Paul, and that he rejected Judaism simply as an historical system of national worship, not because it was a temporary and finished term in the revelation of the true religion. He distinguished, also, far more clearly than Paul had done, between the moral and ritual elements in the Mosaic laws. The substance of Paul's rejection of Judaism he retained. The essential universality of the Gospel he assumed. But the perception of the divine reason for both the enactment and abolition of Judaism was obscured to him, because the whole idea of a progressive revelation was wanting in Justin. He was not even enough of a Jew to enter into Paul's thought of the purpose subserved by that which had been done away.

This brings us to the formal judgment which Justin passes upon Jewish Christians.[1] Trypho asks if a man who believes in and obeys Christ and yet observes the Mosaic ordinances can be saved, — a question which itself shows how completely Justin's Christianity appeared to the Jew as Gentile faith. Justin replies that in his opinion such an one can be saved, provided that he does not strive to persuade Gentile Christians to do the same, nor teach such observances to be necessary to salvation. He admits, however, that some will not have any intercourse with those who observe the law, but states that he thinks differently. "For," he adds, "if some, *because of the weakness* of their mind, besides hoping upon this Christ and keeping the eternal and natural precepts of righteousness and piety, wish also to keep as much as they now can of the Mosaic laws, which we think were ordered on account of the hardness of the people's hearts, and choose to live with the Christians

<small>Justin's formal judgment upon Jewish Christians.</small>

[1] Dial. 47.

and the faithful; as I said before, not persuading them to be either circumcised like themselves, or to sabbatize, or to observe other such rites, — I hold that it is proper to join ourselves to such, and to share all things with them, as with kinsmen and brethren." Moreover, he is even willing to admit that such proselytes as the Jewish Christians may make from the Gentiles will probably [1] be saved. At the same time he would meet any Jewish-Christian refusal to fellowship with Gentiles by a like refusal to fellowship with such Jewish Christians, and declares that those who go over to Judaism itself can certainly not be saved, any more than the Jews themselves who persecute the Christians.

From this passage it is evident that there were differences of opinion in the Christian community, even to the degree of causing the existence of sects. The New Testament, however, testifies to the existence of such differences in the apostolic age itself, though not among the Apostles; and we are only interested to learn whether Justin's description agrees best with the idea that the Church had been radically divided into opposing parties, which had recently combined or were then combining, or with the idea that these sects only represent imperfect or extravagant views, lingering prejudices, and human speculations, — offshoots of Christianity, which were never held by the great body of believers. Various opinions in the Church.

On the one hand, then, Justin speaks of Jewish Christians who continued to observe the Mosaic law. He evidently implies, also, that of these there were two classes, — those who merely held to "the law" themselves, and fellowshipped Two classes of Jewish Christians.

[1] ἴσως; generally translated, "fortasse." Otto inclines to "sine dubio."

with Gentile Christians; and those who considered "the law" binding upon all, and both refused to fellowship with non-observers of it and strove to proselyte them.

Their demands. Justin, it should be noted, describes both classes as wishing to observe "as many things as they now can of the Mosaic ordinances."[1] They had only so far modified the observance of the ritual as their expulsion from Jerusalem had rendered necessary. He distinctly states that they still practised circumcision, and that this was demanded of the Gentiles by those Jewish Christians who sought to proselyte them; so that they had not, as Baur alleges,[2] conceded this point to the Pauline Christians. It is to be observed, also, that he does not say that the Jewish Christians differed in general from the doctrines of the orthodox church. That he knew of Ebionites will appear in a moment, and doubtless they were of the proselyting and exclusive class of Jewish Christians to which he refers in the passage before us. But he also testifies to Jewish Christians who lived in entire harmony with Gentile believers, while preserving their national customs. The Jewish type of Christianity, therefore, was not, except in its extreme form, Ebionitic; nor is there any reason to suppose it had ever been so. If there had been a change in the theology of the Jewish Christians, whereby they had come into closer union with the Gentile Christians, it is fair to suppose that Justin would have mentioned in some way such doctrinal orthodoxy, as one of the conditions of his recognizing the Christianity of such Jews. The fact that he only mentions the matter of the ritual certainly implies that

[1] τὰ ὅσα δύνανται νῦν ἐκ τῶν Μωϋσέως.
[2] The Christianity of the First Three Centuries, vol. i. pp. 106, etc.

it alone was the question between the two parties. But it is also to be noted that while Justin describes the existence of such Jewish Christians, we have already found him speaking of them as comparatively few. In some cases, indeed, they were active proselyters. But they were a small body in comparison with the Christian community as a whole; and the very indifference of Justin to their maintenance of their traditional usages shows of itself how small their number really was. *Their fewness.*

On the other hand, there were some in the Christian community who were so opposed to any form of Judaism as to deny salvation to, and refuse to hold intercourse with, observers of "the law." Perhaps by these Justin meant the Marcionites. He does not call them Christians, though they evidently called themselves by that name; yet neither does he so violently repudiate them as he elsewhere does Marcion and his followers.[1] But allowing that some whom Justin would not have considered heretical were thus violently anti-Jewish, he himself in this passage only expresses his disagreement with them on the question of the salvability and Christian character of the Jewish Christians; he does not dissent from their opposition to Jewish Christianity itself. His own position, here as elsewhere, is distinctly anti-Jewish; but he is lenient in his judgment of those who differ with him. He regards Jewish Christianity as weak-mindedness. He is absolutely opposed to the observance by Christians of the Mosaic ordinances. But he is willing to make allowance for the power of custom and for hon- *The extreme opponents of Jewish Christianity.* *Justin's moderate, but firm, position.*

---

[1] Yet see Dial. 48, where he repudiates the Ebionites as gently, though he considers their doctrines as human teachings.

est differences of opinion, and therefore believes that Christian Jews, though they continue their national usages, should not be excluded from the communion of the Church. To be a disciple of Christ was the saving fact. Questions of ceremonies were of secondary importance.

It would seem perfectly idle, then, to maintain, as the Tübingen critics did, that Justin had any sympathy with Jewish Christianity, or represents a doubtful position between the two sides. Gentile and Jewish Christianity stood, in his view, distinct from each other; and while he covered the latter with the mantle of his charity, he himself occupied no half-way position. It is true that he went further in his charity than Paul had found it possible to do, in admitting the salvation of even those Gentiles who went over to the observance of Jewish rites. But the salvation of individuals is one thing, and the propriety of their opinions and conduct is another. When, moreover, Paul was first establishing the freedom of the Gospel against the previous opinion that Gentiles had to become Jews in order to be Christians, he might well insist that if they were circumcised, Christ would profit them nothing, But if, a century later, the freedom of Gentiles had long been established, there was less need to judge hardly of individual perverts to Jewish Christianity. Justin's charity may have in this instance gone too far; but the change of circumstances from the apostolic age was such that he cannot, on account of his charity, be charged with sympathy with an anti-Pauline type of faith. He is firm in expressing his conviction of the error and weakness of Jewish Christianity, and his very charity is again a proof that this type of religion was too

[marginal note: No sympathy, therefore, with Jewish Christianity.]

GENTILE AND JEWISH CHRISTIANITY. 109

inconsiderable a power in the Church to be seriously feared.

Was Justin, then, in all this, a fair representative of the majority of Christians? That he was disposed to take an ultra-liberal view of even the Ebionites, has been inferred from two passages in his writings. In the Dialogue[1] he argues that even if he should not succeed in proving the pre-existence of Christ, the proof of his Messiahship would yet hold good, and adds that "there are some of our race who confess Him to be Christ, but hold Him to be a man born of men;" and of these, who were manifestly Ebionites,[2] he remarks, "with whom I do not agree." So, in the larger Apology,[3] he says that "the Son of God, called Jesus, even if only a man by ordinary generation, yet on account of His wisdom is worthy to be called the Son of God." But it is fair to explain these expressions as due to Justin's desire to attain the main object of his argument. Fully as he believed in the pre-existent divinity of Christ, he would at least have both pagan and Jew confess His wisdom and Messiahship, if he could persuade them to admit no more. If he referred to Ebionites as of "our race,"— that is, as Christians,— he did but speak according to the name by which they were known to the world; but he rejects their doctrine most strenuously, declaring that not only did he not agree with it, but that most of those who thought as he did — that is, who belonged to the Christian Church — would reject it likewise, since they had been commanded by Christ to put no faith in human

His position that of the majority.

---

[1] Dial. 48.
[2] So it is generally assumed. For the phrase "our race," some editors substitute "your race," but needlessly. Cf. Otto's note.
[3] Ap. i. 22.

doctrines, but only in those taught by the prophets and Himself. These passages therefore indicate, again, no leaning toward Jewish Christianity of any type, but rather show that Justin and the Church stood together in opposition to both Judaizing ceremonies and Ebionite error. And the evidence is strong that Justin did represent the majority of Christians in his day. He specifically claimed to do so,[1] and in most explicit terms separates the heretics, as new and less numerous, from the true and apostolic Church.[2] If so, then we may affirm from him that the great body of Christians in the middle of the second century considered Jewish Christianity as a vanishing type of the faith, to be charitably regarded, indeed, but yet distinctly inferior to the full truth taught by Christ and His Apostles.

We conclude, then, that so far as the formal relations of these two types of Christianity were concerned, there is no reason to infer from Justin that they had recently combined. Both still maintained their existence. But Jewish Christianity was dying fast. The Jewish war had for the second time placed the seal of Providence upon the abrogation of Hebrew rites, and given the final blow to Jewish national influence.[3] Gentile Christianity was not only established, but was assumed by the vast majority of believers to be the natural and apostolic type. Justin and the Church stood positively and uncompromisingly on Gentile ground, and the bitter dispute which had raged between Paul and the Judaizers had long since lost its edge, for the very reason that Gentile Christianity had become so overwhelmingly dominant that the old issues were dead. Such a result,

Bearing of this evidence on the Tübingen scheme.

---

[1] Cf. Dial. 35, 80, etc.   [2] Cf. Lect. VI.
[3] Ap. i. 31, 47.

GENTILE AND JEWISH CHRISTIANITY. 111

be it observed, is just that which we would expect to find, if the course of events in the preceding age had been that which is related in the New Testament.

But, it will be said, was there not a silent but actual fusion of Gentile and Jewish Christianity, in spite of their apparently continued independence? Justin, among others, has been appealed to as evidence that Judaism had imposed certain of its views, and notably its prejudice against Paul, upon the Gentile believers, while it had at the same time accepted in turn from them the Pauline idea of the universality of the Gospel. While thus the results of Paul's missionary work remained, his doctrinal spirit, it is said, was lost in the fusion of his followers with those of the original Apostles. A reaction took place, it is alleged, of Gentile Christianity toward Jewish views. The mere fact of such a reaction may be held without implying doubt of the authenticity of the New Testament books. It may, however, be held with the purpose of explaining the alleged union of the originally divided Christian communities. It is important, therefore, to examine that part of Justin's testimony which has been adduced to show the presence in him of an anti-Pauline or Judaizing spirit, and to inquire whether he does indicate that such a spirit was really at work in the Catholic Church of his day. *Had there been an unconscious fusion?*

1. Appeal has been made to the fact that Justin strongly repudiates the eating of meat which had been offered in sacrifice to idols, and evidently believes that no true Christian would be guilty of such an offence.[1] This has been con- *The abhorrence of meat offered to idols.*

[1] Dial. 34, 35.

trasted with Paul's doctrine of the inherent indifference of such an act,[1] and it has hence been inferred that the adoption in the second century of the absolute unlawfulness of eating meat which had been offered to idols proves that Jewish Christianity had so far imposed its shackles upon the freedom which Paul had claimed for the Gentiles.

It should be observed, also, that this question is mingled with that of the authenticity of the Acts of the Apostles. Holtzmann,[2] for example, assuming that Gal. ii. is inconsistent with the account of the apostolic council given in Acts xv., assigns the latter, with its "decree" of abstinence from meats offered to idols and from blood and from things strangled and from fornication, to the second century, and claims that it represents the fusion of Pauline and Jewish-Christian views to which the Church had gradually come. He admits, indeed, that Paul himself commended, under certain circumstances, abstinence from idol-meat,[3] but sees in Rev. ii. 14, 15, 20, 24, where certain members of Asiatic churches are reproved for eating such meat and for fornication, the first step in the expression by Jewish Christians of the conditions on which they would recognize Gentile Christians. He then points to the prohibition in the pseudo-Clementines,[4] not only of eating idol-meat, but also of the use of things strangled, and blood, and to prohibitions of impurity scattered through the same books; refers to the rebuke administered in the so-called Epistle of Bar-

Connection of this with the authenticity of the Acts.

---

[1] 1 Cor. viii. 4–6; x. 23–26; Rom. xiv. 1–6.
[2] Cf. Zeitschr. für wissensch. Theol., 1883, pp. 159, etc.
[3] 1 Cor. viii. 7–13; x. 28; Rom. xiv. 14, 15.
[4] Hom. vii. 8; Recog. iv. 36.

nabas[1] against those who "rush forward as if proselytes to the Jewish law;" claims incorrectly, as we have seen,[2] that according to Justin the milder Jewish-Christian party demanded of Gentiles these conditions, while the extreme party demanded the observance of the whole law; and finally points to the fact, admitted by all, that in the second century abstinence from idol-meat was characteristic of Christians generally.[3] He accounts for these facts by the "legalistic movement" which in the post-apostolic age took possession of all Christendom, and maintains that by it a *modus vivendi* was gradually established between Pauline and Jewish Christians. The author of the Acts, living not long before Justin, and therefore when this state of things had come about, and supposing that what all believed to be Christian duty must have had apostolic authority, attributed the famous "decree" to the apostolic council. According to Holtzmann,[4] this was done without any conscious intention in the author of the Acts to misrepresent facts, but simply through his ignorant assumption of the prevalent ideas of his day, — a view in which Holtzmann differs from the earlier theory of Baur, Zeller, and others that Acts was a deliberate attempt to reconcile the contending parties by re-

[1] Chapter iii., Lat. vers.

[2] Justin (see above) does not represent any such difference in the demands of the mild and extreme Jewish parties. The real difference was that the milder party claimed the right to observe the law themselves; the extremists insisted on its observance by Gentiles.

[3] He refers to Eus. H. E. v. 1, Just. Dial. 35, Orig. contra Cels. viii. 30, and claims that Judaism, as well as Jewish Christianity, laid stress on these conditions of proselytism rather than on the observance of the whole law.

[4] And Pfleiderer (Paulinism, ii. 228, etc.).

writing the history of the apostolic age so as to give equal honor to Peter and Paul.[1]

Now, we are here concerned with these criticisms of the Acts[2] only so far as they show the significance of Justin's testimony. All admit that the Acts and Justin stand practically on the same ground in this matter. The fact that they do is insisted upon by the "advanced" critics, in order to show that the narrative of the Acts represents the ideas and usages not of the first but of the second century. To prove the authenticity and historical credibility of the Acts would be beyond our purpose. Suffice it to say that traces of the book may be found in the Epistles of Polycarp[3] and of Ignatius,[4] and even in that of Clement of Rome[5] toward the close of the first century. Nor can we here pause to disprove, as has been often done, the fundamental *dictum* of rationalistic criticism, that Gal. ii. is inconsistent with Acts xv. It is sufficient for us to observe that Justin, *unlike* the Acts, clearly shows that the stress laid in his day on abstinence from idol-meats was due to other causes than an inclination to Judaism. He expressly affirms that it was at least partly because of his abhorrence of the Gnostics, some of whom[6] prided themselves on doing this very thing. "They cause us," he says,[7] "who are disciples of the true and pure doctrine of Jesus Christ, to be more faithful and steadfast in the hope announced by Him." Nor were these the Marcionites, who claimed to be special followers of

Justin's abhorrence of "idol-meats" not due to Jewish influences.

---

[1] Holtzmann admits also (p. 164) that the Judaizing source which the author of the Acts used may have already worked up the account of the council.

[2] Cf. Weiss's Einleitung, pp. 560, etc.
[3] Ad Phil. 1.
[4] Smyr. 3, and, perhaps, Mag. 5.
[5] Ad Cor. cc. 2, 13.
[6] Iren. adv. Hær. i. 6. 3.
[7] Dial. 35.

GENTILE AND JEWISH CHRISTIANITY.   115

Paul, for they did not eat meat at all.[1] The action, therefore, of the Christians of the second century would seem in this matter to have been due to their abhorrence of the moral laxity and general worldliness into which heresy often tended, rather than to any reaction from Paulinism to Jewish Christianity. Connected with this was the necessity, as soon as Christianity became a public matter, of making a firm confession of the faith. No way of doing this was so often thrust upon them by their persecutors as the refusing to unite in sacrifice to the gods; and Paul himself recognized[2] the duty under such circumstances of refusing to eat meat which had been offered to idols, since the receiving of it would be considered homage to the false god. It is quite unnecessary, therefore, to see in this prevalent abstinence an anti-Pauline, Judaizing feeling, or to explain it as part of a *modus vivendi* established between Gentile and Jewish believers. The circumstances of the time led the Christian conscience thus to judge of its duty. That by so doing a possible cause of offence to Jewish Christians was removed, is of course obvious; but that the cause of the abstinence lay in the requirements of Jewish Christianity as such, or in the imposition upon the church of a ritualizing and confessedly anti-Pauline doctrine, is a view to which Justin, both by his explanation of the real cause of the abstinence and by his antipathy to Jewish ceremonialism, stands utterly opposed.[3]

[1] Justin (Dial. 35) includes the Marcionites (Μαρκιανοὶ, see Otto's note) and Saturnilians with the Basilideans and Valentinians, not as being eaters of idol-meat, but as being blasphemers of the Maker of all things.

[2] 1 Cor. x. 28. So Orig. contra Cels. viii. 31, gives this as the admitted reason why Christians abstained from idol-meat.

[3] The Clementines do not testify to the opinion of Catholic

2. But we are told that Justin does not mention Paul; nay, that he manifestly avoids mentioning him, and even implicitly repudiates him as an Apostle. Certainly, if this be so, there would be plausibility in the rationalistic theory of the original mutual hostility of the Apostles and division of the Church.

Justin does not mention Paul.

What, then, are in this case the facts? That Justin does not mention Paul, is true; but had he any reason to mention him, and does his silence imply hostility to the Apostle?

He had no reason to mention him.

Anticipating what will more fully appear later,[1] we may say that Justin speaks of the Apostles in general as the messengers sent by Christ to publish His Gospel to the world, as taught by Him and endowed with power from on high, and as having been sent to all nations to be the founders of the Church. They are represented as the authoritative publishers of Christ's doctrine, and the sources from which comes the knowledge of His life and teaching.[2] Of any of them, however, Justin makes mention by name in only three instances, all of which are in the Dialogue. Having affirmed his belief in a visible reign of Christ in Jerusalem, he quotes, first, Isa. lxv. 17–25,

His mention of the Apostles in general.

Christianity, but of the Ebionite sect. They were a veritable "Tendenzschrift;" and the difference between their representation of apostolic history and that of the Acts is as great in tone and spirit as in point of fact. The abstinence from things strangled and from blood, to which, however, Origen and Eusebius (in his report of the letter from Lyons and Vienne) testify, may be explained both by the "decree" of Acts and by the Christians' sensitive abhorrence of brutality. Origen says blood was the food of demons.

[1] Lect. V.
[2] Cf. Ap. i. 31, 33, 39, 40, 42, 45, 49, 50, 61, 66, 67; Dial. 42, 76, 81, 100, 106, 109, 110, 114, 118, 119.

and briefly comments on the passage, alluding also to Ps. xc. 4, and then adds:[1] "And further there was a certain man with us, whose name was John, one of the Apostles of Christ, who prophesied by a revelation that was made to him that those who believed in our Christ would dwell a thousand years in Jerusalem." Again,[2] in the course of an argument to show why Christ is called both Son of Man and Son of God, Justin mentions that He "called one of His disciples — previously known by the name of Simon — Peter; since he recognized Him to be Christ the Son of God by the revelation of the Father." And again[3] he points to the change of Simon's name to Peter and of those of the sons of Zebedee to Boanerges as an indication that Christ was the same who had changed Jacob's name to Israel and Oshea's to Joshua. It is evident that in the last two cases the mention of apostolic names was quite incidental. The mention of John as the author of the Apocalypse is more formal; yet even then the citation from the Apostle is subordinate to that from Isaiah, and it is less as an apostle than as a prophet that mention is made of him at all. In fact, the purpose of Justin's writings called for no special mention of particular Apostles. He was not narrating Christian history. He was arguing for Christianity on ground which he supposed his pagan readers and Jewish hearers would admit. It would have been useless for him to have quoted to them the apostolic epistles or any other Christian authorities, save so far as these were historical witnesses to the facts and teaching of Jesus.

But it is further said that Justin specifically calls the Apostles twelve, and attributes to them all a common mission to all nations. Was not "The twelve."

[1] Dial. 81.   [2] Dial. 100.   [3] Dial. 106.

this an intentional omission of Paul and a transference of his work to the original Apostles? Is not this an indication that Paul had fallen into disrepute even among Gentile Christians, at least among those of them who were in the Catholic Church? Is not Justin's language comparable with the ominous silence of the pseudo-Clementines concerning the same Apostle? It should be remembered, however, that Justin is admitted to have freely used the Epistles of Paul, though without fully reproducing the Apostle's thought.[1] It should be remembered also that he frequently refers, as we shall see,[2] to "the memoirs of the Apostles," and states [3] that these were written by Christ's "Apostles and those who followed them." This expression obviously means that some of the "memoirs" were written by Apostles, and others by their companions. Now, it is certain that Luke's Gospel was included in these "memoirs;" indeed, Justin refers to that Gospel in the very passage in which the above expression occurs. But that Gospel was never referred in all antiquity to an Apostle, and the inference is plain that it was considered by Justin apostolic because of the author's known connection with Paul. In fact, Justin's acceptance of Luke, especially when we remember that Marcion, whom Justin opposed, claimed his amended Luke as the original Pauline Gospel, is of itself sufficient proof of Justin's recognition of Paul's apostleship. Finally, it should be remembered, again, that Justin quotes none of the New Testament Epistles at all, though his acquaintance with most of them can be clearly

Used the Pauline Epistles and Luke.

---

[1] Cf. Otto's Justini Opera, ii. index iii.; and Thoma's exhaustive articles on "Justins literarisches Verhältniss zu Paulus und zum Johannes-Evangelium," Zeitschr. für wissensch. Theol., 1875, pp. 383, 490.

[2] Lect. V.   [3] Dial. 103.

shown. His failure, therefore, to cite from Paul is as consistent with his habit as, in view of the character of his readers, it was natural. His silence about the Apostle is quite a different phenomenon from that of the pseudo-Clementine Homilies and Recognitions, since these pretend to relate the movements and teaching of the principal characters of apostolic history.

When, then, we turn to the passages in which Justin speaks of twelve Apostles, we find them to be only two out of all the many references to the Apostles which occur in his writings. In the one[1] he quotes, as an example of the spirit of prophecy speaking in His own name, Isa. ii. 3, "For out of Zion shall go forth the law, and the word of the Lord from Jerusalem." He then adds: "And that it did so come to pass we can convince you. For from Jerusalem there went out into the world men, twelve in number, and these illiterate and of no ability in speaking; but by the power of God they proclaimed to every race of men that they were sent by Christ to teach to all the word of God." In the other,[2] he is showing how the Mosaic ordinances prefigured Christ and Christianity, and sees in the twelve bells, which he says[3] were hung to the high-priest's robe, a symbol of the twelve Apostles. It seems scarcely credible that these two instances, when Justin often speaks of the Apostles without any specification of number, should be thought to prove an intentional omission of Paul. Nor does the fact that he speaks of the Apostles as sent to all nations prove that he had transferred to the original

---

[1] Ap. i. 39.   [2] Dial. 42.

[3] He probably confounded these with the twelve precious stones in the priestly robe of Aaron. Cf. Otto's note referring to Tert. adv. Marc. iv. 13, where that Father uses the same stones as symbols of the Apostles.

twelve the Gentile work of Paul. It only shows that when Justin wrote, there was no consciousness of the alleged peculiarly Jewish work of the other Apostles. The "memoirs" themselves told him that the mission of the Apostles was to all nations. The established Gentile character of the Christian community rightly confirmed him in regarding this as the apostolic mission. It is almost trifling to assert that Justin's occasional use of the number twelve, which to this day we use without meaning to deny the apostleship of Paul, can be even imagined to contain a slur on the great champion of Gentile Christianity.

Unity of all the Apostles assumed.

3. It remains for me to mention two features of Justin's theology which have been supposed to indicate the influence of later Judaism.

a. The first is his strong Chiliasm. He believed in the triumphant establishment by Christ at the second advent of His kingdom in Jerusalem,[1] and the settlement of the Church in the Holy Land during a thousand years, after which would follow the general resurrection and judgment and the eternal kingdom.[2] Chiliasm has been supposed to have passed over into Christianity from Judaism, and to indicate in its advocates Jewish-Christian sympathies.

Chiliasm.

Upon this point, however, so far as our present investigation is concerned, we need call attention to but the following facts: —

(1) Chiliasm was widely diffused in the second century among Christians of both Gentile and Jewish affinities. Justin states [3] that while he and many others held this view, "many of those Christians who are of the pure and pious opinion do not

Widely diffused.

---

[1] Dial. 32, 35, 40, 51, 80, 81, 110, 113, 121, 138, 139.
[2] Dial. 81, 117, etc.   [3] Dial. 81.

GENTILE AND JEWISH CHRISTIANITY. 121

admit it." We find Chiliasm not only in the "Teaching of the Apostles"[1] and in Papias,[2] but also in Barnabas,[3] as well as later in Irenæus[4] and Tertullian.[5] So widely scattered a belief cannot therefore be considered evidence of Jewish tendencies.

(2) Justin held Chiliasm in a strong anti-Judaic form. He expected no conversion of the Jews as a nation,[6] but believed that the Christian Church as such would inherit the promised land.[7] Nor would Jewish sacrifices ever be restored.[8] Chiliasm indeed, as Dorner says,[9] was anti-Jewish in so far as the millennium was conceived of as only an intermediate state between the present age of suffering and the eternal age of glory which lay still beyond. This is very noticeable in Justin. In the Apology he says nothing of the millennium, and represents the rewards of the righteous as in the highest degree spiritual;[10] and while in the Dialogue he expresses his belief in a literal millennium, he also looks forward to the period after the final judgment as the ultimate object of Christian hope.[11] While, therefore, Chiliasm had certainly affinities with Judaism, its presence among Gentile Christians is no indication of a compromise with Jewish Christians on the points which had distinguished

(margin: Held by Justin in an anti-Judaic form.)

---

[1] c. 16.
[2] Iren. adv. Hær. v. 32.
[3] c. 15.
[4] Adv. Hær. v. 30–36.
[5] Adv. Marc. iii. 24.
[6] Dial. 32.
[7] Dial. 113, 139.
[8] Dial. 118.
[9] History of the Doctrine of the Person of Christ, i. 408, etc., Eng. trans.
[10] Cf. Ap. i. 10, 13, 21, 52. So see his description of the "heavenly kingdom" which Christians expect; Ap. i. 11. Aubé (Saint Justin, pp. 195–199) goes so far as to assert that Justin's idea of the future reward was even negative and philosophical; but he neglects the testimony of the Dialogue.
[11] Dial. 105, 116, 117.

them from one another. We may, with Dorner,[1] regard Chiliasm as an early and crude expression of the belief that Christianity was to conquer the world, or we may infer that it was the original belief of all apostolic Christians. We must certainly recognize that Chiliasm was quite in harmony with that combined literal and mystical method of interpreting Scripture, of which we have given examples from Justin.[2] But we cannot infer that its presence in him and other Gentile Christians was a symptom of sympathy with a Judaizing type of Christianity.

<small>Chiliasm no proof of Jewish sympathies.</small>

b. The other feature of Justin's theology which has been supposed to indicate a Judaizing tendency is his representation of Christianity as the "new law." He declares it to be the new law and covenant which the prophets had predicted and by which the Mosaic had been abolished.[3] Christ is a lawgiver,[4] or else is himself the new law[5] and the new covenant.[6] Justin also often speaks of the way of salvation in a manner which seems to show a legalizing, unevangelical conception. Christians receive indeed in baptism forgiveness of past sins,[7] but pray that, having learned the truth, they may by their works be found keepers of the commandments, and so be saved with an everlasting salvation.[8] Christ will clothe us with prepared garments, if we do His commandments.[9] So, likewise, salvation is represented almost entirely as future. They who can prove to God by their works that they

<small>Christian legalism.</small>

---

[1] Cf. above.

[2] Cf. especially Dial. 81, where Justin fancifully refers Isa. lxv. to the millennium.

[3] Dial. 11, 24, 67, 110, 122.   [4] Dial. 11, 12, 14, 18.
[5] Dial. 11, 43.   [6] Dial. 51, 118, 122.
[7] Ap. i. 61; cf. Dial. 54.   [8] Ap. i. 65.
[9] Dial. 116.

GENTILE AND JEWISH CHRISTIANITY. 123

followed Him will obtain the reward.[1] Hence obedience is predominantly made the condition of salvation. In pagan times Socrates and others were saved through their obedience to reason.[2] In Hebrew times men were saved, if they observed the moral as well as the ritual law.[3] Now, in Christian times "as many as are persuaded that the things taught by us are true, and undertake to be able to live accordingly, are regenerated in baptism,"[4] and afterwards strive to live sinless lives.[5] Repentance, baptism, belief in the revelation of God through Christ, and obedience to Christ's law are the commonly named conditions of salvation.[6] On the ground of these and similar expressions Justin is said to have taught a purely legal way of salvation, and thus to have been far from sharing the Pauline doctrine of salvation through faith. And it must be admitted that this mode of speaking may be fairly said to be characteristic of Justin.[7] We miss in his writings the clear expression of the Pauline doctrine of immediate justification and a full sense of faith as the appropriation of a finished redemption. Yet, on the other hand, we think it possible to collect from Justin other phrases and ideas which imply the evangelical view of the way of salvation. He speaks of it as originating in God's goodness, whereby God was led to send His Son to earth.[8] While emphasizing human liberty, he speaks of Christian life as in some manner based on divine grace to individuals.[9]

[1] Ap. i. 8. So cf. 10, 14, 42, 48, 65.
[2] Ap. i. 5, 10, 46.   [3] Dial. 11–26, 45.
[4] Ap. i. 61.   [5] Dial. 44.
[6] Cf. Dial. 95. "If you repent of your sins and recognize Him to be Christ and observe His commandments, then . . . remission of sins will be yours."
[7] Cf. Lect. IV., where this whole subject is further discussed.
[8] Ap. i. 10.   [9] Dial. 30, 32, 55, 119, 121.

More, also, is made of faith and of Christ's blood than Justin's previous expressions would lead us to expect, or than all of his critics have given him credit for. Isaiah, he says, sends us to that saving bath which is for those who repent and are purified, not by the blood of goats and of sheep, but by faith through the blood of Christ.[1] Abraham was justified and blessed on account of his faith.[2] The Gentiles who have believed on Christ and repented, shall receive the inheritance.[3] The paschal lamb was a type of Christ, "with whose blood they who believe in Him, in proportion to their faith in Him, anoint their houses, i. e. themselves."[4] "All who repent can obtain mercy from God, even as the Scripture foretells, 'Blessed is the man to whom the Lord imputeth not sin.'"[5] "The goodness of God holds him who repents of his sins, as He reveals through Ezekiel, as righteous and free from sin."[6] While, therefore, Justin undoubtedly laid stress on the idea of Christ as a teacher, on faith as the acceptance of truth, and Christian life as obedience, there was evidently another conception of salvation imbedded in his language and thought.

The present question, however, is, To what was his legalistic tendency due? A little earlier we read, in the pseudo-Epistle of Barnabas,[7] of "the new law of our Lord Jesus Christ, which is without the yoke of necessity." A little later than Justin, Athenagoras wrote: "We have a law which makes the measure of righteousness to be dealing with our neighbors as ourselves."[8] The Homily which goes

Its growth in the post-apostolic Church.

---

[1] Dial. 13. πίστει.　　[2] Dial. 23 (διὰ τὴν πίστιν) and 119.
[3] Dial. 26.
[4] Dial. 40. κατὰ τὸν λόγον τῆς εἰς αὐτὸν πίστεως.
[5] Dial. 141.　　[6] Dial. 47.
[7] c. 2.　　[8] Supplic. 32.

GENTILE AND JEWISH CHRISTIANITY. 125

by the name of the Second Epistle of Clement of Rome lays great stress on obedience and good works;[1] while Irenæus[2] and Tertullian[3] speak of the new covenant or new law. These were Gentile Christians. Was the stress thus laid on Christian duty and the employment of apparently legalistic phraseology due to a reaction of Gentile Christianity toward Jewish Christianity, or are we to seek the explanation in other causes? Our full reply to this question must be deferred until with Justin's aid we have studied the influence of paganism on Christianity. But for the present we may observe that, united as this legalism was with a thorough repudiation of Jewish rites, it is at least unnecessary to see in it a sign of the merging of Gentile and Jewish Christianity. It should be remembered that Paul himself spoke of "the law of Christ"[4] and of "the law of the Spirit,"[5] of "waiting by faith for the hope of righteousness,"[6] and of the imperative necessity of good works.[7] It is quite conceivable that in the second age of Christianity practical problems of duty would, in the face of heathenism and persecution, cause the moral side of the Gospel and the necessity of obedience to the Gospel's requirements to be emphasized. It is quite conceivable, also, that Gentile Christianity should not have been able to preserve the strictly evangelical ideas of Paul against the influence of philosophy and the natural tendency of the human mind. It is quite possible that the use of the Old Testament as a book of Christian doctrine, without a just

Its cause.

Not necessarily due to Judaism.

---

[1] cc. 2, 4, 11, etc.
[2] Adv. Hær. iii. 10. 5; iv. 9. 2; 34. 11; etc.
[3] De Præscr. 13; Adv. Jud. 3, 6, 9.
[4] Gal. vi. 2.   [5] Rom. viii. 2.
[6] Gal. v. 5.   [7] Gal. v. 19–25, etc.

sense of the progress of revelation, may have contributed to a revival of the forms of thought which the old dispensation, if superficially understood, was likely to create. But when the authors who represent this tendency vigorously repudiate Judaism, show themselves unable even to appreciate the worth of the Hebrew system, consider Christianity an essentially Gentile institution, and speak of Jewish Christians as weak-minded believers, it may be true that they had themselves lost the clear apprehension of immediate salvation by faith alone, and had thus revived a spirit similar to that of the later Jews; but it is surely not to be inferred that this was a sign of the blending of the body of Gentile Christians with the body of Jewish Christians to which they had formerly been avowedly hostile. We rather infer from the testimony of Justin that Jewish Christianity had become a comparatively small fraction of the Church; that it had, with the exception of the Ebionites, long since been reconciled to the claims of Gentile Christians, and that both Gentile and Jew, with the same exception, acknowledged the authority of all the Apostles. The bulk of Jewish Christians were distinguished from Gentile believers simply by their observance of their national ceremonies, not by repudiation of Paul. But Gentile Christianity was the advancing, growing side of the Church, and the importance to it of the smaller body who still clung to their traditional rites was daily lessening. The Church was grappling with wider questions than that which Jewish Christianity presented to it, and was content to leave the latter to its own course. It was contending for independent right to toleration under Roman law. It was meeting the assaults of heathen tradition and philosophy. To many of its members the

Summary of Justin's testimony.

claims of Judaizing Christianity were perhaps unknown. Certainly the Church believed in no division among the Apostles. The extreme faction of the Ebionites still indeed continued; and the excesses of Gnosticism, notably the undue exaltation of Paul by Marcion, may in some quarters have caused reactions in the opposite direction. In some such way may the anti-Paulinism of the Clementine Homilies and Recognitions be explained. Through the Old Testament also, and, as we shall see, through the Alexandrian philosophy, Judaism entered into the life of Gentile Christianity. But both of these sources of influence must be distinguished from the body of Jewish Christians, who continued to unite Christianity with observance of the ritual law, and who, as the alleged followers of the original Apostles, have been made to play in critical theories so important a part in the formation of the Church. These were in Justin's time a dwindling minority, which was being rapidly swallowed up in the growth of Gentile Christianity; and the theories which would make them to have exerted so great an influence in the second century as to unseat Paul from his apostleship and to recast the Church's remembrance of the apostolic age and to dictate the controlling spirit of the resulting Catholic Church are, we think, in the light of the evidence of the second century itself, entirely baseless.

LECTURE IV.

THE TESTIMONY OF JUSTIN TO THE INFLUENCE OF PHILOSOPHY ON EARLY CHRISTIANITY.

Justin shows the influence of philosophy.
THAT Christianity had come into contact with, and was being affected by, the philosophic thought of the Gentile world, is obvious from the writings of Justin. We have already seen that he pleaded for the toleration of his religion on the ground that it was not only elevating to society but was a philosophy, and should therefore be allowed, like other philosophies, freedom of opinion. We have mentioned, also, that in the Dialogue he formally declares Christianity to be the true philosophy, and himself a philosopher because a Christian.

Contrast with the New Testament.
Such language is in marked contrast with that of the New Testament. In the latter the word "philosophy" is only once used, and then as a probable cause of peril to Christians.[1] The rising heresies, against which the later Epistles of Paul warned the churches, were no doubt Jewish and ritualistic in their immediate origin and character, but were ultimately derived from pagan speculations, and seem to have been the first movements of the mighty current of Gnosticism which afterward poured in upon the Church.[2] Later indications of the same general

[1] Col. ii. 8.
[2] Cf. Col. i. 16; ii. 8, 16, 18, 23; 1 Tim. i. 4; iv. 3, 4; vi. 20; 2 Tim. ii. 16–18; iv. 4; Tit. iii. 9.

PHILOSOPHY AND EARLY CHRISTIANITY. 129

movement may be observed in Second Peter[1] and Jude,[2] in the Apocalypse,[3] and in the Doketism combated in the First Epistle of John.[4] It is true that Paul says "we speak wisdom among them that are perfect," and thereby declares that Christianity already possessed, and implies that eventually it would elaborate, a philosophy of its own; but he adds "yet not the wisdom of this world,"[5] and thereby rejects what was currently known as philosophy in the pagan society of that day. While at Athens he quoted from a Stoic hymn, and expressed ideas with which some of his auditors may have agreed and which seem to show the Apostle's acquaintance with Stoicism; yet even then he spoke of the previous ages as " times of ignorance," and evinced no real sympathy with the popular philosophies themselves.[6] The coincidences which have been often pointed out between Saint Paul's phraseology and that of the later Stoics[7] may show that in Tarsus he had learned at least the ethics of that system, but do not show that pagan thought had moulded any of his conceptions of Christian doctrine.[8] Whether, in addition to this, there are any Alexandrian elements in the Epistle to the Hebrews or not, whether Saint John took his Logos doctrine from Philo or not,[9] it must be admitted that the New Testament writings as a whole belonged to a circle as far removed from the speculations of their day as philosophy itself was as yet

---

[1] 2 Pet. ii. 1, 2, 10, 12, 15, 18, 19.   [2] Jude 4.
[3] Rev. ii. 4, 24.
[4] 1 John i. 1; ii. 22; iv. 2, 3. Cf. Mansel's Gnostic Heresies, Lectt. IV. and V.
[5] 1 Cor. ii. 6.   [6] Acts xvii. 22–31.
[7] Cf. Lightfoot on Philippians, "Saint Paul and Seneca."
[8] Cf. Aubé's Saint Justin, p. 87, note 1.
[9] Cf. Weiss's Einleitung, p. 591, note. He wholly rejects the Philonian source of the Logos doctrine.

either ignorant of the new religion or contemptuously indifferent to it.

But when Gentile Christianity was firmly established, and, conscious of a universal mission, began to meet the habits and thoughts of the pagan world, it was necessarily affected by the currents of the new atmosphere in which it found itself. On the one hand, Gnosticism sought to unite the Christian idea of a revealed redemption with the speculations concerning absolute Being and the origin of evil which had already been elaborated in the Platonic and especially Jewish-Platonic schools and in the religious philosophy of the East.[1] On the other hand, writers who had no sympathy with Gnosticism began to realize the problems which were forced on Christianity by the culture of the age. The new religion had to explain its position toward pagan antiquity as it had already done toward Hebrew antiquity. It began to be defended either by or against philosophy. The way accordingly soon opened for a philosophy of its own, — for an effort to present it in such wise as to satisfy the intellectual needs of converts from thoughtful pagan circles. Already in the so-called Epistle of Barnabas,[2] we may see a Christian reflecting on the deeper meaning of the common faith. The lost Apologies of the Athenians Quadratus and Aristides, presented to the Emperor Trajan, are said by Jerome[3] to have cited the writings of philosophers. If we may place so early the Epistle to Diognetus,[4] we learn from it the interest which a cultivated pagan took in Christianity, while

Beginnings of the union of philosophy and Christianity.

---

[1] Cf. Mansel's Gnostic Heresies, Lect. II.   [2] c. 1.
[3] Letter to Magnus.
[4] Cf. Otto's Justini Opera, tom. ii. proleg. lxii. for account of opinions as to date of the Epistle.

the Epistle itself bears evidence of having been the product of a well-educated man. The author does not indeed follow the philosophers, any more than he does the superstitions of the people or the ritual of the Jews. He is truly scriptural in doctrine, and explains the late appearance of the Saviour by God's determination to let man discover his own helplessness. Yet his description of the benefits which Diognetus would obtain from Christianity — such as the knowledge and love of the Father, and similarity of character with Him — is such as would have appealed most strongly to a religiously inclined philosopher, as will appear from Justin himself.[1] Thus the contact of Christianity and philosophy had begun before Justin wrote. But in him we find it for the first time, among anti-Gnostic writers, openly avowed. He was a student of philosophy as well as of Christianity. He passed from the former to the latter as to a higher stage of culture. He did not break from philosophy in becoming a Christian. He carried into Christianity many of his previous ideas. Paganism was to him not merely the development of evil. It contained also a positive preparation for, and anticipations of, the revelation of Christ. As in the earlier Epistles of Paul we find set forth the difference between the Gospel and the Law, but in the Epistle to the Hebrews the fulfilment of the old economy in the new; so in the Epistle to Diognetus we find paganism set forth as a proof of man's inability to attain to God and righteousness, but in Justin we

In Justin the union avowed.

[1] The last two chapters of the Epistle to Diognetus are probably by a later hand, and are more in Justin's style. They speak of Christianity as not contrary to reason (οὐ παραλόγως ζητῶ), of the author as a teacher of the Gentiles, of the Logos "who appeared as if new and was found old," and of the tree of knowledge as a symbol of the true Christian gnosis.

find the fulfilment by Christianity of the partial truths and gleams of light which in the pagan world had prepared for it.

Let us, first, then recall the condition of pagan thought at this period, and observe Justin's acquaintance with it and the judgments which he passes upon its various types.

Philosophy at this period.

He appears to have been a man of moderate culture. He was certainly not a genius nor an original thinker. He had an inquiring and an impressible mind. He was naturally serious, and anxious to obtain light on the great questions of life and God. He went from one teacher to another, but was soon dissatisfied with all. Yet from nearly all he received ideas which continued to germinate in his mind. He was a true eclectic, and for this very reason is a far better mirror of the intellectual forces to which he was exposed than if he had been an original genius.

Justin's mind.

We should remember that the two marked characteristics of the culture of that age were its eclecticism and its theological spirit. The great schools of Greek philosophy, while still continuing in name, had long ceased to maintain in purity their original doctrines. The age of discovery and conviction had long since been followed by that of doubt, comparison, and mutual approximation. Moreover, the fusion of peoples consequent upon the Roman conquest of the civilized world had caused Greek culture to spread among alien races, who appropriated it in parts and combined it with elements of their own. The result was a search by cultured men for the truth in all schools of thought, together with lurking scepticism as to the possibility of real knowledge; a general acceptance of philosophy as the only guide of life and valuation of the popular

Eclecticism.

religions for political purposes only, together with a refusal to follow exclusively any of the historic philosophical systems. Cicero, who was not unlike Justin in his travels from philosopher to philosopher while searching for truth, exhibits by his scepticism as to absolute knowledge, by his sense of the supreme importance of ethics, and by his deliberate comparison and criticism of the various schools, the rising spirit of the age of the Cæsars. The later Platonists were especially eclectic. They mingled with the doctrines of their master ideas taken from the Stoics and from Aristotle, and sought in this way to build up a system of universal knowledge, and to overthrow the scepticism in which the men of the so-called "Middle Academy" had fallen. At the same time there was no philosophy which exerted greater influence over others than Platonism. It modified and mingled with nearly every other school of thought. The Roman Stoics, depreciating physical inquiries and turning attention to ethical problems, not only approached the same practical spirit which other schools were showing, but often spoke of God and immortality in a manner more Platonic than Stoic. Meanwhile Philo of Alexandria had deliberately fused elements from both Platonism and Stoicism with faith in the Hebrew Scriptures, and had produced a mixed system by which, through the medium of the Hellenistic Jews, Greek thought acted upon the Christian mind of a century later. The Epicureans held most loyally to the tenets of their predecessors; while on the opposite extreme from them such men as Plutarch and Maximus of Tyre stand as the attractive representatives of eclecticism pure and simple, taking from all schools whatever subserved their moral and religious purposes. For the eclecticism of the age of which we are speaking was mainly governed by a desire to serve practical and moral interests. There was a general disposition, in spite of the speculative spirit of some, to regard inquiries concerning the possibility of knowledge and the ultimate nature of things as hopeless and useless. Philosophical doubt was widely diffused, and caused attention to be turned to the direction of conduct. Wherever also the Roman temper was prevalent, there philosophy naturally took a practical turn. Hence Platonist and Stoic alike laid stress on questions of ethics, and sought to exhibit wherein consists a truly rational and noble human life.

Moreover, closely connected with this was the theological aim and religious spirit of the whole period of ancient eclecticism. Many forces united to produce this feature. The influence of Oriental thought, of which Judaism was a part, was a not unimportant factor. The fall of polytheism before the advance of philosophy led to general belief in the unity of God. The influence of scepticism united with the speculative spirit itself not only to lay stress on practical ends, but also to emphasize the divine transcendence and to represent God as the unknowable First Cause. At the same time the sense of dependence and of man's abject need of divine help gave a deeply religious tone to the best writers of the period. The human mind stood on the brink of the impassable gulf which philosophy placed between the finite and the infinite, and inconsistently but necessarily talked of God as if He had been found. It is easy to select from heathen authors passages which seem to utter an almost Christian spirit of faith and resignation.[1] More and more did philosophy itself take a mystical

Theological aim and religious tone of philosophy.

---

[1] Cf. Aubé's Saint Justin, part iii. ch. iii.

PHILOSOPHY AND EARLY CHRISTIANITY. 135

direction, until in Neo-Platonism it actually became a religion. In the second century this varied process was in full movement. In proportion as the Platonic influence was predominant was a real belief in God maintained, yet with an increasing stress on His transcendence and on the need of intermediate beings to reveal Him to mankind. To our minds it appears that the preparation of philosophy for Christianity was complete. The inability of reason clearly to make God known was manifest. The necessity of finding God was equally demonstrated. The truths which had been discovered needed to find a full and orderly exhibition, and to be properly adjusted by the actual revelation of God. The time was ripe for that movement, of which Justin was the earliest representative, by which Christianity was set forth as the reconciliation of the terrible discord between the conclusions of reason and the needs of humanity, and as the expression of all that the human mind had learned to be good and true.[1]

In Justin's writings, then, we recognize the characteristics of the period which we have described. Of his early search for truth in the spirit of eclecticism mention has already been made. He yielded finally to the charms of Platonism.[2]

Justin shows the spirit of the times.

[1] Cf. Zeller's Outlines of Greek Philosophy, pp. 274, etc.; History of Eclecticism, passim; Überweg's History of Philosophy, i. 212–262; Aubé's Saint Justin, part iii.

[2] How far Justin grasped the real system of Plato is a question on which there has been difference of opinion. Doubtless he read into Plato much of later thought as well as of Bible doctrine; but he was certainly acquainted with most of the Platonic books. Reminiscences appear in his Apologies (i. 2, 57, 58; ii. 2) of the Apology of Socrates; and the Introduction to the Dialogue seems to have been moulded after the Socratic Dialogues. We find in Justin, also, clear traces of or quotations from the Republic [Ap. i. 3 (Rep. v. p. 473, ed. Steph.), 44 (Rep. x. p. 617); ii. 3,

But he was acquainted also with Stoicism, and though rejecting its philosophy, praises its ethics, and appears to have taken from the Stoics one of his most characteristic phrases.[1] Most of all, however, does he echo the mind of his age in his conception of philosophy itself. "The duty of philosophy," he says, "is to investigate concerning the divine."[2] "Philosophy leads us to God, and alone commends us."[3] From his Stoic, Peripatetic, and Pythagorean teachers he was unable to learn of God; and hence the pleasure which even before his conversion he found in Plato, since by his aid he expected "henceforth to look upon God," — "for this," he adds, "is the end of the Platonic philosophy."[4] When he was questioned by the aged Christian who was the means of his conversion as to what philosophy is, Justin replied, "Philosophy is the apprehension of the real and the cognition of the true;"[5] and both he and his questioner evidently understood "the real" and "the true" to mean God.[6] So, finally, he was led to accept

10 (Rep. x. p. 595); Dial. 4 (Rep. vii. p. 509)]; the Critias [Ap. i. 68 (Crit. p. 43)]; the Phædo [Dial. 3 (Phæd. p. 85), 4 (Phæd. pp. 65, 66, 67, 72, 76, 92), 5, and Ap. i. 18 (Phæd. p. 107)]; the Gorgias [Ap. i. 8 (Gorg. p. 543)]; the Philebus [Dial. 4 (Phil. p. 30)]; the Timæus [Ap. i. 26; ii. 10 (Tim. p. 28); i. 60 (Tim. p. 36); Dial. 5 (Tim. p. 28)]; the Phædrus [Ap. i. 8 (Phædr. p. 249); Dial. 4 (Phædr. ibid.), 5 (Phædr. p. 246)], and, perhaps, the Laws [Ap. ii. 9 (Legg. ii. 661)]; the Parmenides [Dial. 3 (Parm. p. 127)]; and the Clitophon [Ap. ii. 12 (Clitoph. p. 407)], as well as the second Ps.-Platonic Epistle [Ap. i. 60 (Ep. ii. 312)]. Cf. Otto's Justini Opera, tom. i. index iii. 2.

[1] λόγος σπερματικός. If Justin did not take the phrase from the Stoics, at least it originated with them. Cf. below.

[2] Dial. 1. ἐξετάζειν περὶ τοῦ θείου. [3] Dial. 2.

[4] Ibid.

[5] Dial. 3. ἐπιστήμη τοῦ ὄντος καὶ τοῦ ἀληθοῦς ἐπίγνωσις.

[6] The old man immediately asks, "But what do you call God?" to which Justin replies, "That which always maintains the same

PHILOSOPHY AND EARLY CHRISTIANITY. 137

Christianity because in it he found God revealed.[1] Thus Justin was reared in the idea that philosophy was theology, and that the grand aim of speculation was to attain to the knowledge of God, and so to learn how life should be regulated. He came to Christianity with this strong religious and moral aspiration. He carried over into Christianity the same conception of philosophy, and believed that he had at last found its realization. He affords, therefore, a fair representation of both the eclectic and theological tone of the best culture of the pagan world, and of the natural course by which that culture would, if at all, pass over into Christianity.

When, then, we read the judgments which Justin here and there expresses from his later Christian standpoint upon the various philosophic schools, we find, as we would expect, a free criticism of them combined with evident traces of their continued influence. Of Cynics[2] and Epicureans[3] he speaks only with contempt, and does not appear to have thought teachers of these schools worth seeking. His Peripatetic[4] teacher was more concerned about his fee than about the communication of knowledge to his pupils; but Justin nowhere mentions Aristotle, and betrays little of his influence.[5] Of the Pythagoreans he

His judgments upon the schools.

---

nature, and in the same manner, and is the cause of all other things." Thirlby and Aubé read τὸ ὄν for θεὸν. Otto retains, with most editors, θεὸν.

[1] Dial. 7, 8.   [2] Ap. ii. 3.
[3] Ap. ii. 7, 12, 15.   [4] Dial. 2.
[5] Weizsäcker (Jahrb. für deutsche Theol. xii. 60–119) sees Aristotelian influences in Justin's idea of God dwelling immovably in his own place beyond the heavens (Dial. 127), and in the method of argument concerning the natural mortality of the soul (Dial. 5).

speaks with respect,[1] but objects to the long course of intellectual discipline required by them before their scholars could be even prepared to behold the beautiful and the good.[2] It was, as we have said, Stoicism and still more Platonism which attracted him; and his judgments upon these systems are frequent and often elaborate. He admired the ethics of the former,[3] and appeals to Heraclitus, who has been called[4] "the spiritual ancestor" of the Stoics, and to Musonius Rufus, who was banished by Nero, as examples of those who were hated and put to death because the Logos dwelt in them.[5] He points out also that the Stoics, like the Christians, taught the future destruction of the world by fire.[6] Yet his opposition to the Stoic philosophy was very decided, and he expresses it freely in the Apologies, no doubt remembering the "philosophic Cæsar," who, he hoped, would read his book. He distinguishes the Christian doctrine of the conflagration of the world from that of the Stoics, pointing out that the former represented it as a divine act of judgment, but the latter as a natural and necessary process and including God Himself.[7] He objects to their materialism,[8] but most of all to their doctrine of fate,

Stoicism.

---

[1] Dial. 2, 5.

[2] Justin referred, of course, to the Neo-Pythagoreans who were more a religious sect than a philosophic school, and had borrowed largely from other systems. Cf. Zeller's Outlines of Greek Philosophy, p. 306.

[3] Ap. ii. 7, 8.

[4] Cf. Gildersleeve's note, Apologies of Justin Martyr, p. 221; Zeller's Outlines of Greek Philosophy, p. 233.

[5] Neither Heraclitus nor Musonius was really put to death. This is one of Justin's mistakes.

[6] Ap. i. 20, 60; ii. 7.   [7] Ap. i. 20; ii. 7.

[8] Ap. ii. 7. He distinguishes the Stoic λόγος περὶ ἀρχῶν καὶ ἀσωμάτων from their λόγος περὶ ἠθῶν, and says that the former,

PHILOSOPHY AND EARLY CHRISTIANITY. 139

and declares their philosophy to be destructive of spiritual ideas, to merge God in the changing universe, and to destroy the inherent difference between virtue and vice.[1] In his Stoic instructor Justin found no knowledge of God nor desire to know Him, and his own spiritual aspirations and his deep sense of human responsibility led him to see the radical hostility to these which, in spite of its lofty ethical teaching, the Stoic philosophy logically involved. When, on the other hand, he speaks of Platonism, he is not less free in criticism, but his sympathies are clearly exhibited. Plato, he says, like the Christians, taught a future judgment,[2] and derived his doctrines of creation[3] and of human responsibility[4] and of "the second and third Powers in the universe"[5] from Moses. Justin does not seem to have thought that the Platonic doctrine that God made the world from formless matter was inconsistent with God's absolute authorship of the world. He rather maintains that this was the doctrine of Moses too. Either he did not realize that the eternity of matter was opposed to the Christian doctrine of creation, or he understood Plato to mean by formless matter a practical negation.[6] So also he quotes from the Timæus the statement concerning the World-soul that God "placed it like a χ in the universe," declaring that Plato referred to the Second Power in the

Platonism.

according to which nothing is real which is not material, is inconsistent with the spiritual directions of the latter.

[1] Ap. ii. 7.   [2] Ap. i. 8.   [3] Ap. i. 20, 59.
[4] Ap. i. 44.   [5] Ap. i. 60.

[6] Cf. Zeller's Outlines of Greek Philosophy, pp. 146, etc.; Aubé's Saint Justin, p. 123; Von Engelhardt's Das Christenthum Justins, p. 137. Justin was misled both by his Platonism and by the expression in Gen. i. 2; but he seems to have felt no necessity for the metaphysical doctrine of creation *ex nihilo*.

universe, and took the idea from the account of the brazen serpent.[1] He appears to have considered Plato's "World-soul" as an attempt to teach the doctrine of the personal Logos, thus reading into Plato, as he did into the Old Testament, his Christian ideas, and seeing in that philosopher the one who approached most nearly to the truth.[2] But, on the other hand, he freely differs from Plato. That philosopher, he says, teaches the punishment of the wicked for only a limited period of time and in other bodies than their own, whereas Christians teach the everlasting punishment of the wicked and in the same bodies which they now have. In the introduction to the Dialogue, moreover, Justin evidently indicates his points of conscious departure from Platonism. He no longer imagines, as he did before conversion, that by intellectual discipline alone, or by subduing the hindrances offered by the body, he would be enabled to apprehend God; but he has discovered the moral conditions of this blessedness as they had been taught by revelation and as he now perceives that reason itself teaches.[3] No longer does he believe in the pre-existence of souls, nor even in their natural immortality.[4] The latter he claims to deny on the Platonic principle that whatever is created is perishable. Hence he refers immortality solely to the will of God,[5] — a view which indeed Plato approaches in the Timæus, but which was not his main argument for immortality.[6] Justin ex-

---

[1] Justin says: "Moses took brass and made *it into a cross*, and set it in the holy tabernacle." Ap. i. 60.

[2] So he finds (i. 60) in the obscure expression of the Ps.-Platonic Ep. ii., τὰ δὲ τρίτα περὶ τὸν τρίτον, a reference to the Holy Spirit, likewise taken from Gen. i. 2. Athenagoras (Supplic. 23) quotes the same passage, with apparently the same view of it as Justin's.

[3] Dial. 2, 3.   [4] Dial. 4, 5, 141.   [5] Dial. 6.

[6] Cf. Überweg's History of Philosophy, i. 127, etc.

presses his conscious attitude to Platonism when he says,[1] "I strive to be found a Christian, not because the teachings of Plato are different from those of Christ, but because they are not in all respects similar, as neither are those of the others, Stoics and poets and historians." To him Plato was a theist who had learned much from Moses and had been peculiarly receptive of the divine Logos,— that "light which lighteth every man coming into the world." Despite his quotations from other of Plato's works, it would appear that he knew Platonism mainly as it is represented in the Timæus, and hence cannot be said to have fully grasped the real system of the philosopher.[2] But he found in Platonism, as he understood it, the nearest approach to Christianity, and felt that no break was required with its spirit and principles to pass into the clearer light of Christian revelation.

Justin, then, represents the religious and moral elements of pagan culture finding their satisfaction in the religion of Christ. We see in him what affinities there were between at least one side of paganism and Christianity, and how it was possible for the latter to take into itself ideas and forms of thought which had been elaborated outside of the sphere of revelation. Let us now examine his presentation of Christian theology with the particular purpose of noting the continued influence of the philosophical ideas with which we have found that he approached it.

The influence of philosophy on his theology.

I. First, take his idea of God. This will show the

[1] Ap. ii. 13.
[2] Cf. Jowett's Introduction to the Timæus in his translation of Plato's Dialogues.

intellectual foundation on which his idea of religion was built. To set forth the Christian doctrine of God was required of him, as an Apologist. To show that he had truly found God was, in view of his conception of philosophy, required of him as a philosopher. His Christianity, of course, found in the idea of God its controlling principle. How, then, does Justin represent God?

I. The idea of God.

As against polytheism he sets forth the divine independence. God is not to be worshipped as if He needs anything.[1] On the other hand, against the abstractions of philosophy he sets forth the reality of a living God. Not only do Christians believe in Him more firmly than others,[2] but He is "the most true,"[3] "the real,"[4] having alone life in Himself.[5] He is represented, likewise, as exercising every noble moral quality. He is "the Father of righteousness and temperance and other virtues."[6] In Him "reside temperance and justice and philanthropy."[7] He is "good,"[8] especially toward men;[9] the righteous observer of all things;[10] compassionate and long-suffering.[11] So is He the absolute author of all things. He is called "the Father and Maker of all,"[12] "the Father and Lord of all,"[13] "the Father and King of the heavens,"[14] or simply "the Father of all"[15] including Christ and man as

God's independence.

A living reality.

Moral qualities.

Author of all.

---

[1] Ap. i. 10.
[2] Ap. i. 18.
[3] Ap. i. 6.
[4] Ap. i. 13. τοῦ ὄντως θεοῦ.
[5] Dial. 6.
[6] Ap. i. 6.
[7] Ap. i. 10.
[8] Ap. i. 14, 16.
[9] Ap. i. 10.
[10] Ap. ii. 12.
[11] Dial. 108.
[12] Ap. i. 8; Dial. 140.
[13] Ap. i. 12, 32, 36, 40, 44, 61.
[14] Ap. ii. 12.
[15] Ap. i. 12, 45, 65; ii. 6, 9; Dial. 7, 32, 56, 63, 67, 74, 105, 115, 127.

PHILOSOPHY AND EARLY CHRISTIANITY. 143

well as the universe. He is therefore the Creator,[1] and Cause of all.[2] He knows both the actions and the thoughts of all His creatures.[3] He can do whatever He wills.[4] He foreknows everything; yet not because events are necessary, nor because He has decreed that men shall act as they do or be what they are; but foreseeing all events, He ordains reward or punishment accordingly.[5] His interest in man is unceasing. He is no impassive observer of human life,[6] but is actively concerned in the conduct of His rational creatures,[7] requiring their obedience and enforcing His moral law.[8] He spares the wicked world that more may be saved,[9] and that the hopes of the Christians may be fulfilled.[10] It was out of goodness and for man's sake that He made the world,[11] and it was in accordance with His counsel that Christ came.[12] He cares, finally, not merely for the universe in general, but for each individual in particular.[13] *(Omniscient. Omnipotent. No fatalism. God's interest in man. His goodness. And care of individuals.)*

But at the same time Justin speaks of God in ways which hardly seem consistent with these expressions which have been cited. He is not only specially fond of calling Him the "unbegotten,"[14] the "passionless,"[15] the "incorruptible,"[16] the *(Yet emphasis placed on His transcendence.)*

---

[1] ποιητής or δημιουργός. Ap. i. 13, 16, 57, 58; ii. 5; Dial. 7, 16, 34, 84, 102, 116.
[2] Dial. 5.   [3] Ap. i. 12; ii. 12.
[4] Ap. i. 19; Dial. 5, 6, 16, 84, 142.
[5] Ap. i. 12, 43, 44; ii. 7; Dial. 16, 141.
[6] Ap. i. 28.   [7] Ap. i. 37.
[8] Ap. i. 37; ii. 7, 9.   [9] Ap. i. 28.
[10] Ap. ii. 7.   [11] Ap. i. 10; ii. 4.
[12] Ap. ii. 6.   [13] Dial. 1.
[14] Ap. i. 14, 25, 49, 53; ii. 12; Dial. 5, 114, 126, 127.
[15] ἀπαθής. Ap. i. 12; ii. 12.   [16] Dial. 5.

"unchangeable,"[1] but he describes the divine transcendence in most extreme terms. God is exalted above all the universe, and has an ineffable glory and name.[2] He can be called by no fixed name.[3] In fact, being unbegotten, He has no name.[4] The terms "Father," "God," "Creator," "Lord," and "Master" do not describe what He is, but are mere appellations to set forth His manifested activities.[5] These expressions, it should be observed, are capable of a meaning quite unobjectionable from a New Testament point of view, but they are used by Justin with a partiality which shows that the transcendence of Deity occupied a controlling place in his mind. This appears still more clearly when, in arguing that the God who appeared to Abraham was not the Father and Maker of all, Justin insists[6] that the latter "remains ever in the supercelestial places, visible to none, and never holding intercourse directly[7] with any." He also thinks it absurd to say that the Father and Maker of all, having left the supercelestial places, was visible on a little portion of the earth,[8] and declares that "the ineffable Father and Lord of all neither has come to any place, nor walks, nor sleeps, nor rises up, but remains in his own place, wherever that is, quick to behold and quick to hear, having neither eyes nor ears, but being of indescribable might; and He sees all things, and knows all things, and none of us escapes His observation; and He is not moved or confined to a spot in the whole world, for He existed before the world was made. How, then, could He talk with any one, or be seen by any one, or appear on the smallest portion of the earth?"[9]

[1] Ap. i. 13.
[2] Ap. i. 9; ii. 10, 12, 13.
[3] Ap. i. 10.
[4] Ap. i. 61; ii. 6.
[5] Ap. ii. 6.
[6] Dial. 56.
[7] δι' ἑαυτοῦ.
[8] Dial. 60.
[9] Dial. 127.

God therefore is, according to Justin, the eternal, immovable, unchanging Cause and Ruler of the universe, who resides afar off above the heavens, and is incapable of coming into immediate contact with any of His creatures, but is observant of and interested in them though removed from and unapproachable by them. He is the universal Father, because He is the author of all existences. He is most real, yet most distant; living and active, yet so transcendent in His nature as to act and be known only through an intermediate being. *Distant from creation. Need of intermediate beings.*

We think it evident that two conceptions of Deity were struggling with each other in Justin's mind. God had become a living reality to him. Not only so, but God had become a living factor in human history, a real and known force in human life. Christ had revealed the character and will of the Father of all, and had brought Him practically near to men. But at the same time Justin had not freed himself from the philosophical conception of Deity as simply the unknowable and transcendent Cause. He had not learned the other truth of God's immanence, and had not been able intellectually to adjust the fact, which he nevertheless felt to be true, of God's intimate relation to believers. In the introduction to the Dialogue he defines God as "that which always maintains the same nature, and in the same manner, and is the cause of all other things." [1] He also appeals to Plato's description of that "Being who is the cause of all discerned by the mind, having no color, nor form, nor magnitude, nor anything visible to the eye; but It is something of this sort, that is beyond all essence,[2] unut- *Two conceptions of Deity not harmonized.*

[1] Dial. 3.
[2] ἐπέκεινα πάσης οὐσίας. De Rep. vii. 509.

terable, and inexplicable, but alone beautiful and good, coming suddenly to souls that are naturally well-dispositioned on account of their affinity with, and desire to see Him."[1] It would appear that this conception of Deity, which he obtained from Platonism, and with which he united the Aristotelian idea of the immovability of the First Cause,[2] remained substantially with Justin after he became a Christian, and that his doctrine of the Logos, to which we shall next refer, by occupying the place which would have called forth an expression of the divine immanence and by removing the Supreme Deity from immediate intercourse with men, left the doctrine of the transcendence of God in all its bareness, and unadjusted to that practical revelation of His personal nearness and constant activity in nature and human life which had been given by Christianity. Justin did not merely say, like the fourth Evangelist, that "no man hath seen God at any time." He went further. He did not fully appreciate the other words recorded by the same authority, " He that hath seen me hath seen the Father," nor those of the Apostle to the Gentiles, " In Him we live and move and have our being; for He is not far from any one of us." God is indeed described by him as a person would be. All things issue not from necessity, but from the divine will and for a divine purpose. God is the free and sovereign Creator of the universe. On the one hand, He is a living reality, personally watchful and regulative of His creation, the author of all holiness and salvation as well as of all life. On the other hand, He is far removed from the world, and necessarily disconnected with it, save as He operates through that Logos,

---

[1] Dial. 4. The passage is a summary of Platonic ideas.
[2] Cf. Weizsäcker (Jahrb. für deutsche Theol. xii. 60, etc.).

PHILOSOPHY AND EARLY CHRISTIANITY. 147

whose existence alone bridges the gulf which would otherwise have been impassable and inexplicable. Yet what was more natural than that one coming from Platonism to Christianity should have been unable to adjust the idea of God to which he had been accustomed to the new revelation in which he had believed?[1]

[1] Cf. Weizsäcker, Ibid., pp. 75–77; Von Engelhardt, Ibid., pp. 127–139 and 231–241; Stählin's Justin der Märtyrer und sein neuester Beurtheiler (a criticism of Von Engelhardt from the orthodox side); Hilgenfeld's Die neuorthodox Darstellung Justins (Zeitschr. für wissensch. Theol., 1879, p. 493; a criticism of Von Engelhardt from the rationalistic side). It is the merit of Von Engelhardt to have shown the influence on Justin's theology of his abstract, philosophical conception of God. He does not deny that Justin believed practically in the personality of God, as both Stählin and Hilgenfeld seem to suppose; but he thinks that Justin did not realize the full idea of divine personality. God was to Justin an individual being. I believe that Justin fully recognized God's personality (so Weizsäcker), but had not freed himself from phrases and ideas inconsistent with it. A similar fact may be noticed, not only in Philo, who strove to combine the abstract conception of the Infinite with his Jewish monotheism (cf. Zeller's Outlines of Greek Philosophy, pp. 321, etc.), but also in the Roman Stoics, who spoke as if God were personal, though in fact they merged Him in the universe, and in such writers as Maximus of Tyre, who united the doctrine of divine transcendence with belief in Providence and a most religious spirit. Justin found through Christ a real, personal God; but this affected his previous Platonism only by removing him far from pantheism, and leading him to regard God as a single, independent, but in Himself wholly unknowable being, the author and governor of creation, and yet of whom no predicate, except existence, can be philosophically and absolutely affirmed; while his doctrine of the Logos not only kept him from modalism and emanationism, but increased his sense of the Father's transcendence by making all divine activity to be mediated by the Logos. Von Engelhardt, however, seems to me to understate the Christian element in Justin. Hilgenfeld still clings to the alleged Jewish-Christian character of the Apologist.

II. We pass next to Justin's doctrine of the Logos, which plays so important a part in his system of thought.

II. The Logos.

The term occurs oftenest in the Apologies, but the most important points of the doctrine are brought out in the Dialogue. Justin introduces the word as a familiar one to both Christians and pagans. He uses the doctrine in the Apologies to explain the real nature of Christ, and why He is called Son of God and worshipped as divine by the Christians, as well as to explain the real nature of Christianity and its relation to other truth. He uses it in the Dialogue to show that Christ was the God who appeared to Abraham and Moses.

It is first, then, to be observed that Justin used "Logos" in the sense of "Reason," and conceived of the divine Logos as the personal Reason of God. Thus we read:[1] "Not only among the Greeks through Socrates were these things condemned by reason,[2] but also among the barbarians by the Reason Himself,[3] who took form, and became man, and was called Jesus Christ." So he maintains[4] that those who have lived reasonably[5] were Christians, while those who lived irrationally[6] were wicked. Christians live "according to the knowledge and contemplation of the whole Logos (which is Christ)," being thus superior to those who formerly lived "according to a part of the germinal Logos."[7] Christ is the whole Rationality,[8] the complete Reason. "God begat from Himself a Beginning

"Logos" used in the sense of "Reason."

---

[1] Ap. i. 5.
[2] ὑπὸ λόγου.
[3] ὑπ' αὐτοῦ τοῦ λόγου.
[4] Ap. i. 46.
[5] μετὰ λόγου.
[6] ἄνευ λόγου.
[7] σπερματικοῦ λόγου. Ap. ii. 8: cf. ii. 9, where Christ is said to be the ὀρθὸς λόγος.
[8] τὸ λογικὸν τὸ ὅλον.

before all creatures,[1] a certain rational Power,[2] who is called by the Holy Spirit, Glory of the Lord, Son, Wisdom, Angel, God, Lord, and Logos."[3] The divine Logos, therefore, is essentially akin to reason in man. He is the active, divine power in the universe, which corresponds to and perfectly realizes the rational element in human nature. He is therefore the perfect Reason, of which human reason is the copy. I need hardly observe that this is not the Johannean idea of the Logos. It manifestly was an effort to explain the Johannean doctrine by the philosophical idea of the divine Logos which Philo had elaborated out of Platonism and Stoicism. Justin, as will appear more fully in the next lecture, presupposes John. The philosophical, rationalizing explanation followed the statements of the fourth Evangelist, the absence from whom of this Platonizing conception is notable evidence that the famous Prologue was not the product of the same influences which wrought upon Justin's mind. The latter, on the contrary, already betrays, in this fundamental idea of the Logos as Reason, the philosophical forces which were affecting his intellectual conception of Christianity. *Not the Johannean use of the term.*

As to the nature and work of the Logos, Justin expresses himself as follows: — *The work of the Logos.*

First, as to His relation to God, the Father of all things. Justin teaches that the Logos was begotten by the will and power of God, at a point of time previous to creation. He is the first begotten of God,[4] *His relation to the Father.*

[1] Or, "at the beginning before all creatures" (ἀρχὴν πρὸ πάντων τῶν κτισμάτων).
[2] ὁ θεὸς γεγέννηκε δύναμίν τινα ἐξ ἑαυτοῦ λογικήν.
[3] Dial. 61.
[4] πρῶτον γέννημα. Ap. i. 21. πρωτότοκος. Ap. i. 23, 33; Dial. 84, 85, 100, 116, 125, 138.

a divine Power.¹ He was begotten by the Father's will,² in a peculiar way, out of the Father Himself.³ He is described as proceeding⁴ before all creatures from the Father, by the latter's power and counsel;⁵ the only-begotten by the Father of all things;⁶ the Offspring who was really brought forth from the Father⁷ before all creatures, and who was with the Father,⁸ and with whom the Father communed.⁹ As He was not a creature, so neither was He an emanation from God, like the rays of light from the sun;¹⁰ nor did He proceed from God by abscission,¹¹ so that by begetting Him the substance of the Father was diminished.¹² Justin illustrates the generation of the Logos by the production of a word by speech, and the kindling of fire by fire.¹³ The Logos then, according to Justin, was not personally eternal,¹⁴ but as a person was

---

¹ δύναμις. Ap. i. 23; Dial. 61, 105.
² ἀπὸ τοῦ πατρὸς θελήσει. Dial. 61.
³ ἰδίως ἐξ αὐτοῦ. Dial. 105.
⁴ προελθόντα. ⁵ δυνάμει καὶ βουλῇ. Dial. 100.
⁶ μονογενὴς τῷ πατρὶ τῶν ὅλων. Dial. 105.
⁷ γέννημα τῷ ὄντι ἀπὸ τοῦ πατρὸς προβληθέν.
⁸ συνῆν τῷ πατρί. ⁹ προσομιλεῖ. Dial. 62.
¹⁰ Dial. 128. ¹¹ κατὰ ἀποτομήν.
¹² Dial. 61, 129. ¹³ Dial. 61.
¹⁴ Cf., besides the references given above, Ap. ii. 6 : ὁ Λόγος πρὸ τῶν ποιημάτων καὶ συνὼν καὶ γεννώμενος ὅτε τὴν ἀρχὴν δι' αὐτοῦ πάντα ἔκτισε ... χριστὸς ... λέγεται. This is the most difficult passage in Justin's doctrine of the Logos. The clause ὅτε τὴν κ.τ.λ. may qualify γεννώμενος or λέγεται. If the former, then the Logos was "begotten" at the moment of creation. This view is taken by Semisch and Aubé (Saint Justin, p. 107); and Justin is said to have regarded the Logos as ἐνδιάθετος before creation and προφορικὸς at creation, in quite a Philonian manner. The opposite view is taken by Weizsäcker and Von Engelhardt, who think Justin conceived the Logos to have dwelt in communion with the Father a long time, but not eternally, before creation,

the product of the Father's will at some period before creation. He is "in number"[1] other than the God who made all things, but not "in mind."[2] Yet, as He was not created, but begotten, — as He was not an emanation, nor a mode of appearance, nor a temporary effulgence of divine glory and power,[3] — he must have been to Justin essentially one with the Father of all; and their numerical distinctness from each other must have been as to personality, not as to substance.[4] Hence He is called God,[5] and divine;[6] while at the same time Justin, thinking of the generation of the Logos, speaks of the latter's deity and divine powers as depending on the exercise of the Father's will.[7] The Logos, moreover, is the agent and servant of the Father of all. As, on the one hand, the latter communes with the Logos, so is the Logos the organ of creation, which God "conceived and made by Him."[8] He is also the Father's messenger[9] and min-

Begotten in time by the Father's will,

yet divine.

Agent in creation.

and then ordained to be the agent of creation and redemption. Elsewhere, however, there is nothing said by Justin of a distinction between λόγος ἐνδιάθετος and προφορικὸς, and the sentence does not require that construction here.

[1] ἕτερος ἀριθμῷ. [2] Or will, γνώμη. Dial. 56, 62, 128, 129.
[3] Dial. 128.
[4] Cf. Dorner's History of the Doctrine of the Person of Christ, i. 270-273.
[5] Ap. i. 63; Dial. 34, 36, 37, 56, 63, 76, 86, 87, 113, 115, 125, 126, 128.
[6] Ap. i. 10.
[7] Ap. i. 63. ὃς λόγος καὶ πρωτότοκος ὢν τοῦ θεοῦ καὶ θεὸς ὑπάρχει. Contrast this with John i. 1. So Dial. 129. The Father of all is the Father and God of the Logos, the cause (αἴτιος) of His power and of His being Lord and God.
[8] Ap. i. 64; ii. 6; Dial. 84.
[9] Ap. i. 63; Dial. 34, 56, 58, 86, 93, 126, 128. ἄγγελος. Ap. i. 63. ἀπόστολος.

ister.[1] The Logos is thus the manifested God, who appeared to the patriarchs and spoke through the prophets. He is God, capable of immediate self-revelation to His creatures. He is therefore the medium between the Transcendent One and the finite universe. Consubstantial with the Father of all, He was made numerically distinct from Him, and undertook to carry out His will. He is therefore subordinate to the Father, both as to His person which was begotten in time and as to His office. He is worshipped, says Justin, by the Christians in the second place after God the Father of all.[2]

Such, in brief, was the nature of the Logos according to our author. Such was Justin's effort to explain the doctrine of the divinity of Christ, and His worship by the Christians. His theory evidently contained New Testament elements, and as evidently departed from others. We see in him the earliest effort of the uninspired Church to think out the doctrine of the Trinity; and if Justin made what we consider errors, we should remember the larger amount of what we consider truth which he maintained, and should not expect the earliest theologian to escape all mistakes. But with his relations to the later Trinitarian discussion we are not now concerned. Our point is simply to observe that his doctrine of the Logos was influenced by the philosophical ideas with which his earlier training had brought him into sympathy, and which were widely diffused in his age. Especially was this part of his the-

Effort to explain the divinity of Christ.

The influence of philosophy.

---

[1] Dial. 56, 57, 60, 113, 125, 126. ὑπηρέτης.

[2] Ap. i. 6. "Him and the Son who came from Him and the host of other good angels and the prophetic Spirit we worship." Cf. Lect. VI. Ap. i. 61. δευτέραν μὲν γὰρ χώραν τῷ παρὰ θεοῦ λόγῳ... δίδωσι (scil. Πλάτων). So Ap. i. 13. υἱὸν αὐτοῦ τοῦ ὄντως θεοῦ μαθόντες καὶ ἐν δευτέρᾳ χώρᾳ ἔχοντες.

PHILOSOPHY AND EARLY CHRISTIANITY. 153

ology influenced by the speculations of the Jewish Alexandrian school. That philosophy was sufficiently Platonic to accord with the natural bent of Justin's mind. It was also sufficiently Biblical in its form and pretensions to accord with his valuation of the Old Testament. Furthermore, Philo's doctrine of the Logos was sufficiently like that of the fourth Evangelist — though the two were in reality utterly different[1] — to affect naturally the thought of the Church. It is even probable that Justin was directly familiar with the literature of the Philonian school, and the writings of Philo himself. Dr. E. A. Abbott has pointed out a number of striking literary coincidences between Justin and Philo, all of which can hardly have been accidental.[2] It is indeed true that Justin differs from Philo more than he resembles him. Christianity made that difference, and in its turn deeply affected Justin's use of philosophical thought and language. Nevertheless, an exaggerated idea of di-

especially of Alexandrianism.

---

[1] Cf. Weiss's Einleitung, p. 591, note 5.

[2] Modern Review, July, 1882. The most striking of these coincidences are the use of the phrase λόγος σπερματικὸς, though Justin uses it differently from Philo, and the phrase itself was of Stoical origin (cf. below); the namelessness of God, and the reason for it, namely, that God is older than all other things (Ap. ii. 6); the names applied to the Logos (Dial. 126); the description of the Logos as ἕτερος (Dial. 55) than God, and as τὴν μετὰ τὸν πρῶτον θεὸν δύναμιν (Ap. i. 59) compared with Philo's δεύτερος θεός; and the illustration of the generation of the Logos by the kindling of fire from fire (Dial. 61). The other coincidences mentioned by Dr. Abbott seem to me doubtful. For Dr. Abbott's argument against Justin's use of the Fourth Gospel, see Lect. V. It is enough here to remark again that the presence of these Alexandrian elements in Justin and the absence of them from the Fourth Gospel would seem clearly to indicate that the latter was not the product of the philosophical influences betrayed by the former.

vine Transcendence, and of the need of an intermediate Being or Beings to unite the Infinite and the finite, maintained its hold upon his mind, and led him to introduce into the very foundation of Christianity an element which was not only unchristian itself, but which seriously affected his whole apprehension of his religion. This latter fact will appear, if we next observe the relation in Justin's view of the Logos to man, as we have observed his relation to the divine Father.

The Logos is represented not only as the agent of God in creation, but as the organ of all divine revelation. He is everywhere present and active, but especially makes Himself known to and through the human mind; so that whatever of truth men possess comes from their relation to the divine Logos. What that relation precisely is, Justin expresses very obscurely. He was certainly no pantheist. He did not regard the human reason as the manifestation of the divine. Yet for men to reason well is for them to partake of the divine Logos. We can only say that to Justin the human reason, including the whole rational and moral intelligence of man, was so akin to the divine, and the divine Reason was so universally present with the human, that the dictates of reason were revelations of the Logos himself.[1] But whatever was the nature of this relation, the Logos was the medium of revelation. The theophanies granted to the patriarchs were appearances of the Logos.[2] Still more, it was the Logos who spoke through the prophets. On this latter point, indeed, Justin's expressions vary. He commonly says that the prophetic or Holy Spirit

[1] Cf. Ap. i. 5, 46; ii. 8, 13.
[2] Ap. i. 63; Dial. 55, etc.

spoke through the prophets. But he also speaks of the prophets as inspired by the divine Logos;[1] and while we do not think that Justin meant to deny the personality of the Spirit,[2] and while he doubtless regarded the Spirit as the organ of the Logos, yet the activity of the latter was to him the fundamental fact, and quite threw into the background the work of the Spirit.[3] But more widely still does he teach that the Logos operates. He regards Him as active everywhere, and as having been always present in all nations revealing the truth to receptive minds. Of Him "every race partakes."[4] Through Socrates He condemned the errors of the Greek religion.[5] The Stoic ethics were admirable because of the seed of the Logos which is implanted in every race of men.[6] God teaches men generally through the Logos to imitate Him.[7] "Whatever philosophers and lawgivers said or discovered well was done by them through a partial discovery and contemplation of Reason; but since they did not recognize all the teachings of the Reason,[8] who is Christ, they often contradicted each other."[9] Each philosopher, seeing from a portion of the seminal divine Logos what was congenial to it, spoke well; for through the sowing of the implanted Logos which was in them, all such writers were able dimly to see the realities.[10] This doctrine of the seminal Logos, or Reason,[11] is the one most characteristic of Justin. The term itself was

The seminal Logos.

[1] Ap. i. 33, 36.
[2] Cf. Ap. i. 6, 39, 60, 61, 65. On the other hand, cf. Aubé's Saint Justin, pp. 141, etc.
[3] Cf. Lect. VI.
[4] Ap. i. 46.
[5] Ap. i. 5.
[6] Ap. ii. 8.
[7] Ap. ii. 9.
[8] τὰ τοῦ λόγου.
[9] Ap. ii. 10.
[10] Ap. ii. 13.
[11] λόγος σπερματικὸς.

of Stoical origin,[1] but had been adopted by Philo to designate the copies of the archetypal ideas which exist in the world and, according to him, constitute its reality, — portions, that is, of the manifested Reason of God.[2] Justin uses the term in his own way. The "seed of the Logos" means with him the rational apprehension of truth. He calls it a "seed" or "sowing," because it was but a partial or dim apprehension, yet was capable of germinating into the full truth, namely, Christianity. The Logos, being everywhere diffused and active, Justin calls "seminal," because He imparts these seeds of truth, and because, as apprehended by philosophers and others, He was the formative principle of right knowledge and right living. But, thus modified, the doctrine was to our author the link which united Christianity with all that was good and true in human thought; so that he could claim that it was not a novelty, but rather the perfect revelation of what had previously been known in scattered fragments.

III. When, then, we inquire of our author why men had apprehended so little of the Logos, and had so generally failed to follow the teaching of divine Reason, we not only discover the weakest point in Justin's theology, but perceive still more clearly how much his philosophical premises led him to differ from the teaching of the New Testament.

III. Justin's anthropology.

He declares not only that man was created intelligent and with power to choose the true and do the good,[3] but that he still retains the same ability.[4] Each man

---

[1] Zeller's Outlines of Greek Philosophy, p. 241.
[2] λόγος προφορικὸς. Cf. Überweg's History of Philosophy, i. 230.
[3] Ap. i. 28; Dial. 88, 141. αὐτεξουσίους πρὸς δικαιοπραξίαν.
[4] Ap. i. 10.

by his own free choice does right or wrong.¹ Men are responsible because they have the power to choose.² If they had it not, they could be neither rewarded nor punished; and the fact that they do change from evil to good, and from good to evil, proves that they have the power.³ Justin was arguing against fatalism; but he goes so far to the other extreme that he fails to recognize any responsibility unless founded on full individual ability, and represents man's moral choice as the unassisted work of each individual. Men, he says, have been endowed with rational faculties in which the power of free choice is included;⁴ and the condition of salvation has always been the apprehension and imitation of God,⁵ or the living according to reason.⁶ To inborn depravity there is barely the slightest allusion,⁷ and of a universal guilt he says nothing. Adam's transgression is indeed spoken of as marking the origin of human sin and death, but apparently as the beginning rather than as the cause of it. "Since Adam,⁸ the race has fallen under death and the deceit of the serpent, each man having done evil through his own fault."⁹ Being made like to Adam and Eve, men work out death for themselves, and each by his own fault is what he will appear to be at last.¹⁰ Men differ, it is true, in their power to receive the truth from the Logos,¹¹ and Justin speaks with particular em-

Human freedom and ability.

---

¹ Ap. ii. 7.   ² Ap. ii. 7, 14.
³ Ap. i. 43; ii. 7.   ⁴ Ap. i. 10, 43.
⁵ Ap. i. 10; ii. 1, 2, 4, 8; Dial. 28.
⁶ Ap. i. 5, 46; Dial. 141.
⁷ Ap. i. 10, where he says the demons have as their ally τὴν ἐν ἑκάστῳ κακὴν πρὸς πάντα καὶ ποικίλην φύσει ἐπιθυμίαν.
⁸ ἀπὸ τοῦ Ἀδάμ.
⁹ Dial. 88. παρὰ τὴν ἰδίαν αἰτιὰν. Cf. also Dial. 100.
¹⁰ Dial, 124, 140, 141.   ¹¹ Ap. ii. 13. κατὰ δύναμιν.

phasis of some who "cannot rise from the earth," and are therefore easy victims of the demons.¹ But these are individual variations. Of a guilty world, of sin as destroying man's ability to please God, he says nothing. The possession of reason, on the contrary, involves the power of moral choice; and since reason is possessed by all men, all men stand or fall according to their individual conduct.²

What, then, was the origin of human wickedness and hostility to the truth? Justin replies that it was caused by the power of the evil angels, and their offspring, the demons. He is the first of the Church Fathers to accept the legend, founded on Gen. vi. 1, 2, of the union of the angels who had been placed by God over the world with the daughters of men.³ These fallen angels and demons

The demons originated evil.

---

¹ Ap. i. 58.   ² Ap. i. 10.

³ Ap. ii. 6. This interpretation of Genesis had been adopted by the Alexandrian Jews. Philo found in it another point of connection between Judaism and heathenism. It is elaborated in the apocryphal book of Enoch, and is represented in some of the manuscripts of the LXX. Cf. Commentaries on Gen. vi.; also Lenormant's Les Origines de l'histoire, ch. vii. The legend naturally accorded with Justin's desire to show analogies between Christian and heathen traditions, as well as with his recognition of the at least partly historical character of the latter. Moreover, as Aubé (Saint Justin, iii. ch. vii.) shows, pagan philosophy made belief in δαίμονες very prominent. Justin coincides with this belief, but makes the demons wicked because opposed to Christ. He believes also in good angels (Ap. i. 6), but says little of them, since the Logos occupies his thought as mediator between God and man. Aubé is certainly wrong in making demonology to have passed to the Christians from the Persians. The form in which it appears in Justin came to the Christians from the Alexandrian Jews, and was confirmed by the popular paganism; but Christ and the Apostles taught the reality of evil spirits, and declared them to be the great foes of the Gospel. It

appeared to men, overcame them with fear, subdued them by magical writings, taught them to offer sacrifices, blinded Reason by terror, and were adored by the people, and sung by the poets, as gods.[1] The demons thus originated polytheism, and have ever waged war against Reason, or the Logos.[2] Having learned from the prophets of the coming Christ, they taught to their followers stories, and themselves performed deeds in imitation of what the Christ would do. Hence the analogies between Christianity and paganism.[3] Hence, too, their hostility to the Christians, which they expressed by raising impostors and heretics, and by fomenting persecution.[4] Had it not been for them, the Logos would have restrained men from evil;[5] and the utter unreasonableness of the way in which Christians are treated proves the demoniacal origin of persecution.[6]

To Justin, therefore, the world of spirits was very real. He considered the stories of the poets largely historical, and referring to actual apparitions from the spirit-world.[7] At any rate, polytheism was the product of the demons.[8] He appeals to frequent exorcisms of demons by Christians, as proof of the truth of Christianity.[9]

is noteworthy that the Clem. Recogg. (i. 19) interpret "the sons of God" as "righteous men who had lived the life of angels," thus showing what the Ebionite view was; though the Homilies (viii. 13) represent them as angels in human form. Both Recognitions and Homilies also make the offspring "giants," not "demons."

[1] Ap. i. 5; ii. 5.
[2] Ap. i. 5, 12, 14, 21, 23, 25, 56, 57, 58; ii. 7, 9, 13; Dial. 79, 83.
[3] Ap. i. 23, 26.   [4] Ap. i. 50, 57, 58; ii. 13.
[5] Ap. i. 10.   [6] Ap. i. 5, 12; ii. 1.
[7] Ap. i. 5.   [8] Ap. i. 23, 54, 64; ii. 5, 10.
[9] Ap. ii. 6, 8; Dial. 30, 76, 85. In Ap. i. 18, he speaks of the popular belief that souls of the dead took possession of men, and

But at the same time the dominion of the demons is represented as due to the terror caused by their appearances, to the blinding of reason by passion at their suggestion, and to man's ignorance of the real nature of the supposed gods.[1] And hence reason can break the fetters which the demons have imposed. If all knew the truth, none would choose wickedness.[2] In short, the evil under which humanity suffers is not inherited guilt, or corruption, but ignorance and fear.

<small>Their dominion due to human fear and ignorance.</small>

It must thus, we think, be again manifest that Justin's conceptions of human freedom and need were determined by his conception of the Logos as reason. His view of man is essentially that to which a rationalizing theology usually comes. It thus, again, testifies that the influences which modified Justin's Christianity were philosophical. Even his demonology, unphilosophical as it appears to modern eyes, was in his age shared in various forms by writers of nearly all schools.[3]

IV. With, then, these premises in his mind, it was inevitable that Justin would represent Christianity in a correspondingly defective and one-sided way. To him

---

he apparently shared in this belief himself; but probably he regarded these souls as themselves under the power of demons. Cf. Kaye's Justin Martyr, p. 111. In Dial. 105, he says that in ancient times the souls of the prophets and the righteous fell at death under the dominion of evil angels, but that Christians are delivered from such. The righteous ancients, however, will be saved through Christ in the resurrection (Dial. 45). Christ went to Hades, but did not remain there (Dial. 99); but of His then delivering the Hebrew saints, Justin says nothing. Apparently they were not to be delivered until the resurrection. Cf., on the contrary, Ignatius ad Mag. ix.

[1] Ap. i. 5; ii. 5.   [2] Ap. i. 12.
[3] Aubé's Saint Justin, pp. 224, etc.

PHILOSOPHY AND EARLY CHRISTIANITY. 161

the grand fact of Christianity was the incarnation of the divine Logos. In a real incarnation he most positively believed.[1] The Logos who had previously appeared to the patriarchs, and spoken through the prophets, and been partially known to all mankind, had voluntarily[2] and according to the will of the Father[3] become incarnate in the Virgin Mary. The whole Logos had thus revealed himself.[4] The full manifestation of truth, therefore, had at last been made.

IV. Justin's one-sided representation of Christianity.

Consequently the object of Christ's coming was, in Justin's thought, primarily to teach. This, indeed, was not its only object. He came to destroy the power of the demons.[5] By dying and rising, He conquered death.[6] By His suffering He saves us.[7] By His blood He cleanses believers.[8] He endured all things for our sakes[9] and on account of our sins.[10] God has mercy, through the mystery of Him that was crucified, on all races of believing men.[11] By His blood He bought us.[12] But while these and similar expressions are frequent, the greatest stress is laid by Justin on Christ as a teacher. Becoming man, He taught us for the conversion and restoration of the human race.[13] Our teacher is Jesus Christ, who was

Christ's coming was primarily to teach.

---

[1] Ap. i. 5, 23, 32, 33, 63, 66; ii. 6, 10, 13; Dial. 34, 43, 45, 48, 54, 63, 64, 66, 68, 75, 84, 88, 98, 99, 100, 103, 105, 113.

[2] Ap. i. 33; Dial. 88.   [3] Ap. i. 23; ii. 6.
[4] Ap. ii. 10.   [5] Ap. i. 46; ii. 6; Dial. 91, 131.
[6] Ap. i. 63.   [7] Dial. 74.
[8] Ap. i. 32; Dial. 13, 40, 54.
[9] Ap. i. 50, 70, 103.   [10] Dial. 63.
[11] Dial. 105.
[12] Dial. 134. δι' αἵματος καὶ μυστηρίου τοῦ σταυροῦ κτησάμενος αὐτοῖς.
[13] Ap. i. 23.

born for this very purpose.[1] He is the true lawgiver[2] and law,[3] and Christianity is therefore the complete revelation of truth. While previous "writers were able to see realities darkly through the sowing of the implanted Logos," Christians possess the participation[4] and active imitation[5] of the Logos Himself, according to the grace which is from Him.[6]

Moreover, expressions which apparently belonged to another type of theology are often rationalized by Justin into harmony with his own mode of thought. When he says[7] that "Christ through sharing our suffering brings us healing," the context makes it clear that this healing was conceived of by Justin as the correction of our errors through giving us the truth. When he says[8] that "God persuades and leads us to faith," he seems again, from the context, to refer not to the work of the Spirit in the heart, but to the exhortations and revelations of the Logos made externally to us. The clean raiment of the saints is not the robe of imputed righteousness, but the future reward with which we shall be invested if we do His commandments.[9] If he quotes[10] the Psalm, "Blessed is the man to whom the Lord imputeth not sin," he also understands[11] the remission of sin to be received in baptism, and to include only the sins previously committed.[12] So, too,

---

[1] Ap. i. 13. So cf. Ap. i. 14, 22, 32; ii. 2, 8, 10, 13; Dial. 8, 9, 11, 76, 83, 100, 102, 113, 116, 121.

[2] Dial. 11, 12, 14, 18.   [3] Dial. 11, 43.

[4] μετουσία.

[5] μίμησις, opposed to μίμημα, which the heathen had.

[6] Ap. ii. 13; cf. i. 20.   [7] Ap. ii. 13.

[8] Ap. i. 10.   [9] Dial. 116.

[10] Dial. 141.   [11] Ap. i. 61.

[12] Cf. also Thoma's article in the Zeitschr. für wissensch. Theol., xviii. 383, etc. He proves Justin's use of Paul's epistles, but

Christ's power is chiefly represented as consisting in His mighty word.[1] Justin certainly believed that Christ by His death and resurrection had won a victory, in which His people are to share, over the evil spirits and over death. He believed also that Christ is a King, and actually reigning in the unseen world.[2] But in spite of such expressions the manifest tendency of his thought was to find the real centre of Christianity in its being the revelation of truth, and its power in the power of truth.

This tendency affected, finally, his idea of salvation itself. He commonly represents it as future. The Christian is not so much a saved man as one who hopes to be saved through belief in Christ's teaching, baptism for the remission of past sins, and subsequent obedience.[3] Faith is belief in the truth of Christ's word rather than the acceptance of a finished redemption; and with it not merely repentance but

<small>*His idea of salvation.*</small>

---

contends that he rationalizes their thought. We admit his proof, though we think that he points out many resemblances which are doubtful; but we think that he gives the wrong reason for Justin's modifications of Pauline doctrine. Cf. Lectt. III. and VI. The passage (Dial. 95, 96) where Justin explains the sentence "Cursed is every one that hangeth on a tree" as fulfilled when the Jews cursed Christ, and as not meaning that Christ was cursed by God, is no rationalizing of the Pauline doctrine, for Justin teaches the same doctrine himself in the same passage ("The Father caused him to suffer these things in behalf of the human family"), but was due to Justin's desire to meet an obvious Jewish misapplication of the phrase. At the same time his explanation harmonizes with his disposition to find *external* items of the fulfilment of prophecy, and with his inability really to appreciate the Hebrew economy.

[1] Dial. 102, 113, 121; Ap. ii. 10.

[2] Ap. i. 40-42, 45, 51; Dial. 36, 74.

[3] Ap. i. 8, 10, 14, 42, 65; ii. 1, 2; Dial. 35, 44, 53, 92, 100, 111, 116.

obedience is joined as the condition of obtaining the future reward.¹ Most notably does this appear in Justin's account of the sacraments: "As many as are persuaded and believe that what we teach is true, and *undertake to be able to live accordingly*, are instructed to pray and to entreat God, with fasting, *for the remission of their sins that are past*. Then they are brought by us where there is water, and are regenerated ² in the same manner in which we ourselves were." ³ The "illumination" ⁴ of those who learned the Christian doctrines was evidently the sense in which they were "made new through Christ." ⁵ Then, "after we have thus washed him who has been convinced and has assented to our teaching, we bring him to the place where the brethren are assembled, that we may offer prayers, . . . that we may be counted worthy, now that we have learned the truth, by our works also to be found good citizens and keepers of the commandments, so that we may be saved with an everlasting salvation." ⁶ Making allowance for Justin's evident effort to represent the Christian doctrines and ceremonies in the way most likely to commend them to his pagan readers, we yet cannot but see that his whole idea of the way of salvation was strongly affected by what we may fairly term his rationalistic tendency. To be sure, as has been already said, expressions can be quoted which seem quite inconsistent with his prevailing theory. Of this side of his theology we shall speak hereafter;⁷ but

---

[1] Ap. i. 8, 19, 28, 32, 65, 66; ii. 1, 4, 8, 12; Dial. 13, 15, 28, 41, 44, 47, 129.

[2] ἀναγεννῶνται. Cf. Lect. VI.

[3] Ap. i. 61.   [4] φωτισμός.

[5] καινοποιηθέντες διὰ τοῦ χριστοῦ.   [6] Ap. i. 65.

[7] Cf. Lect. VI.

PHILOSOPHY AND EARLY CHRISTIANITY. 165

our very point is that he was thus inconsistent in his presentation of Christianity. Two elements coexist in his language, but the dominating traits of his theology were as we have stated. These were the channels into which his own thought ran. These were the utterances of his real intellectual self. And these all followed from the fundamental conception of the Logos as the Reason of God mediating between transcendent Deity and the created universe, and the kindred philosophical premises with which Justin approached Christianity.

As now we review these features of Justin's theology, several inferences bearing on the history of early Christianity seem to be warranted. *We infer:*

(1) The first is that Justin's theology evidently contained two elements which did not entirely harmonize. One was the philosophical element, which we have studied. We recognize it as a well-known type of speculation. We see in it the influence on early Christianity of the mixed philosophical systems of that day, and particularly of Platonism and Jewish Alexandrianism. Justin is not the first orthodox Christian writer who betrays these influences. The prologue of the Fourth Gospel implies their existence in the churches of Asia at the end of the first century, though we hold that it was not their product. The so-called Epistle of Barnabas contains Alexandrian elements, though it does not enter the region of theology proper. But in Justin these philosophical influences appear in full vigor, as we have found both his exegesis and his theology to testify. By what road they entered into combination with Gentile Christianity is, amid the paucity of evidence, a difficult question to answer. Doubtless the more liberal Hellenistic Jews, who freely

(1) Justin's theology contained two elements.

united at their conversion with Gentile churches, were the principal means of the combination; while, as regards Justin himself, we know that he wrote against the Valentinian and Basilidean heresies, and so must have become acquainted with other forms of Egyptian speculation. We have found reason, also, to infer that he was acquainted with the writings of Philo or the teaching of that school. He does not, however, write like a man who was consciously introducing novelties into Christian thought;[1] and while his own studies may have augmented the influence of philosophy upon him, the same influence was clearly at work quite widely in the Church. However we may explain the means of contact, the fact is certain that this philosophical element, which even in its Alexandrian form was quite a different force from the attachment of Jewish Christianity to historical Judaism, had entered to modify the faith of the Church. But whence did Justin obtain the other element of his theology? It was certainly not the product of philosophy, for to explain it was the very object of his philosophizing. It must have preceded in Christianity the philosophical tendency. It was, therefore, the genuinely Christian element; it was the belief of the Church handed down from a previous age. Hence Justin, together with the whole philosophical movement in the early Church to which he belonged, testifies, by his manifest effort to explain Christian doctrine philosophically, to the previous existence of the non-philosophical beliefs of which he affords us a sight as the original faith of the Christian Church.

(2) But, furthermore, the tendency of Justin's theology provides, we think, the key to the modifications

[1] Cf. Lect. VI.

PHILOSOPHY AND EARLY CHRISTIANITY. 167

of Pauline, or, to speak correctly, of apostolic doctrine in the second century. Justin came, as we have seen, to a legalistic theology through the influence, not of Judaism, but of philosophy. He renders it, therefore, highly proba- (2) Philosophy modified his apprehension of Christianity. ble that the forces which operated to change apostolic doctrine were derived from paganism. We do not mean, of course, that the influences betrayed by him were the only ones in operation. He is only an illustration of his times, but, we think, a typical one. But we may infer from him that the habits of thought which the Gentiles brought into the Church are sufficient to explain the corruptions of apostolic doctrine which began in the post-apostolic age. Legalism is not a peculiarly Jewish thing. Natural religion is legalistic; and when the vast majority of the Church became composed of converted heathen, their very inability to appreciate the real worth of the Hebrew economy — an inability which, as we have seen, Justin shared — would tend to blunt their perception of the difference between "law" and "grace," which in the apostolic age was so strongly felt. That the prevalent view of the Old Testament as a book of perfect Christian doctrine aided this tendency, and also helped to impose a hierarchy on the Church, may be admitted. That Alexandrian Judaism, with its philosophical, rationalizing spirit, affected the post-apostolic church, is certain; but Alexandrian Judaism, so far at least as it affected Christianity, is to be reckoned a Gentile rather than a Jewish influence. The phenomena, therefore, do not require us to suppose a blending of anti-Jewish and Jewish Christianity, nor that the latter, as a type of Christian life, came to exert a controlling influence on the former. On the contrary, pagan thought, the political and speculative ideas of the day, the new circumstances which called for stress to be laid on Christian morals in opposition to heathen manners, — these and similar causes may be most probably assigned as the real causes of the failure of the second century to carry on the complete doctrinal ideas of the first. Nothing was more natural than this. To say nothing of inspiration, the training of the Apostles in the Hebrew system must have led them to definitions of religious truth which Gentile converts, wholly without these inherited ideas, could only slowly and partly appreciate. It was when the apostolic age ended that the development of Christian thought toward the apostolic standard and fulness began; and the superiority of the teaching of the Apostles appears most plain when we observe the fall to a lower and fragmentary apprehension of it which immediately followed. Justin, we think, testifies most clearly to the direction in which we are to look for the causes which modified original Christianity in the succeeding period.

(3) Finally, it is impossible not to see exemplified in Justin the fact that Christianity was and is not only a gospel for the lost, but also the practical realization of the unattained ideals and unsatisfied longings of the human soul. Humanity had failed really to find God, and to reach the social righteousness and inward peace of which it so sorely felt the need. But humanity had at least discovered that its need was God, and had learned to distrust its ability to find Him. If in Seneca and Epictetus, in Plutarch and Maximus of Tyre, we read sentiments which seem almost Christian, we are to infer that the dawn of a better day was drawing near, and these exceptional spirits were like high mountain-peaks

(3) Christianity the realization of the best aspirations of paganism.

which catch the first glow from the rising sun. It is very certain, indeed, that Christianity was not the *product* of the forces which moulded them, save in that larger sense which Justin crudely taught when he spake of the Logos of which all men partake. Justin, as we have seen, implies the already established belief in the Church of those doctrines which his philosophy strove to understand and explain; and as we shall see hereafter, those beliefs originated among the Christians in the apostolic age itself. But while the spiritual side of paganism did not aid in the creation of Christianity, the latter was the satisfaction of the hitherto unsatisfied needs of paganism, and is thus witnessed by Justin as the truth for which a thinking moral world as well as a guilty lost world was unconsciously waiting. Certainly the path by which Justin came to the new religion was trodden by others; and if these Gentile believers sometimes brought error into Christianity, they also discovered in it the divine light whose dim reflections and broken gleams had already awakened, but had failed to satisfy, their loftiest and purest thoughts.

LECTURE V.

THE TESTIMONY OF JUSTIN TO THE NEW TESTAMENT.

THE next phase of Justin's testimony which demands our attention is its bearing upon the New Testament. Standing, as he does, midway in the second century; describing the customs and defending the beliefs of the Christians; speaking for the Roman Church, which was itself the best mirror of the whole Christian community, yet also acquainted by travel with the churches of other cities; the first post-apostolic author whose writings are of any considerable size, — Justin is naturally a witness of first importance on this most important subject.

Justin's position makes him an important witness to the New Testament.

It is generally admitted that at the close of the second century our four Gospels and nearly all the remaining books of the New Testament were universally regarded by the Church as apostolic and authoritative, and were placed on a level with the sacred scriptures of the Old Testament.[1] Was this a new opinion? Had there been a fusion of originally antagonistic parties into a Catholic Church, and a corresponding blending of their respective literatures into one sacred collection? Are any of these books unauthentic, and did the reception of them as authentic

The problem.

---

[1] Cf. Reuss's History of the Canon, pp. 103–116; Westcott's Canon of the New Testament, pp. 303, etc.

grow out of a mistaken view of the real course of apostolic history? Or can we find evidence of the existence and recognized authority of these books at a much earlier period, so as to be warranted in concluding that the opinion which prevailed at the close of the second century had always been the substantial opinion of the Church? Did Christian life and thought in the second half of the second century lay in order the foundations of the Church out of the stones which a previous age, animated by quite different ideas, had quarried and cast in confusion on the ground; or did it build upon a foundation already laid by apostles and apostolic men? For the answer to this question we eagerly interrogate Justin. Does he show that in his day other Gospels than our four were used, either in such wise as to indicate that our four were not known at all, or, if known and used, were held to be no more authoritative than others? Did he recognize the apostolic authorship of the Fourth Gospel? More widely still, did he recognize the authority of apostles, and does he testify to the existence of a sacred Christian literature comparable with the Old Testament? It is manifestly of the utmost value to examine accurately and interpret fairly his testimony upon these points.

This phase of Justin's testimony, however, and especially the question whether he used our Synoptic Gospels, has been that which has in modern times attracted the most attention. Justin refers frequently to certain books, which he describes as "memoirs of the Apostles," but which, he says, were "called Gospels,"[1] and were read in the weekly assembly of the Christians interchangeably with "the prophets,"[2] and from which he adduces events of Christ's life and examples of His

[1] Ap. i. 66.   [2] Ap. i. 67.

teaching; and the question of the identity of these books with our Gospels has been one of the great critical battles of the present century. The identity had previously been denied by several writers;[1] but Eichhorn, in 1794, was the first to give wide currency to the denial. He maintained that our Synoptics were secondary recensions of an original Aramaic Gospel, and that Justin's quotations are from a previous recension of the same.[2] Similar views were introduced about the same time into England by Bishop Marsh;[3] while, in Germany, Paulus and others sought to solve the problem by maintaining that Justin took his citations from a harmony of at least Mark and Luke.[4] Interest in the question increased after the publication, in 1832, of Credner's "Essays,"[5] in which he held that while Justin knew our Gospels, he used chiefly the "Gospel of Peter," a reference to which Credner claimed to find in the Dialogue.[6] The new views were answered by Bindemann[7] and Semisch[8] in Germany, and by Bishop Kaye[9] in England; but the

Modern criticism.

---

[1] Cf. Norton's Genuineness of the Gospels, p. 2, referring to Bolingbroke. In 1777 Stroth maintained that Justin's citations were from the Gospel according to the Hebrews (cf. Weiss's Einleitung in das N. T., p. 41).

[2] Cf. his "Allgemeine Bibliothek d. bibl. Lit.," 1794, quoted in Credner's Einleitung (1836), p. 176; also Eichhorn's later "Einleitung."

[3] Marsh's Michaelis, 1795. Cf. Kaye's Justin Martyr, in reply.

[4] Paulus was among the first to maintain that the Gospels were based on oral tradition; while Gratz simplified Eichhorn's theory of an original written Gospel (Credner's Einleitung, pp. 177, 178).

[5] Beiträge zur Einleit. in d. bibl. Schrr., 1832.

[6] Cf. below.

[7] Studien und Kritiken, 1842.

[8] Die apostol. Denkwürdigkeiten des M. J., 1848.

[9] Justin Martyr, 1853, 3d ed.

subject was so intimately involved with the theories of the Tübingen school of criticism, according to which the Gospels were written in the interest of certain "tendencies" the operation of which was alleged to have extended far into the second century, that after the appearance of that school the controversy became sharper than ever. Baur himself merely remarks that while Justin was acquainted with one or more of our Gospels, he has named none of them;[1] but Schwegler[2] denied that Justin knew our Gospels at all, alleging that he used only the Gospel of Peter, which Schwegler identified with the Gospel according to the Hebrews. More moderate views, however, began in time to prevail. It was generally admitted that Justin knew our Synoptics, and only the question remained whether he had also used one or more extra-canonical Gospels, and if so, whether he had relied on them chiefly or merely incidentally. Hilgenfeld, while maintaining Justin's principal use of the Gospel according to Peter, recognized his use also of the canonical Gospels, and has reproved[3] the author of "Supernatural Religion" for denying the fact. On the other hand, Bleek,[4] to take an example from the more conservative writers, declared that "Justin meant by 'the memoirs' our Gospels, two of which he used, but that we still find him to have had recourse to another evangelic history, probably the Gospel according to the Hebrews." In England, Dr. Sanday[5] has defended Justin's use of the canonical Gospels, against the denials of the author of "Supernatural Religion," though

[1] Christian Church of the First Three Centuries, Eng. trans., i. 147.
[2] Nachapost. Zeitalter, 1846.
[3] Zeitschr. für wissensch. Theol., 1875, p. 584.
[4] Introd. to New Test., T. & T. Clark, 1861, i. 335; ii. 240.
[5] Gospels in the Second Century, 1876.

still inclined to think that he also followed an extra-canonical source; while Westcott[1] holds that the canonical Gospels alone, together with oral tradition, supplied Justin with his knowledge of the evangelic history. Finally, it has been suggested that the problem of Justin's quotations may be solved by supposing him to have used a Gospel harmony. Long since, as we have stated, Paulus advanced this view, alleging Justin's harmony to have been formed from Mark and Luke. Credner, also, in his "History of the Canon,"[2] supposed that the Gospel of Peter was a harmony of evangelic sources, with apocryphal additions; and Von Engelhardt[3] now maintains not only that Justin used a harmony, but that this was none other than a harmony based on our Synoptics themselves.[4]

Justin's quotations from the "memoirs" have thus been intimately connected with the larger questions of the origin and mutual relations of the Gospels, and of the rise of the Catholic Church itself; and the approximate solution of the difficulties suggested by earlier criticism concerning his quotations has contributed much to the overthrow of the rationalistic theories of early Christianity. So much, however, has been written in accessible books upon this part of my subject, that, in view of the limits of a single lecture within which I am confined, I shall discuss, as briefly as possible, Justin's testimony to the first three Gospels, in order to obtain space to notice his testimony to the Fourth Gospel, — the discussion of which has lately assumed an interesting phase, — and his testimony to the way in

---

[1] Canon of the New Test., 1855, pp. 66–70.   [2] 1852.
[3] Das Christenthum Justins, p. 345.
[4] Sanday also (Gospels in the Second Century, p. 136, note) thinks the hypothesis of a harmony plausible.

which apostolic literature, in part or in whole, was regarded by the Church of his age.

I. The data by which Justin's relation to our Synoptic Gospels must be determined are, then, briefly as follows:— *I. Justin's use of the Synoptic Gospels.*

Once in the longer Apology, and seven times in the Dialogue, he mentions the "memoirs of the, or of His, Apostles."[1] Four times, in the Dialogue, he speaks simply of "the memoirs."[2] Elsewhere he uses other expressions descriptive of the character or origin of these books. Speaking of the Annunciation to the Virgin, he says: "As those who related all things concerning our Saviour Jesus Christ taught."[3] Again: "The Apostles, in the memoirs composed by them, which are called Gospels, thus handed down."[4] Again: "The Apostles wrote[5] that the Holy Spirit as a dove flew upon" Jesus after His baptism.[6] Still again: "In the memoirs which I say were composed by His Apostles and those who followed them."[7] Finally, speaking of the change of Simon's name to Peter, Justin says, "It is written in his memoirs that it so happened,"[8] by which, if the text be correct, we must understand "Peter's memoirs." This term, "the memoirs," was a descriptive one. Justin is the only writer known to *The "memoirs."*

---

[1] Ap. i. 67; Dial. 100–104, 106 (twice). τὰ ἀπομνημονεύματα τῶν ἀποστόλων.

[2] Dial. 105 (three times), 107.

[3] Ap. i. 33. ὡς οἱ ἀπομνημονεύσαντες πάντα τὰ περὶ τοῦ σωτῆρος ἡμῶν Ἰ. Χ. ἐδίδαξαν.

[4] Ap. i. 66. οἱ ἀπόστολοι ἐν τοῖς γενομένοις ὑπ' αὐτῶν ἀπομνημονεύμασιν, ἃ καλεῖται εὐαγγέλια, οὕτως περέδωκαν κ.τ.λ.

[5] ἔγραψαν.   [6] Dial. 88.

[7] Dial. 103. ἐν τοῖς ἀπομνημονεύμασιν ἅ φημι ὑπὸ τῶν ἀποστόλων αὐτοῦ καὶ τῶν ἐκείνοις παρακολουθησάντων συντετάχθαι.

[8] Dial. 106. γεγράφθαι ἐν τοῖς ἀπομνημονεύμασιν αὐτοῦ γεγενημένον καὶ τοῦτο.

have applied it to the evangelic narratives, though the corresponding verb was used by Papias to describe the composition of Mark's Gospel;[1] and Tatian, Justin's pupil, appears to have been familiar with his master's terminology.[2] Most probably Justin took the phrase from the well-known "Memoirs" of Xenophon,[3] which he quotes in his Apologies,[4] and the resemblance between which and the Gospels must have impressed his own mind, in view of his frequent comparison of Socrates with Christ. The term, also, would well describe to his pagan readers what these Christian narratives really were.[5] If so, then we may assume that the term "Gospels" was the usual one employed by the Christians themselves. Justin says, "the memoirs, which are called Gospels."[6] The latter term was evidently well established; and its use by Justin is the more noteworthy because the plural, "Gospels," is not found, with probably one exception,

"Gospels."

---

[1] Eus. H. E. iii. 39. Μάρκος μὲν ἑρμηνευτὴς Πέτρου γενόμενος ὅσα ἐμνημόνευσεν ἀκριβῶς ἔγραψεν ... ὥστε οὐδὲν ἥμαρτε Μάρκος οὕτως ἔνια γράψας ὡς ἀπομνημόνευσεν. Cf. too Clem. Recog. ii. 1, where Peter says: "In consuetudine habui, verba Domini mei, quæ ab ipso audieram, revocare in memoriam." The term is also used by Eusebius (H. E. v. 8; vi. 25), though not of the Gospels.

[2] Orat. ad Græc. 21, where he bids the Greeks look at their own ἀπομνημονεύματα, apparently in contrast to those of the Christians. Cf. Von Engelhardt's Das Christenthum, etc., p. 337. Von Engelhardt, however, is not justified in saying (p. 336) that this term for the Gospels was widely diffused.

[3] Ξενοφῶντος Ἀπομνημονεύματα.

[4] ii. 11; cf. also i. 5; ii. 10.

[5] Justin's use of the term in the Dialogue, as well as in the Apology, shows that he did not merely use it for the sake of his pagan readers, but that it was his own favorite term.

[6] Ap. i. 66. It is perfectly arbitrary to regard the words as spurious.

JUSTIN ON THE NEW TESTAMENT. 177

in earlier writers. We frequently find, before Justin, "the Gospel" spoken of, meaning the Christian revelation, or message, and gradually having attached to it the idea of a written document.[1] Our Apologist, however, testifies that in his day the term was commonly applied in the Church to the single written narratives of Christ's life, as it ever since has continued to be. True, in the Dialogue, we find the singular also employed.

[1] In the New Testament, we find only the singular, and in the sense of the Gospel message or dispensation. In Clem. Rom. ad Cor. 47, we read τί πρῶτον ὑμῖν ἐν ἀρχῇ τοῦ εὐαγγελίου (Παῦλος) ἔγραψεν, where there is evident reference to Phil. iv. 15, and εὐαγ. is used in both places in the same sense. In Ignatius we find only the singular (cf. Philad. 5, 8, 9; Smyr. 5, 7), but, except in Phil. 9, with evident consciousness that the Gospel was written (cf. Bib. Sacra, July, 1885, "Descriptive Names applied to N. T. Books by Earliest Writers," B. B. Warfield. Polycarp's collection of Ignatius's Epistles surely proves also the valuation of Christian literature by the earliest churches. If they desired the Epistles of Ignatius, much more would they use and collect the writings of the Apostles). In the Didache, we find the singular four times, — c. 15 : "Reprove one another in peace, ὡς ἔχετε ἐν τῷ εὐαγγελίῳ." "Your prayers and alms, etc., so do, ὡς ἔχετε ἐν τῷ εὐαγγελίῳ τοῦ κυρίου ἡμῶν." c. 8 : "Do not pray as the hypocrites, but ὡς ἐκέλευσεν ὁ κύριος ἐν τῷ εὐαγγελίῳ αὐτοῦ, οὕτω προσεύχεσθε." Then follows the Lord's Prayer. c. 11 : "As to Apostles and prophets so do, κατὰ τὸ δόγμα τοῦ εὐαγγελίου; and let every Apostle coming to you be received as the Lord " (cf. Matt. x. 40). These seem to imply a written Gospel, though Harnack (sub cap. 15) denies it. In Barnabas we find only the singular (v. and viii.), where it means the message given to the Apostles to preach. In Hermas the word does not occur, nor in the fragments from Papias. In the Epistle to Diognetus, c. xi. (where we read εὐαγγελίων πίστις ἵδρυται) is an addition to the Epistle. The Epistle itself, however, is probably later than Justin. From Hippol. adv. Hær. vii. 10, we learn that Basilides quoted John i. 9, as τὸ λεγόμενον ἐν τοῖς εὐαγγελίοις. If this be, as is probable, Basilides's language, he furnishes the earliest example of the plural, and, be it observed, applies it to the Fourth Gospel.

Trypho states[1] that he had "read the precepts in the so-called Gospel;" and Justin himself says[2] that "in the Gospel it is written that Christ said, 'All things are delivered unto me by my Father.'" Thus the term "Gospel" was already commonly used to describe the *collection* of written memoirs, as well as the particular memoirs themselves. In Justin's time this nomenclature was fully established, precisely as we find it in Irenæus[3] and all subsequent writers.

The "memoirs of the Apostles" were, then, several evangelic narratives believed to have been "composed by apostles or their followers."[4] This expression of Justin's, while he does not say how many memoirs there were, nor how many were written by apostles, exactly tallies with our four Gospels, though it cannot be used as proof unless supported by other evidence. The names of the authors of the memoirs he nowhere gives, unless in the single instance in which he seems to speak of Peter's memoirs.[5] This was the passage on which Credner based his theory that Justin used an uncanonical Gospel of Peter. But inasmuch as the earliest antiquity made Mark the interpreter of Peter, and Mark's Gospel the recital of Peter's preaching;[6] and inasmuch as Justin immediately quotes as from the

[1] Dial. 10. [2] Dial. 100.
[3] Adv. Hær. iii. 5. 1; iii. 11. 7. [4] Dial. 103.
[5] Dial. 106. Speaking of the change of Simon's name to Peter, Justin says, "It is written ἐν τοῖς ἀπομνημονεύμασιν αὐτοῦ that this happened." Otto thinks αὐτοῦ an error for αὐτῶν or τῶν ἀποστόλων αὐτοῦ. Others refer αὐτοῦ to Christ; but it is fatal to this that Justin elsewhere uses the genitive after "memoirs" for the authors.
[6] So Papias, in Eus. H. E. iii. 39. Μάρκος μὲν ἑρμηνευτὴς Πέτρου γενόμενος ὅσα ἐμνημόνευσεν ἀκριβῶς ἔγραψεν. So Iren. adv. Hær. iii. 1. 1.

same memoirs an incident [1] which is now only found in the Gospel of Mark, it is at least equally credible, even so far as the mere wording is concerned, that by Peter's memoirs he meant the second canonical Gospel. These memoirs, however, were the sources to which Justin appealed for information as to Christ's life. In them were related "all things concerning our Saviour Jesus Christ." [2] To them Justin appeals for examples of Christ's teaching [3] and for events of His life.[4] They were regularly read in the Church, and commented upon by the presiding officer,[5] and were therefore well-known and generally accepted public documents. Both Justin and the Church relied upon them without question as apostolic narratives of the teaching and life of Jesus.

We have next to examine Justin's account of Christ's life and teaching, as it is disclosed by the statements scattered through his writings, and compare it with the account given by the Synoptical Gospels. *His account of Christ's life.*

Summarizing the results of such an examination,[6] we discover, —

(1) That *his account of the life of Christ is remarkably full.* We learn from him Christ's birth from the Vir-

[1] The naming of Zebedee's sons Boanerges. On the apocryphal Gospel of Peter, see Westcott's Canon, p. 90, note 2; Fisher's The Supernatural Origin of Christianity, p. 198.

[2] Ap. i. 33, though the πάντα need not be pressed too rigidly, so as to exclude, for example, oral tradition. Perhaps, as Westcott suggests (Canon, p. 101, note 1), Justin had in mind Luke i. 3, or Acts i. 1.

[3] Cf. Ap. i. 15-17, 66; Dial. 105, 107.

[4] Ap. i. 33; Dial. 88, 100-104, 106.   [5] Ap. i. 67.

[6] Cf. Westcott's Canon, pp. 91-94; Sanday's Gospels in the Second Century, pp. 91-98; Charteris's Canonicity, for similar summaries.

gin,[1] and the events of His infancy;[2] His waiting in obscurity "until about thirty years of age;"[3] the mission of John the Baptist,[4] together with the baptism[5] and temptation[6] of Jesus; the characteristic features of Christ's teaching;[7] the fact and variety of His miracles;[8] quotations from or references to the accounts of the healing of the centurion's servant[9] and Matthew's feast;[10] the choosing of the Twelve;[11] the naming of Zebedee's sons;[12] the commission of the Apostles;[13] the discourse after the departure of John's messengers;[14] the sign of the prophet Jonas;[15] the parable of the Sower;[16] the confession

(1) Remarkably full.

---

[1] Cf. Ap. i. 21, 22, 32, 33, 46; Dial. 43, 66, 75, 76, 84, 100.

[2] Born under Cyrenius, one hundred and fifty years ago (Ap. i. 46); visit of Magi; annunciation to Joseph; journey to Bethlehem at the time of the census; Jesus born in a cave near Bethlehem; laid in a manger, where the Magi found Him; flight to Egypt; massacre of the children in Bethlehem by Herod (Dial. 78, 102); the star of the Magi (Dial. 106); the circumcision (Dial. 67).

[3] Dial. 88 ("He grew up like other men, and waited thirty years more or less till John appeared").

[4] John, the last of the Jewish prophets; Matt. iii. 11, 12, quoted; John imprisoned and beheaded by Herod (Dial. 49); Christ ended John's ministry (Dial. 51); John, the herald of Christ (Dial. 88).

[5] Dial. 88.   [6] Dial. 103, 125.

[7] Brief and concise utterances (Ap. i. 14); power of His word, by which He confuted the Scribes and Pharisees (Dial. 102).

[8] Dial. 49; Ap. i. 22 (healed the lame and paralytic and blind from birth (ἐκ γενετῆς πονηροὺς; cf. below, p. 185), and raised the dead). So Ap. i. 30, 31, 48; Dial. 69.

[9] Dial. 76, 120, 140 ("Many shall come from the East and West," etc.).

[10] Ap. i. 15 ("I came not to call the righteous," etc.).

[11] Ap. i. 39; Dial. 42.   [12] Dial. 106.

[13] Ap. i. 16, 19, 63; Dial. 35, 82.

[14] Ap. i. 63; Dial. 51, 100, 106.

[15] Dial. 107.   [16] Dial. 125.

JUSTIN ON THE NEW TESTAMENT. 181

of Peter;[1] the announcement of the Passion;[2] while of the later period, and especially the last week of Christ's life, and of the events which immediately followed the resurrection, Justin speaks with still greater fulness.[3] In fact, we may obtain from him passages which correspond in substance to portions of every chapter of Matthew's Gospel, and sometimes to portions of considerable size;[4] also to portions of all but seven of the chapters of Luke's Gospel.[5] The evidence, therefore, upon which to base a comparison of Justin's account of Christ's life with that of the Synoptists is larger than might have been expected, and sufficient to yield positive results.

(2) Now, *with the exception of a few items to be mentioned presently, Justin's account of Christ's life agrees in*

[1] Dial. 100.   [2] Dial. 51, 106.

[3] We find references to, or quotations from, the triumphal entry (Ap. i. 35; Dial. 53); the second cleansing of the temple (Dial. 17, "My house shall be called a house of prayer," etc.); the tribute money (Ap. i. 17); the two commandments (Dial. 93); the rebukes of the Pharisees (Dial. 17, 95, 112, 122); the discourse on the Mount of Olives (Ap. i. 16, 28; Dial. 35, 51, 76, 82, 116, 125); the institution of the Supper (Ap. i. 66); the agony (Dial. 99, 103); the trial before the Sanhedrim (Dial. 103); Christ's silence at His trial (Dial. 102, 103); Pilate's sending Him to Herod (Dial. 103); His crucifixion under Pontius Pilate (Ap. i. 13, 35; ii. 6; Dial. 30, 85); the parting of His garments (Ap. i. 35; Dial. 97, 103); the mockery of the Jews (Dial. 101); the cry on the Cross (Dial. 99); the resurrection on the first day of the week (Ap. i. 67; Dial. 41); the report of the Jews that Christ's body was stolen (Dial. 108); His last commission (Ap. i. 31, Apostles sent to all nations; 61, baptism in the name of the Trinity); and His ascension (Ap. i. 21).

[4] As, e. g., Matt. ii. 5, 6, 11–23 (Ap. i. 34; Dial. 78, 103); v. 16, 20, 22, 28, 29, 32, 34, 37, 39, 40–42, 44–46 (Ap. i. 1, 15, 16; Dial. 85, 96, 105, 133); xxiii. 6, 7, 13, 15, 16, 23, 24, 27, 31 (Dial. 17, 95, 112, 122).

[5] Cf. Otto's Justini Opera, tom. i. index iii.

substance and so far as the events narrated are concerned precisely with the account given by our first three Gospels. His language is not always identical with theirs, as we shall see; but his story is, with a few trifling exceptions, exactly the same as theirs: so that we may already affirm that if his "memoirs" were not our Gospels, they at least related substantially the same story of Christ's life.

(2) Agrees, with a few exceptions, substantially with that of our Gospels.

(3) Furthermore, the agreement between Justin's account taken from the "memoirs" with that of our Gospels often extends *to small particulars,* which are the more significant because of their very smallness. Thus his account of Christ's infancy, unlike that given in the early apocrypha, is identical with that of our Gospels, save that he states that Christ was born in a cave near Bethlehem, and that the Magi were from Arabia.[1] He refers to the enrolment under Cyrenius.[2] He speaks of Christ's natural growth from infancy to manhood,[3] and says that at His baptism He was thirty years old, "more or less."[4] So the naming of the sons of Zebedee,[5] Christ's silence at His trial,[6] Pilate's sending Him to Herod,[7] and the Jews' story that He was stolen from the tomb by His disciples,[8] are examples of the slight

(3) The agreement extends to small particulars.

---

[1] Dial. 78.

[2] Ap. i. 34, 46. When he appeals (Ap. i. 34) to the "registers which were made under Cyrenius" (τῶν ἀπογραφῶν τῶν γενομένων ἐπὶ Κυρηνίου) for proof that "there is a certain village in the land of the Jews, thirty-five stadia from Jerusalem, in which Jesus Christ was born," he probably merely takes for granted that such registers had been preserved by the Government. So when he appeals to the "Acta Pilati" (i. 35, 48).

[3] Dial. 88.   [4] Cf. ὡσεὶ, Luke iii. 23.
[5] Dial. 106.   [6] Dial. 102, 103.
[7] Dial. 103.   [8] Dial. 108.

coincidences in matters of fact which continually occur in the accounts of Justin and the Synoptists.

(4) *The differences between the two accounts are the following.*[1] Justin says that Cyrenius was the first procurator of Judæa;[2] that Joseph was "of Bethlehem;"[3] that Jesus was born *in a cave* near Bethlehem;[4] that the Magi were from Ara- (4) The differences from our Gospels.

[1] It is hardly fair with Sanday (Gospels in the Second Century, p. 91) to infer from the fact that Justin derives Christ's Davidic descent through Mary (Ap. i. 32; Dial. 100, 120), that he had a genealogy of Christ different from those of Matthew and Luke; for he may have understood one or both of these to give Mary's pedigree. Clement of Alexandria (Strom. i. 21, quoted by Westcott's Canon, p. 91, note 1, though Westcott goes too far in saying that Clement "distinctly refers the genealogy to Mary") apparently understood even Matthew to give Mary's pedigree (if not her lineal, at least her legal, pedigree). Her Davidic descent, which may be defended from Acts ii. 30; Rom. i. 3; Luke i. 32, was universally believed in the early Church (cf. Andrew's Life of Our Lord, p. 52); and while the explanation of the Gospel genealogies adopted by Africanus (Eus. H. E. i. 7) referred both to Joseph, Mary was supposed and is expressly said by Africanus to have been of the same tribe. Justin refers to none of Mary's ancestors later than David, and mentions as her ancestors, David, Jesse, Phares, Judah, Jacob, Isaac, and Abraham, all which names occur in both Matthew and Luke, while his reference to Adam as the ancestor of these patriarchs, in giving his reason why Christ called himself the Son of Man (Dial. 100), points to Luke iii. 38. Of the course of descent from David to Mary, Justin is silent.

[2] Ap. i. 34. ἐπιτρόπου. Cyrenius, whatever his precise office, was not the first "governor." Luke ii. 2, has αὕτη ἀπογραφὴ πρώτη ἐγένετο ἡγεμονεύοντος τῆς Συρίας Κυρηνίου.

[3] Dial. 78. "He went up from Nazareth, where he dwelt, to Bethlehem, ὅθεν ἦν." This is obviously a reference to Luke ii. 4: "διὰ τὸ εἶναι αὐτὸν ἐξ οἴκου καὶ πατριᾶς Δαυείδ;" but the fact is stated by Justin so as to apparently imply that Joseph had lived in Bethlehem previously.

[4] Dial. 78. "Since he could not find lodging in the village." Caves were often used as stables, and Justin says the Magi found Jesus laid in a manger.

bia;[1] and that Jesus was deformed, or not of comely aspect, as had been predicted.[2] He speaks of John the Baptist "sitting" by the Jordan,[3] and states that when Jesus went down to the water to be baptized, a fire was kindled in the Jordan,[4] and that the Voice from heaven

[1] Dial. 78. Sanday (Gospels in the Second Century, p. 93) makes Justin say that Herod "ordered a massacre of *all* the children in Bethlehem." So he does in Dial. 78; but in Dial. 103, he says that Herod, "when He [Christ] was born, slew all the children born in Bethlehem about that time (ἐκείνου τοῦ καιροῦ);" cf. Matt. ii. 16, "from two years old and under."

[2] Dial. 14, 49, 85, 88, 100, 110, 121, referring to Isa. liii. 2, 3. ἀειδής.

[3] Dial. 51, 88. καθεζομένου.

[4] Dial. 88. κατελθόντος τοῦ Ἰησοῦ ἐπὶ τὸ ὕδωρ καὶ πῦρ ἀνήφθη ἐν τῷ Ἰορδάνῃ. Cf. Otto, *sub loco*. The same legend was found in the Predicatio Pauli by the author of the tract De Rebaptismate (ascribed by some to Ursinus, a monk of the fourth century; by others to Cyprian. Cf. Ante-Nic. Fathers, Amer. ed. v. 665), "cum baptizaretur, ignem super aquam esse visum." In the Gospel of the Ebionites (according to Epiphanius, Hær. xxx. 13), when Jesus *came up* from the water a great light (φῶς) shone round the place (περιέλαμψε τὸν τόπον); and the old Latin Codex a (Vercellensis) adds to Matt. iii. 15, "et cum baptizaretur lumen ingens circumfulsit de aqua ita ut timerent omnes qui advenerant" (cf. Sanday, Ibid., p. 108. He adds that there is a similar addition in g' (San Germanensis)). Otto also cites Oracc. Sibyll. vii. 82–84 : —

> Ὡς σε λόγον γέννησε πατήρ, πνεῦμ' ὄρνιν ἀφῆκε,
> Ὀξὺν ἀπαγγελτῆρα λόγων, λόγος, ὕδασιν ἁγνοῖς
> Ῥαίνων σὸν βάπτισμα, δι' οὗ πυρὸς ἐξεφαάνθης,

and the Liturgy of the Syrians, which, in the narrative of the baptism, has "quo tempore adscendit ab aquis, sol inclinavit radios suos." In this last case we may perhaps see the original form of the legend. Justin does not say that the "memoirs" related this legend. His language is, "When Jesus had gone to the river Jordan, where John was baptizing, and when He had stepped into the water, a fire was kindled in the Jordan; and the Apostles of this very Christ of ours wrote that when He came out of

which followed the baptism repeated the words of the Second Psalm, "Thou art my Son; this day have I begotten thee."¹ He states that Christ healed those who "from birth were blind, dumb, and lame,"² but

the water the Holy Spirit as a dove lighted on Him." Thus he carefully makes the "memoirs" responsible only for the descent of the Spirit as a dove.

¹ Dial. 88, 103. These words are found in Luke iii. 22, according to D. and lat. mss. a, b, c, ff₂' l. The Gospel of the Ebionites (Epiphan. xxx. 13) had "Thou art my beloved Son; in Thee I am well pleased. And again, To-day I have begotten Thee." The words of the Psalm are referred to the baptism by Clement of Alexandria (Pædag. i. 6); Methodius (Conviv. virgg. Discourse viii. ch. 9); Lactantius (Instt. Div. iv. 15); Juvencus (Hist. Ev. i. 363); and Augustine (Enchiridion, c. 49). (Cf. Otto, sub Dial. 88, where the quotations are given. He also refers to Acta Petri et Pauli, c. 29; but there seems in that place to be no reference of the words to the baptism.) Augustine, however (Harmony of the Gospels, ii. 14) says the reading was found in some codices of Luke, but was said not to be found in the more ancient codices. Either Justin's manuscript had this Western corruption, or he had heard it thus quoted and relied on his memory.

² Ap. i. 22. Our Gospels contain no examples of the healing of those dumb or lame from birth. The manuscripts of Justin read " χωλοὺς καὶ παραλυτικοὺς καὶ ἐκ γενετῆς πονηροὺς." Most editions substitute for πονηροὺς πηροὺς, following Dial. 69, where we read, "τοὺς ἐκ γενετῆς καὶ κατὰ τὴν σάρκα πηροὺς καὶ κωφοὺς καὶ χωλοὺς ἰάσατο, τὸν μὲν ἄλλεσθαι, τὸν δὲ καὶ ἀκούειν, τὸν δὲ καὶ ὁρᾶν τῷ λόγῳ αὐτοῦ ποιήσας." In Ap. i. 22, Gildersleeve substitutes ἀναπήρους. Whatever the reading, it should be noted that Justin connects ἐκ γενετῆς only with πονηροὺς in Ap. i. 22, and chiefly with πηροὺς in Dial. 69; and from the latter passage it is clear that Justin meant by πηροὺς (and therefore probably in Ap. i. 22 by πονηροὺς = suffering), the blind. Hence I infer he had in mind John ix. 1, and that he includes the dumb and lame by a pardonable inexactness of statement. In Mark ix. 21, however, the "lunatic" boy is said to have been afflicted ἐκ παιδιόθεν. Could Justin have had in mind, also, Acts iii. 2, and confused it with Christ's miracles?

that the Jews ascribed these miracles to magic;[1] also that the ass's colt used at the triumphal entry was found by the disciples "bound *to a vine* at the entrance of a village."[2] He cites from the "memoirs" that in Gethsemane *Christ's sweat fell like drops* when He was praying;[3] that the Jews came upon Christ "*from the Mount of Olives*,"[4] and that there was not a man to aid Him.[5] Pilate sent Him *bound* to Herod *as a compliment;*[6] and Justin apparently represents Herod Antipas as a successor of Archelaus in the dominion of Herod the Great.[7] He says that His persecutors placed Christ on the judgment-seat, and said, "Judge us;"[8] and that at the crucifixion the

[1] Dial. 69. καὶ γὰρ μάγον εἶναι αὐτὸν ἐτόλμων λέγειν καὶ λαοπλάνον. In Clem. Recog. i. 58, a scribe declares that Christ performed "signa et prodigia ut magus non ut propheta." So in the report of Pilate, incorporated in the Acts of Peter and Paul, we read that the Jews asserted Jesus "magum esse et contra eorum legem agere." In Ap. i. 30, Justin undertakes to prove that Christ did not do miracles μαγικῇ τέχνῃ. Celsus (Orig. contra Cels. ii. 48) attributed them to sorcery. This charge was, in fact, substantially the same with that mentioned in the Gospels (Matt. ix. 34; xi. 24, etc.), that he cast out devils by Beelzebub. For λαοπλάνον, see Matt. xxvii. 63 and John vii. 12.

[2] Ap. i. 32.

[3] Dial. 103. Justin significantly cites it "from the memoirs, which I say were composed by the Apostles and their followers;" thus no doubt referring the story to Luke's Gospel. On the spuriousness, however, of Luke xxii. 43, 44, see Notes on Select Readings in Westcott and Hort's Greek Testament; and on the bearing of Justin's text on the age of the Gospels, see below. Justin, however, has only θρόμβοι, not θρόμβοι αἵματος. Tatian, in his Diatessaron, had the passage, which is translated by Mœsinger from Ephraem's Commentary, "et factus est sudor ejus ut guttæ sanguinis."

[4] Dial. 103. ἀπὸ.
[5] Dial. 103.
[6] Dial. 103. χαριζόμενος.
[7] Dial. 103.
[8] Ap. i. 35. κρῖνον ἡμῖν.

JUSTIN ON THE NEW TESTAMENT. 187

mocking bystanders not only shook their heads and shot out their lips,[1] but "twisted their noses to each other,"[2] and cried, "Let Him who raised the dead deliver Himself;"[3] and "He called Himself Son of God; let Him come down and walk; let God save Him."[4] *After* He was crucified, *all* His acquaintances forsook Him, having denied Him.[5] To these items are to be added two sayings of Christ's, reported by Justin, but not found in our Gospels. These are, "In whatsoever things I take you, in these will I also judge;"[6] and "There shall be schisms and heresies."[7] But with these we have enumerated all the substantial

[1] Ap. i. 38; Dial. 101.
[2] Dial. 103. τοῖς μυξωτῆρσιν ἐν ἀλλήλοις διαρρινοῦν.
[3] Ap. i. 38. ὁ νεκροὺς ἀνεγείρας ῥυσάσθω ἑαυτόν.
[4] Dial. 103. [5] Ap. i. 50.
[6] Dial. 47. Διὸ καὶ ὁ ἡμέτερος κύριος Ἰ. Χ. εἶπεν· 'Ἐν οἷς ἂν ὑμᾶς καταλάβω, ἐν τούτοις καὶ κρινῶ. We find this nowhere else attributed to Christ. Clement of Alexandria (Quis Div. Salv. c. 40) quotes it, with a slight variation of text, without indicating its source. Otto refers to Hippolytus (Περὶ τῆς τοῦ παντὸς αἰτίας, 2) "whatever manner of persons they [were when they] lived without faith, as such they shall be faithfully judged" (Ante-Nic. Fathers, Amer. trans. v. 222); but Hippolytus seems merely to state a similar idea. By John Climachus (died 606), it was attributed to Ezekiel (cf. Otto). Apocryphal or interpolated writings of Ezekiel were known in the early Church; and J. B. Lightfoot (Clem. Rom. ad Cor. viii. note 12) supposes that Justin obtained it from that source, and from lapse of memory ascribed it to Christ, perhaps confusing it with John v. 30. Others (Grabe, Credner, etc.) suppose that Justin obtained it from the Gospel according to the Hebrews. Others consider it an inaccurate quotation of John v. 30, or Matt. xxiv. 30, and xxv. 1, etc.; or an oral tradition; or perhaps a gloss (Otto), summarizing these passages.
[7] Dial. 35. Justin cites, as words of Christ, ἔσονται σχίσματα καὶ αἱρέσεις." Cf. 1 Cor. xi. 18, 19. The sentence is found nowhere else attributed to Christ; but similar summaries to the same effect are numerous. Cf. Tertullian, Clement of Alexandria, Clem. Recog., quoted by Otto.

differences between Justin's account of Christ's life and that of the canonical Gospels.[1]

If, then, we review these items, it must be evident that in comparison with the large amount of agreement between Justin and the canonical Gospels, *the differences are most trifling.* It is to be noted, moreover, that for none of the points in which he differs from our Gospels, except the "bloody sweat," does Justin cite the authority of the "memoirs." Indeed, he seems carefully to avoid doing so, as may be seen in his account of the baptism, where, while relating that a fire

<small>The differences are trifling,</small>

<small>and not cited from the "memoirs,"</small>

---

[1] Justin (Dial. 88) states that Jesus was a carpenter by trade, and made "ploughs and yokes by which He taught the symbols of righteousness and an active life." Mark vi. 3, however, according to the correct text, reads οὐχ οὗτός ἐστιν ὁ τέκτων; The tradition that He made ploughs and yokes evidently grew, as Justin's own language shows, from the desire to exhibit the symbolical import of His work. In Dial. 51, he says that Christ came and put an end to (ἔπαυσε) John's preaching and baptizing. But this can hardly be called a divergence from our Gospels; for though John did not immediately cease working after Christ's baptism, yet Christ did not enter on His Galilean ministry till John was imprisoned. Cf. Luke iii. 19, 20; John iii. 26-30. Dr. Sanday says (Gospels in the Second Century, p. 98): "There is nothing in Justin (as in Luke xxiv.) to show that the ascension did not take place on the same day as the resurrection." But neither is there anything in either Luke or Justin to show that it did; and Justin speaks of Christ's instructing the disciples in the true meaning of the Old Testament after His resurrection (Ap. i. 50; Dial. 106), which would seem to imply that some time elapsed between the resurrection and the ascension. In Dial. 35, Justin makes Christ say, "Many false Christs and *false apostles* shall arise;" and in Dial. 51, that He preached, "saying that the kingdom of heaven is at hand and that He must ... be crucified, and on the third day rise again, and *would appear again in Jerusalem* and *would eat and drink with His disciples;*" but these passages are so easily explained as amplifications of the statements of our Gospels that they can scarcely be cited as extra-canonical sayings.

appeared on the Jordan, he makes the Apostles responsible only for the fact of the descent of the Spirit like a dove. As to the differences themselves, and may be some are obvious mistakes, as when he makes Cyrenius first procurator of Judæa, and when he states that the Jews went to arrest Christ *from* the Mount of Olives, and when he shows ignorance of the civil positions held under the Romans by the Herods. Others are inferences which may be drawn from the Gospels, as that Joseph was "from Bethlehem," and that Pilate sent Jesus bound to Herod as a compliment. Others are general statements with perhaps a mixture of exaggeration, as when he seems to say that Christ healed not only the blind from birth, but also those born lame and deaf. In other cases his recital is colored by his desire to show the fulfilment of prophecy. Thus he probably represented Christ's persecutors as saying "Judge us," because he read in Isaiah (lviii. 2,) "They ask of me judgment;" and Christ Himself as deformed, because he read (Isa. liii. 2), "He was without form and comeliness." In two cases Justin conforms to textual errors which are still represented in manuscripts of our Gospels; namely, in the case of the bloody sweat and the words spoken from heaven at the baptism. Of all these differences from the canonical Gospels, only two can be plausibly adduced as evidence for Justin's use of an extra-canonical document. These are his account of the fire in the Jordan, and the words spoken at the baptism. Both were found with variations, according to Epiphanius, in the Gospel of the Ebionites, but they are also found scattered in other works; and while the words spoken at the baptism are doubtless to be regarded as an early textual corruption of the canonical account, the story of the fire was probably a mere tradition current in various quarters. Its earliest form seems to appear in the Syrian Liturgy, which states that when Christ ascended from the water, "the sun bended its rays."

As to the two extra-canonical sayings of our Lord, neither is elsewhere found attributed to Him. The first — "In whatsoever things I take you, in these I will judge" — is repeated by Clement of Alexandria, but without hint of its source, and by a later writer is attributed to Ezekiel. Interpolated writings of Ezekiel are known to have been current in the early Church, and Justin may have confused this phrase with our Lord's warnings to the disciples of the suddenness and decisiveness of the second advent. The second saying — "There shall be schisms and heresies" — reminds us of Paul's words,[1] — "I hear that there are schisms among you, and I partly believe it; for there must be heresies among you," — and looks like a substantial expression in Paul's language of Christ's warnings against false prophets. So Justin shortly after adds to Christ's prediction that "many false prophets shall arise,"[2] the words "and false apostles." Similar warnings, in various phraseology taken from later times, are attributed to Christ by several early writers.

Of course it is possible that Justin obtained these items from some document. If he did, however, it influenced him but slightly, and must have been a document which merely added to the common canonical narrative a few legendary details. But while this is possible, oral tradition, together with corruption of the Gospel text, is quite sufficient to explain all the points of difference. The marvel is that so little legendary matter is found in Justin.

Oral tradition and textual corruption.

[1] 1 Cor. xi. 18, 19.   [2] Matt. xxiv. 11.

When, for example, we compare his account of the Magi with the fanciful account given forty years earlier by Ignatius of the Star of Bethlehem,[1] we cannot but remark the sobriety of Justin's narrative. In the same way his account differs from the fragments of Papias,[2] and always in the direction of the simple, unadorned story of the Gospels.

It is certain, therefore, that the extra-canonical element in Justin, so far as it concerns matters of fact, is so insignificant that it does not in the least affect the inference which we are forced to draw from his agreement with our Gospels, that these latter were identical with the "memoirs." This general and really conclusive argument should not be forgotten in subsequent questions of the relations of texts to one another. We are sure that Justin used narratives of Christ's life which claimed the authorship of apostles or their companions, which were publicly used in the Church, and which gave the same story that is preserved in our Gospels; and since, in the generation immediately following his, our four Gospels were, by the testimony of Irenæus and others, recognized as apostolic and universal authorities in the same way in which they are now recognized, it is absurd to suppose that in so short a time they had displaced others which had already received the veneration and moulded the faith of believers. The facts which Justin presents throw the whole burden of proof on those who venture to deny the identity of his "memoirs" with the canonical Gospels.

The force of this substantial agreement with our Gospels.

On what, then, is such a denial based? It is based

[1] Ad Eph. 19.
[2] Iren. adv. Hær. v. 32, and, perhaps, v. 36.

on the *textual* differences between Justin's quotations from the "memoirs" and the narrative of the Synoptic Gospels, and on the alleged *textual* agreement of his quotations with those found in certain early uncanonical writings. I can only give the results of an examination of the evidence upon these points, with a few illustrations.

The textual differences.

(1) It is, then, a fact that Justin's quotations from the "memoirs" differ considerably from the text of our Gospels. In the first Apology, for example, there are, as I reckon, thirty-six passages which may be regarded as taken from the "memoirs," because either citing some instance of Christ's teaching or relating some event of His life. But only two of these agree exactly with the language of our Gospels.[1] The rest differ from it, sometimes slightly, sometimes considerably; and the question arises whether the variations are such as to lead us to suppose that Justin used another Gospel, either alone or in addition to ours, from which he took this variant text, and which he therefore regarded as an apostolic and authoritative source.

They are considerable.

To answer this question we have to inquire into Justin's method of quotation elsewhere, and to ask if, assuming his use of our Gospels, that

Justin's habit of quotation.

---

[1] Ap. i. 16 : Οὐχὶ πᾶς ὁ λέγων μοι Κύριε, κύριε, εἰσελεύσεται εἰς τὴν βασιλείαν τῶν οὐρανῶν, ἀλλ' ὁ ποιῶν τὸ θέλημα τοῦ πατρός μου τοῦ ἐν τοῖς οὐρανοῖς. Cf. Matt. vii. 21. Ap. i. 19 : Τὰ ἀδύνατα παρὰ ἀνθρώποις δυνατὰ παρὰ θεῷ. Cf. Luke xviii. 27 (... παρὰ τῷ θεῷ ἐστιν). Sanday (Gospels, etc., p. 113) cites Ap. i. 15, Οὐκ ἦλθον καλέσαι δικαίους ἀλλὰ ἁμαρτωλοὺς εἰς μετάνοιαν; but the correct text of Matt. ix. 13 omits εἰς μετάνοιαν, and Luke v. 32 reads οὐκ ἐλήλυθα. He also (p. 115) cites Ap. i. 35, where Justin quotes Zech. ix. 9, in part as in Matt. xxi. 5; but I include only quotations from the "memoirs."

method will explain his variations from the canonical text.

Fortunately we may test his method, since his writings contain a few quotations from well-known classic authors and abound in long quotations from the Old Testament. Examining these, I have obtained the following results: —

In the two Apologies there are nine quotations from the classics, — six from Plato, two from Xenophon, and one from Euripides. Five of these are mere phrases, very short, and most of them quite familiar; and these Justin repeats accurately. Another, though a familiar passage from Plato, is quoted very freely, and its author is simply called "a certain one of the ancients."[2] Again Justin quotes even his favorite Timæus loosely,[3] and varies the text of still another Platonic sentence.[4] The familiar opening paragraph of Xenophon's Memoirs he cites inaccurately,[5] and gives

His classical quotations.

---

[1] Ap. i. 5. λέγοντες " καινὰ εἰσφέρειν αὐτὸν δαιμόνια." Xen. Mem. i. 1. Ap. i. 39. "ἡ γλῶσσ' ὀμώμοκεν, ἡ δὲ φρὴν ἀνώμοτος." Eur. Hippol. 607. Ap. i. 44. ὥστε καὶ Πλάτων εἰπών· " Αἰτία ἑλομένου, θεὸς δ' ἀναίτιος." De Rep. 10, 617 E. Ap. ii. 3. "'Αλλ' οὔτι γε πρὸ τῆς ἀληθείας τιμητέος ἀνήρ." De Rep. 10, 595 C (Plato has ἀλλ' οὐ γὰρ πρό γε ἀληθείας, etc.). Ap. i. 60. "ἐχίασεν αὐτὸν ἐν τῷ παντί." Plato, Tim. 36.

[2] Ap. i. 3. ἔφη γάρ που καί τις τῶν παλαιῶν · "Αν μὴ οἱ ἄρχοντες φιλοσοφήσωσι καὶ οἱ ἀρχόμενοι, οὐκ ἂν εἴη τὰς πόλεις εὐδαιμονῆσαι. De Rep. 5, 473 D. ἐὰν μὴ ἢ οἱ φιλόσοφοι βασιλεύσωσιν ἐν ταῖς πόλεσιν ἢ οἱ βασιλεῖς . . . φιλοσοφήσωσιν, οὐκ ἔστι κακῶν παῦλα ταῖς πόλεσιν. The same sentiment is expressed in Ep. vii. 326 B.

[3] Ap. ii. 10. Socrates said, "τὸν δὲ πατέρα καὶ δημιουργὸν πάντων οὔθ' εὑρεῖν ῥᾴδιον οὔθ' εὑρόντα εἰς πάντας εἰπεῖν ἀσφαλές." Tim. 28 C. τὸν μὲν οὖν ποιητὴν καὶ πατέρα τοῦδε τοῦ παντὸς εὑρεῖν τε ἔργον καὶ εὑρόντα εἰς πάντας ἀδύνατον λέγειν.

[4] Ap. i. 60. τὰ δὲ τρίτα περὶ τὸν τρίτον. Ps.-Ep. ii. 312 E. καὶ τρίτον περὶ τὰ τρίτα.

[5] Ap. ii. 10. Justin changes the order of the clauses as well as the tense, and for οὐ νομίζειν substitutes μὴ ἡγεῖσθαι.

from the same book a condensed account of "Hercules's choice."[1] It thus appears that whenever he cites from a Greek author a passage of more than a few words, he fails to reproduce the exact text of the original.

It is more important, however, to examine Justin's quotations from the Old Testament. These were, of course, taken from the Septuagint translation; and while the text of the Septuagint is itself sometimes uncertain, yet results may be reached with approximate accuracy.

Quotations from the Old Testament.

Confining our examination still to the Apology, which is sufficient to test Justin's method, I have found forty-seven quotations from the Old Testament. Of these, six agree exactly with Van Ess's text of the Septuagint,[2] and in eight the variation is so slight[3] that the quotations may be fairly called accurate. Twenty-two[4] may be classed as more or less variant in text;

---

[1] Ap. ii. 11. Cf. Xen. Mem. ii. 1, 21, etc. To the above passages might be added Ap. i. 2. ὑμεῖς δ' ἀποκτεῖναι μὲν δύνασθε, βλάψαι δ' οὔ. On this Gildersleeve's note is, "The *sentiment* is found in Plato. Socrates says (Apol. 30 C): ἐμὲ μὲν γὰρ οὐδὲν ἂν βλάψειεν οὔτε Μέλητος οὔτε Ἄνυτος· οὐδὲ γὰρ ἂν δύναιτο. The *language*, with its effective rhetorical position, is traditional. 'Εμὲ δὲ Ἄνυτος καὶ Μέλητος ἀποκτεῖναι μὲν δύνανται, βλάψαι δὲ οὔ. Epict. Enchir. 53. 3 ; Diss. 1. 29. 18 ; 2. 2. 15 ; 3. 3. 21."

[2] Ap. i. 33 (Isa. vii. 14), translating, however, "Immanuel;" i. 38 (Isa. l. 6); i. 53 (Isa. liv. 1); i. 63 (Isa. i. 3), twice; i. 64 (Gen. i. 2).

[3] Ap. i. 37, differing in only one word from Isa. i. 3; i. 37, differing in order of clauses from Isa. lxvi. 1; i. 40 (Ps. xix. 2); i. 40 (Pss. i. and ii.); i. 45 (Ps. cx. 13); i. 48 (Isa. lvii. 1); i. 54 (Ps. xix. 15), introducing ἰσχυρός as explanatory; i. 55 (Lam. iv. 20); i. 59 (Gen. i. 1–3), οὕτως for the second φῶς.

[4] Ap. i. 32 (Gen. xlix. 10, though here Justin may have used a different text of the LXX.); i. 35 (Isa. ix. 6, νεανίσκος ἡμῖν ἀπεδόθη for υἱὸς καὶ ἐδόθη ἡμῖν); i. 35 (Isa. lxv. 2, and lviii. 2, with several verbal differences); i. 35 (Ps. xxi. 17, 18, with slight variations); i. 37 (Isa. i. 11–15), a very mixed quotation of clauses in confused

eight [1] as very free quotations; and three [2] are manifest cases of free combination of different passages. In

order; i. 38 (Isa. lxv. 2, with slight variations); i. 38 (Ps. xxi. 17, 19), two clauses united as in i. 35, but in opposite order, and in both places reading "feet and hands" for "hands and feet" of the LXX.; i. 38 (Ps. iii. 6, with ἀνέστην for ἐξεγέρθη, and ἀντελάβετο for ἀντιλήψεται); i. 38 (Ps. xxi. 8, 9, with slight variations); i. 39 (Isa. ii. 3, with slight variations); i. 41 (Ps. xcvi. quoted freely, though Justin's text may have varied from ours. He seems to have combined verse 5 with 1 Chron. xvi. 5 ("idols of demons"). Did he combine them, or were they combined in his text? He claims also that the Jews had cut out the last verse of the Psalm, "ὁ κύριος ἐβασίλευσεν ἀπὸ τοῦ ξύλου." There is, however, no manuscript authority for the verse in the LXX. The Christians may have used a Targum written in the Christian interest. Cf. Sanday's Gospels, etc., p. 47); i. 44 (Isa. i. 16, with slight variations, indicating lapses of memory); i. 47 (Isa. lxiv. 10-12, with slight variations); i. 49 (Isa. lv. 1-3, with slight variations); i. 50, 51 (Isa. liii. 12; lii. 13-15; liii. 1-12, quoted with unusual accuracy for the most part, but in c. 50, Isa. liii. 12 differs from the LXX. and from the quotation of the same verse in c. 51); i. 51 (Ps. xxiv. 7, 8, with several variations); i. 51 (Dan. vii. 13, referred by Justin to Jeremiah. The quotation also slightly varies from our text of Daniel; and Justin adds "καὶ οἱ ἄγγελοι αὐτοῦ σὺν αὐτῷ," probably from Matt. xxv. 31. The text of Daniel, however, was specially variable); i. 52 (Isa. lxvi. 24, with παυθήσεται for τελευτήσει); i. 53 (Isa. i. 9, with slight variations); i. 53 (Jer. ix. 26, quoted as from Isaiah, with variations of text and transposition of clauses); i. 54 (Gen. xlix. 10, 11, with slight variations from the quotation in c. 32); i. 61 (Isa. i. 16-20, with the same variations as in c. 44).

[1] Ap. i. 37 (Isa. lviii. 6, 7); i. 44 (Deut. xxx. 15, 19, quoted very freely and said to have been spoken by God to Adam); i. 47 (Isa. i. 7, quoted freely and mixed with a reminiscence of Jer. l. 3); i. 49 (Isa. v. 20); i. 60 (a free recital of the story of the brazen serpent (Numb. xxi. 6-9), introducing τύπῳ and πιστεύητε); i. 60 (Deut. xxxii. 22); i. 62 (Ex. iii. 5); i. 63 (Ex. iii. 2, 5, 14, quoted three times freely, but retaining the important words of the original).

[2] Ap. i. 32 (Isa. xi. 1, mixed with Numb. xxiv. 17); i. 52 (Ez. xxxvii. 7, quoted freely and followed by Isa. xlv. 23, with varia-

196 JUSTIN MARTYR.

five of these instances,[1] also, the quotation appears to have been modified by the remembrance of some passage in the Gospels, usually itself a quotation of the same Old Testament text; and several evident slips of memory occur.[2] It thus appears that while the agreement of Justin's quotations with the text of the Septuagint is greater than with our text of the Gospels, yet there is more variation than agreement, and an evident dependence in many cases upon memory. The quotations from the Old Testament in the Dialogue are more numerous and longer and somewhat more accurate than in the Apology;[3] but the same general characteristics prevail in them. If, however, there is so much freedom in Justin's quotations from the Old Testament, which he declared to be inspired, and from even the verbiage of which he drew predictions of Christian truth and history, we ought not to be surprised at still more freedom in his use of the Gospel narratives, since three of these are Synoptic accounts and therefore specially liable to be commingled, and since he lived near enough to the apostolic age for oral tradition to render less necessary

His textual variations from our Gospels not surprising,

---

tions, as if it formed part of Ezekiel); i. 52 (where a passage is quoted as if from Zechariah, which is a mixture of Zech. ii. 6, with reminiscences of Isa. xliii. 5, 6, and xi. 12; and Zech. xii. 10-12, quoted as in John xix. 37, with additions from Isa. lxiii. 17, and lxiv. 11).

[1] Ap. i. 34 (Mic. v. 2, as Matt. ii. 6, but omitting τὸν Ἰσραήλ); i. 35 (Zech. ix. 9, as Matt. xxi. 5); i. 51 (Dan. vii. 13, influenced by Matt. xxv. 31); i. 48 (Isa. xxxv. 6, with reminiscence of Matt. xi. 5); i. 52 (Zech. xii. 10-12, as John xix. 37).

[2] Such as the reference of Zech. ix. 9, to Zephaniah (Ap. i. 35); of Dan. vii. 13, to Jeremiah (Ap. i. 51); of Jer. ix. 26, to Isaiah (Ap. i. 53); and the statement that Deut. xxx. 15, 19, was spoken by God to Adam (Ap. i. 44).

[3] Cf. Sanday's Table, based on Credner (Gospels, etc., p. 41).

the exact quotation of the Gospels than a later age would require.

Of, then, the thirty-four variant quotations from the "memoirs" contained in the Apology, fifteen [1] may be explained as textual variations of passages in our Gospels, quite similar to the variations found in many quotations from the Old Testament, and indicating that Justin quoted the Gospels from memory or else changed the language to express more briefly or clearly the sense; fifteen [2] ex-

and may be explained

by dependence on memory,

---

[1] Ap. i. 15 (Matt. v. 28, with verbal variations, but the principal words retained, and παρὰ τῷ θεῷ added to make the meaning clearer); i. 15 (Matt. v. 32, using the same words, but putting the indicative for the subjunctive tense, and adding ἀφ' ἑτέρου ἀνδρὸς for clearness); i. 15 (Matt. xix. 12, with the order of the first two clauses changed, εὐνοῦχοι repeated, and the clause " Let him who can receive it," etc. paraphrased); i. 15 (Matt. vi. 19, 20, with very slight variations); i. 15 (Matt. vi. 1, with μὴ ποιεῖτε ταῦτα πρὸς τὸ θεαθῆναι ὑπὸ τῶν ἀνθρώπων for προσέχετε τὴν δικαιοσύνην ὑμῶν μὴ ποιεῖν ἔμπροσθεν τῶν ἀνθρώπων πρὸς τὸ θεαθῆναι αὐτοῖς. The following clause is the same in Justin and Matthew); i. 16 (Luke vi. 29, with slight variations, and χιτῶνα and ἱμάτιον transposed as in Matt. v. 39); i. 16 (Matt. v. 22 abbreviated, yet so as to give the substantial meaning); i. 16 (Matt. v. 41, with slight verbal variation); i. 16 (Matt. v. 16, with slight verbal variations, and "let your good works shine," instead of " let your light shine "); i. 16 (Matt. v. 34, influenced by Jas. v. 12, but agreeing with Matthew in "τὸ δὲ περισσὸν τούτων ἐκ τοῦ πονηροῦ"); i. 16 (Luke xviii. 18; Mark x. 17, with ὁ ποιήσας τὰ πάντα added to ὁ θεὸς (the correct text of Matt. xix. 16 reads, " Master, what good thing shall I do," etc.)); i. 17 (Matt. xxii. 17-20; Mark xii. 14-17; Luke xx. 22-25, with verbal variations, but the last verse nearly exact); i. 17 (Luke xii. 48, quoted quite freely); i. 63, twice (Matt. xi. 27, quoted with ἔγνω for ἐπιγινώσκει, the clauses transposed, and οἷς ἂν ὁ υἱὸς ἀποκαλύψῃ for ᾧ ἐὰν βούληται ὁ υἱὸς ἀποκαλύψαι. In Dial. 100, Justin has γινώσκει. Cf. below, for the various readings of this verse).

[2] A good example of this class is found in Ap. i. 16: "But many will say to me, Lord, Lord, did we not eat and drink and

or by combination. plain themselves as a combination of parallel passages in the Gospels, due to an intentional

perform miracles in Thy name? And then will I say to them, Depart from me, workers of lawlessness. There shall be wailing and gnashing of teeth, when the righteous shine as the sun and the wicked are sent into the eternal fire," where we have a combination of Matt. vii. 22, 23, and Luke xiii. 26–28, followed by a reminiscence of Matt. xiii. 42, 43. So cf. Ap. i. 15 (a combination of elements from Matt. v. 29, 30; xviii. 8, 9; Mark ix. 47: "If thy right eye offend thee," etc.); i. 15 (quotes Matt. ix. 13, with εἰς μετάνοιαν from Luke v. 32, or the latter with ἐλήυθα changed to ἦλθον from Matthew, though Justin's text agrees with D in Luke. Either he combined the two Gospels, or they had already been combined in his copies. Justin adds, as if also spoken by Christ, "For the heavenly Father wisheth the repentance of the sinner rather than his punishment," a reminiscence of both Old and New Testament passages (Ez. xviii. 23; xxiii. 11; Rom. ii. 4; 1 Tim. ii. 4; and 2 Pet. iii. 9), which gives the spirit of Christ's ministry); i. 15 ('Εγὼ δὲ ὑμῖν λέγω· Εὔχεσθε ὑπὲρ τῶν ἐχθρῶν ὑμῶν καὶ ἀγαπᾶτε τοὺς μισοῦντας ὑμᾶς καὶ εὐλογεῖτε τοὺς καταρωμένους ὑμῖν καὶ εὔχεσθε ὑπὲρ τῶν ἐπηρεαζόντων ὑμᾶς. Justin's text is most like Luke vi. 27, 28. That this passage was early confused and variously cited, appears from the Didache, c. 1; Polyc. ad Phil. xii.; Athenag. Supplic. xi., who, though introducing a clause from Luke, follows Matthew; Cl. Hom. iii. 19; xi. 32; xii. 32, where the quotations vary from each other and from Justin and from the Gospels; Apost. Constt. i. 1, 2. Matthew's text was early corrupted from Luke, and the patristic quotations were freely and variously made. In Dial. 133, Justin himself omits the fourth clause, which he gives in the Apology; and in Dial. 85, he has, "Jesus commanded us ἀγαπᾶν καὶ τοὺς ἐχθρούς); i. 15 (Matt. v. 42, 46, and Luke vi. 30); i. 15 (Matt. xvi. 26, with ὠφελεῖται and ἀπολέσῃ, apparently from Luke ix. 25. In Matthew, however, D and latt. also have ὠφελεῖται); i. 15 (Luke vi. 35, 36, and Matt. vi. 45); i. 16 (combination of Matt. xxii. 37; Luke x. 27; Mark xii. 29; Matt. vi. 10); i. 16, 63 (Matt. vii. 24, or Luke vi. 47, with Matt. x. 40 or Luke x. 16, and, perhaps, John xiv. 24); i. 16 (combination of Matt. xxiv. 5 with vii. 15 (freely cited), 16 (with ἐκ for ἀπὸ), and 19); i. 19 (μὴ φοβεῖσθε κ.τ.λ. Matt. x. 28 and Luke xii. 4, with variations); i. 33 (combination of Luke i. 31, 32, and Matt. i. 21, attributing all to the angel who appeared

or unintentional mingling of their language. In one instance a variation from the text of our Gospels is introduced, the cause of which can be probably assigned, and which may serve to show the freedom with which Justin quoted. He cites[1] our Lord's language thus: "If ye love them who love you, what *new thing* do ye?" and it is not improbable that he was led to do this by the thought, which he had just expressed in the preceding chapter, of the new morality which Christianity had introduced.[2] So, when he continues, "For even *the fornicators* do this,"[3] we recall the mention of Christian chastity with which he had opened his description of the new morality.[4] On the other hand, no particular reason can be assigned for the phrase, in which Justin stands alone, "Where the treasure is, there also is *the mind* of the man."[5] But if we add two instances[6] in which he appears to give merely

or by other reasons.

to Mary. So too reads the Protevangelium of James (c. 11), which also has, "Thou shalt conceive of His word" (cf. Justin's Ap. i. 33), or "according to His word" (cf. Sanday's Gospels, etc., p. 129); i. 61 (John iii. 3 and Matt. xviii. 3, with variations: see below, on Justin's use of John); i. 66 (in the account of the institution of the Eucharist, Justin combines Matt. xxvi. 26–28 (Mark xiv. 22–24) with Luke xxii. 17–20, or 1 Cor. xi. 23, 25: see below, on Justin's testimony to corruptions of the text).

[1] Ap. i. 15. Εἰ ἀγαπᾶτε τοὺς ἀγαπῶντας ὑμᾶς, τί καινὸν ποιεῖτε;
[2] So Westcott's Canon, p. 124.
[3] καὶ γὰρ οἱ πόρνοι τοῦτο ποιοῦσιν.
[4] Also, in quoting (Ap. i. 34) the words of Micah (v. 2) from Matthew (ii. 6), "who shall rule my people," he omits the closing words τὸν Ἰσραήλ, fearing, no doubt, that they might be interpreted of the Jewish people. So cf. i. 15, ἀφ' ἑτέρου ἀνδρός, added to ὃς γαμεῖ ἀπολελυμένην for clearness, and i. 16, ὁ ποιήσας τὰ πάντα, added to οὐδεὶς ἀγαθός, εἰ μὴ μόνος ὁ θεός, perhaps a trace of his anti-Marcionism.
[5] Ap. i. 15. ὅπου γὰρ ὁ θησαυρός ἐστιν, ἐκεῖ καὶ ὁ νοῦς τοῦ ἀνθρώπου.
[6] Ap. i. 35, "Judge us;" fulfilling, as Justin points out, Isa.

a summary of events recorded in the Gospels, and in which, through the desire to show the fulfilment of prophecy, he makes the language of Christ's persecutors conform more to the Old Testament than to our Gospels, we shall have classified the various types of quotations from the "memoirs" found in the Apology.

It thus certainly appears that Justin is more exact in his quotations from the Old Testament than in those from the Gospels, if we suppose these to have been identical with his "memoirs;" but it also as certainly appears that if we extend to the Gospels the same methods of quotation which he used with the Old Testament, and if we take into consideration the verbal agreements and disagreements of the Synoptic Gospels themselves (which must have contributed then, as they do now, to inaccuracy of quotation), and if we remember that Justin's object did not call so much for the precise repetition of the words of the "memoirs" as for their substantial sense, all his variations from the text of the Gospels may be reasonably explained while maintaining his principal use of them and their identity with the "memoirs." In giving merely a statement of the results obtained from a comparison of his quotations with the canonical texts, we have necessarily failed to show, as would appear from a study of the evidence itself, the large amount of matter which Justin has in common with the first three Gospels. Partial agreements with the texts given by Matthew and Luke are continual.[1] The variations we have noted imply

The textual variations therefore do not overthrow the argument from the substantial agreement of Justin with our Gospels.

lviii. 2 ("ask of me judgment"); i. 38, the mockery of Christ on the Cross, where Justin's language is determined by the wish to show the fulfilment of Ps. xxi. 7.

[1] Cf. Sanday's Gospels, etc., pp. 118-128.

that the element common to both is much larger than that which is peculiar to each. Agreements with Mark alone are indeed much less frequent, because that Gospel has itself so much in common with the other two; but even they are not wholly wanting.[1] At any rate, Justin gives us a text which has so much in common with our Synoptic Gospels that it may clearly have been derived from them. The variations cannot be used, therefore, to overthrow the conclusion already drawn from their agreement in substance, — that his "memoirs" were our Gospels.

(2) But what is to be said of the alleged fact that in the peculiarities of his quotations Justin agrees with a Gospel text used by other early writers? This fact has been often affirmed so strongly [2] as to convey the impression that Justin usually and closely represents a different type of text from that of our Gospels; and the infer-

(2) Are said to agree with other post-apostolic writings,

---

[1] Besides the mention of the naming of Zebedee's sons (Dial. 103), which is rather an agreement in matter than in language, we note an agreement with Mark ix. 47 in Justin's quotation (Ap. i. 15): "It is better for thee with one eye to enter *into the kingdom of heaven*" (though Mark has "kingdom of God"); and with Mark xii. 30, in the quotation (Ap. i. 16; Dial. 93): "Thou shalt worship the Lord thy God . . . with all thy heart and with all thy strength ($\dot{\epsilon}\xi$ ὅλης τῆς ἰσχύος σου). Perhaps, too (i. 45), the expression, "the mighty word which from Jerusalem *His Apostles*, having gone out everywhere, preached," is a reminiscence of Mark xvi. 20, "and they, having gone out everywhere, preached, the Lord working with them," etc. If so, it would follow that Justin had the conclusion to Mark's Gospel, which has become canonical. See below, on Justin's testimony to corruptions of the Gospel text. Mark vi. 3 has also, "Is not this the carpenter?" So Justin (Dial. 103) says Jesus was reckoned as a carpenter; but as he adds that He made ploughs and yokes, he would seem to have also relied in this instance on tradition.

[2] Cf. Reuss's History of the Canon, pp. 46, etc.

ence has been drawn that the latter do not give the original narratives upon which the faith of the Church was built. Especially have Justin's agreements with the Pseudo-Clementine Homilies and Recognitions been emphasized. Even Von Engelhardt[1] thinks these sufficient to imply the use by Justin of a written source other than our Gospels. Yet the fact is that the quotations in Justin and those in the Clementines differ as much as they agree. That there are a few instances of striking agreement, is true.[2] One of the best examples of this is the form in which both cite the saying, "Let your yea be yea and your nay nay, for that which is more than these is of the evil one."[3] But the modification of Matthew's language evidently came from James v. 12, "Let your yea be yea, and your nay nay,"— a sentence, indeed, which is quoted by Clement of Alexandria as our Lord's words;[4] while, as Dr. Sanday has observed,[5] the second clause has no force when joined to the language of James, and it corresponds exactly with the expression reported by Matthew. Another example is Justin's quotation[6] of Christ's reply to the rich young man, "Why callest thou me good? One is good, *my Father who is in heaven.*" The Homilist has:[7] "Do not call me good: for the Good is one, *the Father who is*

especially with the Ps.- Clementines.

How far this is so.

---

[1] Das Christenthum Justins, pp. 343, 344.
[2] Cf. Examples 2, 8, 9, 11, 13, on pages 205-207.
[3] Ap. i. 16; Clem. Hom. iii. 55; cf. Matt. v. 37. Justin has, περὶ δὲ τοῦ μὴ ὀμνύναι ὅλως, τἀληθῆ δὲ λέγειν ἀεί, οὕτως παρεκελεύσατο (χρ.)· Μὴ ὀμόσητε ὅλως. Ἔστω δὲ ὑμῶν τὸ ναὶ ναί, καὶ τὸ οὒ οὔ· τὸ δὲ περισσὸν τούτων ἐκ τοῦ πονηροῦ. So the Homilist gives it, ἔστω ὑμῶν τὸ ναὶ ναί, καὶ τὸ οὒ οὔ· τὸ γὰρ περισσὸν τούτων ἐκ τοῦ πονηροῦ ἐστιν.
[4] Strom. v. 14.
[5] Gospels, etc., p. 122.
[6] Dial. 101.
[7] Hom. iii. 57; xviii. 3.

in heaven." But not only do the first clauses differ in the two quotations, but traces of the last and most peculiar clause are widely scattered in early Christian literature;[1] so that it is not improbable that both Justin and the Homilist found it in their text of Matthew.

But however striking these occasional agreements, by the side of them can be placed examples of difference which effectually disprove the theory that Justin and the Clementines followed a common uncanonical source. Thus Justin[2] has, "For your heavenly Father knoweth that ye have need of these things;" the Clementine Homilist[3] has, "For your heavenly Father knoweth that ye need all these things before ye ask Him." Justin three times[4] has, "They shall come from the East and West, and shall sit down with Abraham and Isaac and Jacob in the kingdom of heaven, but the sons of the kingdom shall be cast out into the outer darkness;"[5] the Homilist has,[6] "Many shall come from the East and from the West, the North and the South, and shall recline *on the bosoms* of Abraham and Isaac and Jacob," omitting the concluding clause. In citing the saying reported in Matt. xi. 27, "No one knoweth the Son save the Father," etc., Justin reverses the first two clauses, twice[7] has "No

The agreements of Justin and the Ps.-Clem. balanced by differences.

[1] Cf. p. 206, note, (9).
[2] Ap. i. 15, quoting Matt. vi. 32, with slight variations.
[3] Hom. iii. 55, mingling Matt. vi. 32 and 8.
[4] Dial. 76, 120, 140.
[5] "Ἥξουσιν ἀπὸ ἀνατολῶν καὶ δυσμῶν καὶ ἀνακλιθήσονται μετὰ Ἀβραὰμ καὶ Ἰσαὰκ καὶ Ἰακὼβ ἐν τῇ βασιλείᾳ τῶν οὐρανῶν· οἱ δὲ υἱοὶ τῆς βασιλείας ἐκβληθήσονται εἰς τὸ σκότος τὸ ἐξώτερον.
[6] Hom. viii. 4. πολλοὶ ἐλεύσονται ἀπὸ ἀνατολῶν καὶ δυσμῶν, ἄρκτου τε καὶ μεσημβρίας, καὶ ἀνακλιθήσονται εἰς κόλπους Ἀβραὰμ καὶ Ἰσαὰκ καὶ Ἰακώβ.
[7] Ap. i. 63.

one *knew*[1] the Father," and gives the final clause " and to whom the Son may reveal Him;"[2] the Homilist[3] likewise reverses the clauses, and reads " knew " for " knoweth," but gives the last clause[4] " to whomsoever the Son may will to reveal Him."

Thus the agreements and differences between Justin and the Clementines fairly balance each other, and we certainly cannot conclude that Justin depended on an uncanonical Gospel which was also used by the Homilist, and which was the source of their variations from the canonical text. It is far more probable that the variations from the Gospel text which are scattered throughout these early writers are to be explained either by corruption of the current text, or by the copying of one writer by another, or by traditional modes of expression which had arisen in the Church. Sometimes, also, the phenomena appear to present mere coincidences. In some instances these variations found their way into apocryphal Gospels ;[5] but the relation of Justin's text to that of such contemporaneous writings as we are able to compare with it does not by any means

---

[1] ἔγνω. In Dial. 100, Justin has γινώσκει.
[2] οἷς ἂν ὁ υἱὸς ἀποκαλύψῃ.
[3] Hom. xvii. 4; xviii. 4.
[4] οἷς ἐὰν βούληται ὁ υἱὸς ἀποκαλύψαι. Cf. note below.
[5] Thus, in the Protevangelium of James (c. 11), Luke i. 31, 32, 35, and Matt. i. 21 are united as they are by Justin (Ap. i. 33). The Protevangelium also has the phrase " Thou shalt conceive *according to His word*," and Justin (Ibid.) explains the " power " which "overshadowed" Mary as the Logos. Tischendorf ("When were our Gospels written?" p. 88) thinks Justin used the Protevangelium; but the mingling of Matthew and Luke was too easy to prove this, and the reference of the " Word " in the Protevangelium was to prophecy, while Justin meant the personal Logos. The Protevangelium also (c. 18) places the birth of Jesus in a cave.

point to the use of an extra-canonical document, so that we may again affirm that the few instances in which he differs from our text and agrees with other authors do not weaken the conclusion to which we have been already led, that his "memoirs" were identical with our Gospels.[1]

---

[1] The evidence for Justin's relation to the Clementines will appear more clearly by an examination of the following passages, which he has in common with the Homilies: —

(1) Matt. iv. 10; Hom. viii. 21; Dial. 103, 125. Justin agrees with Matthew. The Homilist has, "Thou shalt *fear* the Lord thy God (Κύριον τὸν θεόν σου φοβηθήσῃ καὶ αὐτῷ λατρεύσεις μόνῳ)."

(2) Matt. v. 34, 37; Hom. iii. 5; xix. 2; Ap. i. 16. Justin and the Homilist agree. Both combine Jas. v. 12 with Matthew. Clement of Alexandria (Strom. v. 14) and Epiphanius (adv. Hær. i. 20) also quote, "Let your yea be yea," etc., as Christ's word. It was an easy error. See p. 202, note 3.

(3) Matt. v. 39, 40 (Luke vi. 29); Hom. xv. 5; Ap. i. 16. Justin follows Luke mainly, but combines with Matthew. The Homilist gives a free recital rather than a precise quotation, but substitutes μαφόριον (a head covering) for χιτῶνα (tunic).

(4) Matt. vi. 8, 32; Hom. iii. 55; Ap. i. 15. Justin agrees with Matt. vi. 32, with variations. The Homilist combines Matt. vi. 8 and 32. See p. 203.

(5) Matt. vii. 15; Hom. xi. 35; Ap. i. 16; Dial. 35. Justin, in Ap. i. 16, combines Matt. xxiv. 5 with vii. 15, 16, but with variations (Πολλοὶ γὰρ ἥξουσιν ἐπὶ τῷ ὀνόματί μου, ἔξωθεν μὲν ἐνδεδυμένοι δέρματα προβάτων, ἔσωθεν δὲ ὄντες λύκοι ἅρπαγες· ἐκ τῶν ἔργων αὐτῶν ἐπιγνώσεσθε αὐτούς). So in Dial. 35, except ἐλεύσονται (as Matt. xxiv. 5) for ἥξουσιν. The Homilist has "πολλοὶ ἐλεύσονται πρός με ἐν ἐνδύμασι προβάτων, ἔσωθεν δέ εἰσι λύκοι ἅρπαγες· ἀπὸ τῶν καρπῶν αὐτῶν ἐπιγνώσεσθε αὐτούς. Justin is thus here much freer in his quotation than the Homilist; but the latter, by introducing πρός με, seems to show a reminiscence of Matt. vii. 22 (πολλοὶ ἐροῦσίν μοι ἐν ἐκείνῃ τῇ ἡμέρᾳ κ.τ.λ.).

(6) Matt. viii. 11; Hom. viii. 4; Dial. 76, 120, 140. Justin agrees with Matthew. The Homilist has ἐλεύσονται for ἥξουσιν, adds "from the North and the South," substitutes ἀνακλιθήσονται εἰς κόλπους Ἀβραάμ for ἀνακλιθήσονται μετὰ Ἀβραάμ, and omits the last clause. See p. 203, notes 5 and 6.

(7) Matt. x. 28 (Luke xii. 4); Hom. xvii. 5; Ap. i. 19. Justin

(3) Our discussion, however, must take a further step before exhausting Justin's testimony to the Synoptic combines Matthew and Luke, with variations, taking the form of sentence rather from Luke; thus, Μὴ φοβεῖσθε τοὺς ἀναιροῦντας ὑμᾶς καὶ μετὰ ταῦτα μὴ δυναμένους τι ποιῆσαι, φοβήθητε δὲ τὸν μετὰ τὸ ἀποθανεῖν δυνάμενον καὶ ψυχὴν καὶ σῶμα εἰς γέενναν ἐμβαλεῖν. The Homilist, likewise, combines Matthew and Luke, but follows Matthew more closely, though still with variations, substitutes "him that killeth (i. e., the Demiurge)" for "them that kill," and adds "of fire;" thus, Μὴ φοβηθῆτε ἀπὸ τοῦ ἀποκτείνοντος τὸ σῶμα, τῇ δὲ ψυχῇ μὴ δυναμένου τι ποιῆσαι· φοβήθητε δὲ τὸν δυνάμενον καὶ σῶμα καὶ ψυχὴν εἰς τὴν γέενναν τοῦ πυρὸς βαλεῖν Ναὶ λέγω ὑμῖν, τοῦτον φοβήθητε.

(8) Matt. xi. 27; Hom. xvii. 4; xviii. 4; Ap. i. 63; Dial. 100. Justin reverses the first two clauses; reads in his first clause in the Apology, ἔγνω; in the Dialogue, γινώσκει; and gives the last clause, οἷς ἂν ὁ υἱὸς ἀποκαλύψῃ. The Homilist likewise reverses the first two clauses: reads ἔγνω in the first, and gives the last clause (nearly as Matthew) οἷς ἂν βούληται ὁ υἱὸς ἀποκαλύψαι. This sentence is variously quoted by writers of all types; and no inference for the existence of an uncanonical documentary source can be drawn from the agreement (such as it is) between Justin and the Homilist in regard to it. See Westcott's Canon, p. 120. See, especially, the various forms in which the verse is quoted by Iren. adv. Hær. iv. 6.

(9) Matt. xix. 16, 17 (Mark x. 18; Luke xviii. 18, 19); Hom. iii. 57; xviii. 3; Ap. i. 16; Dial. 101. In the Apology Justin agrees nearly with Mark and Luke, but adds ὁ ποιήσας τὰ πάντα; thus, Προσελθόντος αὐτῷ τινος καὶ εἰπόντος· Διδάσκαλε ἀγαθέ, ἀπεκρίνατο λέγων· Οὐδεὶς ἀγαθός, εἰ μὴ μόνος ὁ θεὸς ὁ ποιήσας τὰ πάντα. In the Dialogue he combines Luke (Mark) with Matthew, and adds "My Father who is in heaven;" thus, λέγοντος αὐτῷ τινος Διδάσκαλε ἀγαθέ, ἀπεκρίνατο· Τί με λέγεις ἀγαθόν; Εἷς ἐστιν ἀγαθός, ὁ πατήρ μου ὁ ἐν τοῖς οὐρανοῖς. The Homilist, in iii. 57, has Μή με λέγετε ἀγαθόν· ὁ γὰρ ἀγαθὸς εἷς ἐστιν, and in xviii. 3, Μή με λέγε ἀγαθόν· ὁ γὰρ ἀγαθὸς εἷς ἐστιν, ὁ πατὴρ ὁ ἐν τοῖς οὐρανοῖς. The Marcosians also (Iren. i. 20. 2) read the passage with the same addition; but various additions were early made to the seemingly incomplete text of Matthew. Marcion (Epiph. adv. Hær. xlii.) read "ὁ πατήρ." Clement of Alexandria (Pædog. i. 8) read "ὁ πατήρ μου ὁ ἐν τοῖς οὐρανοῖς." Origen (de Princip. ii. 5;

Gospels. It is not only incredible on histori- (3) Did he
cal grounds that these latter should have re- use a Har-
placed in the estimation of the Church the mony?
"memoirs" of which Justin speaks, but it is impossible

adv. Cels. v. 11) read "ὁ θεὸς ὁ πατήρ." Early Latin manuscripts and Syriac versions and later uncial manuscripts added "ὁ θεύς." Nothing, therefore, can be inferred from Justin's agreement with the Homilist, except that both followed a widely spread reading.

(10) Matt. xxv. 41; Hom. xix. 2; Dial. 76. Justin substitutes ὑπάγετε for πορεύεσθε; τὸ σκότος τὸ ἐξώτερον for τὸ πῦρ τὸ αἰώνιον; ὃ ἡτοίμασεν ὁ πατήρ for τὸ ἡτοιμασμένον; and τῷ σατανᾷ for τῷ διαβόλῳ. So the Homilist, except that he retains διαβόλῳ. But both ὑπάγετε and ὃ ἡτοίμασεν ὁ πατήρ have ancient Western manuscript authority for them in Matthew, while τὸ σκότος τὸ ἐξώτερον is not without later attestation by confusion with e. g. Matt. v. 30 (see Westcott and Hort's Notes on Select Readings, p. 18), and was an easy error. Textual corruption, therefore, will account for the texts both of Justin and of the Homilist. In Dial. 103, Justin says the devil was called Satan by Christ; hence, perhaps, his introduction of the word here.

(11) Luke vi. 36; Hom. iii. 37; Ap. i. 15; Dial. 96. Both Justin and the Homilist have "χρηστοὶ καὶ οἰκτίρμονες;" but as Luke vi. 35 has "χρηστός," the union of the two words was easy.

(12) Luke xi. 51; Hom. iii. 18; Dial. 17. Justin says, "Woe unto you, Scribes; for ye have the keys (τὰς κλεῖς ἔχετε), and ye do not enter in yourselves, and them that are entering ye hinder" (τοὺς εἰσερχομένους κωλύετε). The Homilist speaks of the Scribes and Pharisees as having been intrusted with the key of the kingdom, which is knowledge, and adds, 'Ἀλλὰ ναὶ, φησὶν (χρ.), κρατοῦσι μὲν τὴν κλεῖν, τοῖς δὲ βουλομένοις εἰσελθεῖν οὐ παρέχουσιν. Both refer to Luke, but in quite independent ways.

(13) John iii. 3, 5; Hom. xi. 26; Ap. i. 61. Both read ἀναγεννηθῆτε and τὴν βασιλείαν τῶν οὐρανῶν; but the Homilist adds, after ἀναγεννηθῆτε, ὕδατι ζῶντι εἰς ὄνομα πατρὸς υἱοῦ ἁγίου πνεύματος. Recog. vi. 9 has: Amen dico vobis, nisi quis denuo renatus fuerit ex aqua, non introibit in regna coelorum. Both show John varied by fusion with Synoptists and by the influence of technical theological language. See below, on Justin and John.

N. B. The above note is based on the list of parallel passages given by Westcott (Canon, p. 160), with some corrections and additions.

on textual grounds to regard them as later recensions of the evangelical narrative witnessed to by Justin. For, as we have seen, his quotations bear all the marks of combination and addition. As the few statements of fact which he adds to the narrative of the Gospels are manifestly legendary accretions, so his textual peculiarities show as clearly a later stage of narration than our Gospels. To suppose that out of the evangelical account as represented by Justin, the Synoptic narratives were made, is to reverse all that we know of the tendencies of the second century as well as the laws of literary relationship.

Justin, then, presupposes our Synoptic Gospels. But did he combine them himself in his own memory and recital, or did he follow in his combinations and variations some previous work? He certainly testifies to their use by the Church; but is there any reason to believe that in his quotations he followed a written form which was based upon them and yet varied from them in text, and which contained such slight additions to their historical matter as we have found in his statements? This is the view of Von Engelhardt.[1] He supposes the existence of a brief Gospel Harmony, which was based chiefly on Matthew, and was a "practical aid for the use of the three evangelical writings," and which had received some few legendary additions. From this he believes that Justin took his quotations and statements. This theory makes Justin testify not merely to the existence of our Synoptics, but also to the fact that they were already in his time so old and so well established as to have been made the foundation of a Harmony. The theory is certainly not in itself incredible. The

The supposition not incredible.

[1] Das Christenthum Justins, p. 345.

JUSTIN ON THE NEW TESTAMENT. 209

Diatessaron of Tatian may have had less complete predecessors.

More recently, also, the attempt has been made by Dr. Charles Taylor[1] to show that Justin was acquainted with the substance of the lately recovered "Teaching of the Apostles;" and he certainly succeeds in pointing out a few striking points of contact between our Apologist and the earlier chapters of this ancient manual.[2] In any view Justin throws

Justin and the "Teaching."

---

[1] Cf., most recently, "The Expositor," November, 1887.

[2] The most evident are the following. Ap. i. 16: "The greatest commandment is, Thou shalt worship the Lord thy God, and Him only shalt thou serve with all thy heart and with all thy strength, κύριον τὸν θεὸν τὸν ποιήσαντά σε." Cf. Διδ. i.: "The way of life is this: first, thou shalt love τὸν θεὸν τὸν ποιήσαντά σε." So Barn. c. 19: 'Αγαπήσεις τόν σε ποιήσαντα. In Dial. 93, Justin seems to show a knowledge of the negative form of the Golden Rule, and says: "He that loves his neighbor will both pray and endeavor that the same things *may happen* (γενέσθαι) to his neighbor as to himself." Cf. Διδ. i.: "Secondly, thy neighbor as thyself: πάντα δὲ ὅσα ἐὰν θελήσῃς μὴ γίνεσθαί σοι καὶ σὺ ἄλλῳ μὴ ποίει." In Barnabas (19) we read, "Thou shalt not take evil counsel against thy neighbor," and "Thou shalt love thy neighbor more than [Cod. Sin. reads "as"] thine own soul." In Dial. 93, Justin unites the Great Commandments with the Golden Rule, as the "Teaching" does (c. i.), but as the Gospels do not. In Ap. i. 15, we read, εὔχεσθε ὑπὲρ τῶν ἐχθρῶν ὑμῶν καὶ ἀγαπᾶτε τοὺς μισοῦντας ὑμᾶς καὶ εὐλογεῖτε τοὺς καταρωμένους ὑμῖν, which is not found precisely in the Gospels (Luke vi. 28 has τοὺς καταρωμένους ὑμᾶς), but is found in the "Teaching" (c. i.) in a different order, but in nearly the same words (προσεύχεσθε instead of εὔχεσθε). The "Teaching" adds, however, "fast for those who persecute you." Cf., also, Prof. Rendel Harris's notes on p. 36 of his edition of the "Teaching" ("The Teaching of the Apostles, Newly Edited, with Fac-simile Text and a Commentary for the Johns Hopkins University," Baltimore, 1887). He doubts whether we have any direct quotation from the "Teaching" in Justin, yet thinks that Dial. 35 ("From the fact that there are such men who call themselves Christians and confess the crucified Jesus to be both Lord

14

not a little light upon the "Teaching," and the latter upon Justin. The relation, also, which exists between Justin and the so-called Epistle of Barnabas [1] is at least in favor of the Apologist's knowledge of such a summary of instructions as is found in the "Teaching." Yet the evidence for Justin's use of the "Teaching" is, after all, very slight, and in even the passages where he connects with it he also differs from it. Of course, also, the "Teaching" could not have been itself the source from which he derived his quotations, since it contains but few of them. It can only illustrate the supposition that he used a manual based on our Gospels.

But it is a serious objection to this theory that we have no notice in early writers of the existence of such a Harmony. The "Teaching" was obviously not such; and even Tatian's Diatessaron, written later in the century, does not appear to have been known in the early Western churches.[2] Moreover, Justin quotes differently in different places the same Gospel passages. Thus, in the Apology[3] he gives as Christ's reply to the rich young man, "*None is good but*

Objections to the theory.

and Christ, and yet do not teach His doctrines (μὴ τὰ ἐκείνου διδάγματα διδάσκοντες), . . . we, the disciples of the true and pure teaching of Jesus Christ (τῆς ἀληθινῆς Ἰησοῦ Χριστοῦ καὶ καθαρᾶς διδασκαλίας) are made more confident," etc.) implies that Justin knew a written Διδαχὴ τοῦ κυρίου. But there is no reason to assert that it was a *written* Teaching. Again, he thinks that Dial. 111 (ὁ οὖν παθητὸς ἡμῶν καὶ σταυρωθεὶς Χριστὸς οὐ κατηράθη ὑπὸ τοῦ νόμου ἀλλὰ μόνος σώσειν τοὺς μὴ ἀφισταμένους τῆς πίστεως αὐτοῦ ἐδήλου) was a "memory" of Διδ. xvi. (τότε ἥξει ἡ κτίσις τῶν ἀνθρώπων εἰς τὴν πύρωσιν τῆς δοκιμασίας καὶ σκανδαλισθήσονται πολλοὶ καὶ ἀπολοῦνται. οἱ δὲ ὑπομείναντες ἐν τῇ πίστει αὐτῶν σωθήσονται ὑπ' αὐτοῦ τοῦ καταθέματος); but the "curse" in the two passages refers to very different things.

[1] Cf. Von Engelhardt's Das Christenthum Justins, pp. 379, etc.
[2] Cf. Zahn's Tatian's Diatessaron, pp. 3–12.
[3] Ap. i. 16.

God alone, who made all things;" in the Dialogue,[1] "*Why callest thou me good? One is good, my Father who is in heaven.*" In the Apology[2] we read, "Thou shalt *worship the Lord thy God, and Him only shalt thou serve,* with all thy heart and with all thy strength, *the Lord God who made thee;*" in the Dialogue,[3] "Thou shalt *love* the Lord thy God with all thy heart and with all thy strength, *and thy neighbor as thyself.*"[4] It is, indeed, not impossible that some of the parallel passages in the Synoptic Gospels may have come to be traditionally harmonized. It is possible that Justin's pen may have been sometimes guided by the remembrance of expressions which were connected with the Gospel text in books used for purposes of instruction or worship in the Church. It is possible that in this may occasionally lie the explanation of his agreement in quotation with other uncanonical writers. But we think that the phenomena of his quotations are more consistent with the view that he cited freely and from memory. It is certain that if he used any other written document than our Gospels, that document was itself based upon the latter; but while the possibility of his occasional use of such a document cannot be positively denied, there appears to be need of assuming nothing but the Gospels themselves, allowance being made for the corruption of their texts, together with oral tradition and the operation of Justin's own mind, in order to account for the form of his quotations.

[1] c. 101.   [2] Ap. i. 16.   [3] c. 93.

[4] So Ap. i. 16: "I say unto you, Pray for your enemies," etc., which agrees with Dial. 96 and 133, but differs from Dial. 85, where we read, "Jesus commanded us to *love* even our enemies." Cf. also Ap. i. 15 (γίνεσθε δὲ χρηστοὶ καὶ οἰκτίρμονες κ.τ.λ.) with Dial. 96, and Ap. i. 16 (πολλοὶ δὲ ἐροῦσί μοι· Κύριε, Κύριε κ.τ.λ.) with Dial. 76, and Ap. i. 16 (ὃς γὰρ ἀκούει μου κ.τ.λ.) with Ap. i. 63, etc.

(4) But whether Justin used a Harmony or not, his quotations testify not only to the existence, but also to the already considerable antiquity of our Synoptic Gospels. They do this by the fact that, as we have several times observed, they contain what appear to be corruptions of the original text. They correspond not infrequently to "various readings" of the Gospels which are attested by other early evidence, but which certainly were textual corruptions. Sometimes they agree with readings given by the Codex Bezæ; sometimes with readings given by "old Latin" manuscripts. The report, for example, which Justin gives of the words spoken from heaven at Christ's baptism is found in Luke iii. 22, according to these very authorities.[1] Other examples of probable corruption may be found in the reference to the "bloody sweat," which Justin explicitly says [2] was mentioned in the "memoirs," but which Westcott and Hort expunge from Luke as a Western corruption;[3] and in Justin's evident dependence, in his account of the institution of the Eucharist, upon Luke xxii. 19 b, 20, although these verses appear to have been introduced into Luke from 1 Cor. xi. 23–25.[4] He seems, also,[5] to show acquaintance with the verses which

(4) His quotations show the Synoptic Gospels already ancient books.

Textual corruption.

[1] D. and lat. mss. a, b, c, ff$_2'$ 1; cf. above, note, p. 185.

[2] Dial. 103.

[3] See Westcott and Hort's New Testament Notes on Select Readings, p. 64.

[4] See Ibid., p. 63. Justin, however (Ap. i. 66), may have himself combined 1 Cor. xi. 23, etc., with his remembrance of the account in the "memoirs;" cf. "the Apostles in the Memoirs composed by them, which are called Gospels, οὕτως παρέδωκαν ἐντετάλθαι αὐτοῖς· τὸν Ἰησοῦν λαβόντα ἄρτον κ.τ.λ.," with 1 Cor. xi. 23, ἐγὼ γὰρ παρέλαβον ἀπὸ τοῦ κυρίου ὃ καὶ παρέδωκα ὑμῖν κ.τ.λ.

[5] Ap. i. 45 (τοῦ λόγου τοῦ ἰσχυροῦ ὃν ἀπὸ Ἰερουσαλὴμ οἱ ἀπόστολοι αὐτοῦ ἐξελθόντες πανταχοῦ ἐκήρυξαν) compared with Mark xvi. 15–18.

JUSTIN ON THE NEW TESTAMENT. 213

were early added as a conclusion to Mark's Gospel. We do not mean that Justin's text is now represented in its entirety by any one manuscript or class of manuscripts, but that he gives evidence of that corruption of the canonical texts which, according to abundant testimony, took place even in the century immediately succeeding that in which they were written, and which most plainly appears in those manuscripts which textual critics have classified as "Western." If, however, this be so, then Justin not only testifies that our Synoptic Gospels existed in his day, and were used by the Church as public documents, and were regarded as apostolic and authoritative records of the life of Christ, but he also proves, by the incidental character of his quotations and by their very variations from the text of our Gospels, that these latter were in the middle of the second century already ancient books, handed down from the apostolic age. No more explicit testimony to our Synoptic Gospels could well be asked of him; and the very difficulties which at first sight present themselves in his quotations, in the end confirm his evidence for their apostolic authority.

II. So far we have said nothing of Justin's relation to the Fourth Gospel. The vast majority of his evangelical references were undoubtedly derived from the first three Gospels; and as we have seen, he testifies plainly to their antiquity and established use in the Church. But what witness does he bear to that other Gospel which we find in the next generation placed by all the Church side by side with the Synoptics as their apostolic complement? *II. Justin and the Fourth Gospel.*

It may be fairly said that Justin's use of the Fourth

Gospel is now generally admitted. The views of the early Tübingen critics, which placed the composition of that Gospel in the middle or even in the second half of the second century, have been generally abandoned. The historical evidence for its existence and use has gradually pushed the date assigned for its origin farther back. Critics, of course, still differ among themselves; but few will be now found who do not assign it to a date considerably earlier than the writings of Justin. In fact, from the rationalistic side has come of late the most energetic assertion of Justin's use of it. Albrecht Thoma[1] goes to the extreme limit in maintaining the influence of this Gospel on our Apologist. He declares that their relation is such as to amount to "a literary community of goods." He holds that Justin comments on and amplifies the statements of the Fourth Gospel. At the same time he declares that Justin never formally quotes from it; that he never uses it as historical material, but even avoids doing so; that he did not include it among "the memoirs of the Apostles," and therefore did not believe in its apostolic authorship; in short, that to Justin the Fourth Gospel was a book of doctrine, not of history, with whose forms of thought and expression he was saturated, but which he and the Church were far from regarding as a trustworthy narrative of Christ's life.

Similar views have also been advocated in England by Dr. Edwin A. Abbott, who maintains that while Justin was acquainted either with the Fourth Gospel or with the "Ephesian tradition" out of which the Gospel grew, he carefully avoided citing it as

[1] Justins literarisches Verhältniss zu Paulus und zum Johannes-Evangelium: Zeitschr. für wissensch. Theol., 1875. See, also, his Die Genesis des Johannes-Evangelium, 1882.

JUSTIN ON THE NEW TESTAMENT. 215

he cites the "memoirs," and did not regard it as apostolic or authoritative.[1]

So far as Justin's use of the Fourth Gospel is concerned, Thoma errs, we think, both in many instances where he affirms it, and in several where he denies it;[2] and similarly strained

Evidence for Justin's use of the Fourth Gospel.

---

[1] See "Justin's Use of the Fourth Gospel," Modern Review, July and October, 1882. Dr. Abbott summarizes the results of his study, thus: " That (1) Justin knew of the existence of the Gospel or parts of the Gospel in some form; (2) he never avowedly quotes it as a Gospel or as authoritative; (3) although it is one of his main purposes to prove Christ's divinity and pre-existence previous to the incarnation, he yet never borrows thoughts or arguments from that Gospel which alone enunciates these doctrines; (4) although he agrees with the Fourth Gospel in identifying the Logos with Christ, he differs from the Gospel, and approximates to the Jewish philosopher Philo in his expression of his views of the Logos; (5) where he treats of topics peculiar to the Fourth Gospel (as distinguished from the Synoptics), namely, the mystery of the brazen serpent and the appearance of God to Abraham, he differs from the Gospel and agrees with Philo; (6) in all these points, and especially in his doctrine of the Logos, his doctrine is more Alexandrine and less Christian, or, in other words, less developed than that of the Gospel; (7) he repeatedly associates references to the Fourth Gospel with teaching from apocryphal or traditional sources; (8) even where he is said by modern critics to be 'remembering' or 'referring to' passages in Saint John's Gospel, it is admitted by these same critics that he never quotes those passages, but quotes the Synoptists by preference; (9) even when he declares that he will show how Jesus 'revealed' His pre-existence and divinity, he quotes the words of Jesus, not from the Fourth Gospel, but from those Gospels which, as Canon Westcott truly says, 'do not declare Christ's pre-existence.'" The truth or falsity of these criticisms will appear as we proceed.

[2] Thus, for example, when Justin (Dial. 53), speaking of Christ's entry into Jerusalem, sees in the ass a symbol of Jews and in the colt a symbol of the as yet untrained Gentiles, Thoma finds acquaintance with the fact mentioned immediately after the entry in John xii. 20, that certain Greeks desired to see Jesus.

references have been pointed out by others;[1] but the fact of his use of it may be said to have been demonstrated. First of all, we would maintain that Justin's doctrine of the Logos presupposes acquaintance with that of the Fourth Gospel. As we found in the last lecture, Justin's doctrine is strongly tinctured by philosophy; that of the Fourth Gospel is markedly devoid of this; and it would be a strange phenomenon, if, at a time when such influences as those which Justin shows were abroad in the Church, a work were composed, involving the same theme, but without the impress of the prevailing philosophy. Moreover, Justin's theory, while influenced by philosophy, differed essentially from Philo's in precisely those points which he had in common with the Fourth Gospel. Everything, however, is against the supposition that he knew himself to be introducing novelties into Christian doctrine. He not only declares his beliefs to be those of the Church,[2] but in his theology the philosophical and Christian elements often conflict, showing that he tried to build on that which he had received.[3] Some Christian authority is required to provide the basis on which Justin argued, and the Fourth Gospel alone supplies this. Thus, because the Fourth Gospel lacks the philosophical element found in Justin but contains the Chris-

From his doctrine of the Logos.

So when Justin (Dial. 97) quotes from Isa. lvii. 2, "I stretch out my hands to an unbelieving and gainsaying people," Thoma finds it suggested by John xii. 32, 33, "I, if I be lifted up, will draw," etc. Justin does indeed understand Isaiah to refer to the crucifixion, but there is surely no need to assume a reference to John's narrative. Critics have repeatedly refused such evidence of literary dependence when used by "apologists."

[1] See the passages cited, and sometimes successfully refuted, by Dr. Abbott; e. g., pp. 723 (g), 725 (j), 730, 733, etc.

[2] See Lect. VI.   [3] See Lectt. IV. and VI.

tian element on which his philosophizing theology rested, it cannot be regarded as the further development of the movement of thought represented by Justin, but must be regarded as an earlier authority from which the Apologist partly diverged, but on which at the same time he built. This general fact creates of itself the presumption that Justin was not only acquainted with the Gospel, but also accepted its doctrine as apostolic.[1]

Passing, however, this general consideration, let us turn to the literary evidence for Justin's use of the Fourth Gospel, apart from those passages which involve the question of his direct citation of it. *From literary coincidences.* This evidence consists of certain words or phrases which are so similar to the language of the Gospel as, when taken all together, to create a strong probability that they were derived from it. He calls Christ " the only spotless and just *Light sent to men from God.*"[2] Christ is " *the only begotten* " of the Father, — a

---

[1] The reversal of this general argument appears to be Dr. Abbott's fundamental error. He insists that the Fourth Gospel was the complete and self-consistent Christian elaboration of the philosophical ideas received from Alexandrianism and partially worked up by Justin. Justin, therefore, represents a middle stage between Philo and the Fourth Gospel. But the philosophical movement shown in Justin certainly did not tend to throw off philosophy, but just the contrary; and hence the production by it of the Fourth Gospel is incredible. It is far more in accordance with the known tendency of the age to suppose that the Gospel preceded the philosophical movement in the Church; which movement took that Gospel for its point of departure, but actually departed from its views or reproduced them imperfectly.

esides, the evidence of Basilides (Hippol. Refut. vii. 10) and of Irenæus (adv. Hær. iii. 11), if not of Polycarp (ad Phil. vii., since the Gospel and the First Epistle stand and fall together) and Papias (see Dr. Lightfoot's article, "Papias," Contemporary Review, October, 1875), is decisive for the earlier date for the Gospel.

[2] Dial. 17. κατὰ οὖν τοῦ μόνου ἀμώμου καὶ δικαίου φωτός, τοῖς

term applied to Him in the New Testament only by the Fourth Evangelist and in the First Epistle of John.[1] He is "the good Rock which causes *living water to break out from the hearts of those* who through Him have loved the Father of all, and who *gives to drink to those who will the water of life.*"[2] "We from Christ who begat us unto God *are both called and are the true children of God, who keep the commandments of Christ.*"[3] "He that knoweth not Him [i. e. Christ], knoweth not the counsel of God; and he that *revileth and hateth Him, manifestly revileth and hateth Him that sent Him.*"[4] It was predicted that

ἀνθρώποις πεμφθέντος παρὰ τοῦ θεοῦ κ.τ.λ. True, Justin has just quoted Isa. v. 20, "Woe to you who make light darkness and darkness light;" but his language is at least in striking accord with John i. 9; viii. 12; xii. 46, etc.

[1] Dial. 105. Μονογενὴς γὰρ ὅτι ἦν τῷ πατρὶ τῶν ὅλων οὗτος, ἰδίως ἐξ αὐτοῦ λόγος καὶ δύναμις γεγεννημένος κ.τ.λ. So Ap. i. 23. I. X. μόνος ἰδίως υἱὸς τῷ θεῷ γεγέννηται. Ap. ii. 6. ὁ μόνος λεγόμενος κυρίως υἱός. The fact that Justin does not cite John to prove the generation of the Logos does not invalidate the evidence of his language for his acquaintance with John's Gospel.

[2] Dial. 114. ὡς καὶ χαίρειν ἀποθνήσκοντας διὰ τὸ ὄνομα τὸ τῆς καλῆς πέτρας καὶ ζῶν ὕδωρ ταῖς καρδίαις τῶν δι' αὐτοῦ ἀγαπησάντων τὸν πατέρα τῶν ὅλων βρυούσης καὶ ποτιζούσης τοὺς βουλομένους τὸ τῆς ζωῆς ὕδωρ πιεῖν. See John iv. 10; vii. 38; Rev. vi. 17; xxi. 6.

[3] Dial. 123. οὕτως καὶ ἡμεῖς ἀπὸ τοῦ γεννήσαντος ἡμᾶς εἰς θεὸν χριστοῦ ... καὶ θεοῦ τεκνα ἀληθινὰ καλούμεθα καὶ ἐσμέν, οἱ τὰς ἐντολὰς τοῦ χριστοῦ φυλάσσοντες. See John i. 12; xiv. 15; and, still more, 1 John iii. 1, 2; v. 2. Abbott (p. 736) argues that Justin and the First Epistle borrowed from a common source, and appeals to the antithesis made by Philo between "being" and "being called," and to the natural exhortation of the Christians to one another to be not merely "called," but to be God's children. But this is merely an effort to escape from the evident coincidence of Justin's and John's language. The whole phrase, "θεοῦ ... φυλάσσοντες," is Johannean in all its parts.

[4] Dial. 136. Ὁ γὰρ τοῦτον ἀγνοῶν ἀγνοεῖ καὶ τὴν βουλὴν τοῦ θεοῦ καὶ ὁ τοῦτον ὑβρίζων καὶ μισῶν καὶ τὸν πέμψαντα δηλονότι καὶ

Christ would rise from the dead, "*which*," adds Justin, "*he has received* from His Father."[1] Moses said to the people, when he erected the brazen serpent, "If ye look to this image and *believe in it*, ye shall be saved."[2] So the statement, "The true God and His Son and the prophetic Spirit we worship and adore, *honoring them in reason and truth*,"[3] certainly must remind us of John iv. 24, "They that worship Him must worship Him in spirit and truth," "spirit" being changed to "reason" quite after Justin's habit of speech. The argument, also, against Judaizing — that God governs the world on the Sabbath as on other days — is at least in striking agreement with Christ's reply to the Jews, "My Father worketh hitherto."[4] So, where Justin says of the Logos

μισεῖ καὶ ὑβρίζει. See John v. 23. Justin merely intensifies John's expression. He adds, also, καὶ εἰ οὐ πιστεύει τις εἰς αὐτόν, οὐ πιστεύει τοῖς τῶν προφητῶν κηρύγμασι τοῖς αὐτὸν εὐαγγελισαμένοις καὶ κηρύξασιν εἰς πάντας, with which compare John v. 46.

[1] Dial. 100. ὃ ἀπὸ τοῦ πατρὸς αὐτοῦ λαβὼν ἔχει. See John. x. 18. ταύτην τὴν ἐντολὴν ἔλαβον παρὰ τοῦ πατρός μου. Dr. Abbott (p. 724) mistakes Justin's purpose in immediately quoting Matt. xi. 27. Justin regarded the saying in Matthew as a general statement (πάντα) of the particular fact reported by John. Hence his quotation of the former does not invalidate the evidence of his language that he remembered John x. 18.

[2] Ap. i. 60. 'Ἀναγέγραπται . . . λαβεῖν τὸν Μωϋσέα χαλκὸν καὶ ποιῆσαι τύπον σταυροῦ . . . καὶ εἰπεῖν τῷ λαῷ· ἐὰν προσβλέπητε τῷ τύπῳ τούτῳ καὶ πιστεύητε ἐν αὐτῷ, σωθήσεσθε. So, also, Dial. 94. See John iii. 15. Abbott (p. 575) quotes Philo (Allegories, ii. 20): "If the mind, when bitten by Pleasure, Eve's serpent, is able to discern with the soul the beauty of Temperance, the serpent of Moses, and, through this, God Himself, he will live;" but this is insufficient to account for Justin's application of the brazen serpent to Christ crucified and his emphasis on πιστεύητε.

[3] Ap. i. 6. λόγῳ καὶ ἀληθείᾳ τιμῶντες.

[4] Dial. 29. See John v. 17. Abbott (p. 577) quotes Philo (Allegories, i. 155): "That which rests is one thing only, God. But by rest I do not mean inaction, since that which is by nature

that "He has never done or said anything but what He who made the universe ... has willed Him to do and speak," we remember Christ's declaration reported by the fourth Evangelist, "I did not speak of myself, but the Father who sent me, He hath given me a commandment what I should say and what I should speak;"[1] and Justin's use of the same participle which the Fourth Gospel employs to designate the "sending" of Christ by the Father into the world — a usage which is peculiar to that Gospel among the books of the New Testament — is a point of evidence none the less strong for being small.[2] The fact, likewise, that he five times

active, that which is the Cause of all things, can never desist from doing what is most excellent." But not only is the application of the thought the same in both Justin and John, but Justin adds, " and the priests, as on other days, so on this, are ordered to offer sacrifices," which is so evidently an echo of Matt. xii. 5, that the presumption is that in the previous clause, also, he follows an evangelical authority.

[1] Dial. 56. οὐδὲν γάρ φημι αὐτὸν πεπραχέναι ποτὲ ἢ ὡμιληκέναι [ἢ ὡμιλ. is wanting in the manuscripts, but restored by Otto] ἢ ἅπερ αὐτὸν ὁ τὸν κόσμον ποιήσας, ὑπὲρ ὃν ἄλλος οὐκ ἔστι θεός, βεβούληται καὶ πρᾶξαι καὶ ὁμιλῆσαι. See John xii. 49. Abbott (p. 723) says that Justin's language was a natural remark, in order to guard against a polytheistic inference from the doctrine of the Logos ; which is true, but does not invalidate the inference to be drawn from the agreement of his thoughts with that of the Fourth Gospel. Nor is this inference invalidated by Justin's use of ὁμιλεῖν; for it is characteristic of him to deviate freely from the terminology of even those New Testament books which he certainly knew.

[2] Dial. 17. "The only spotless and just Light, τοῖς ἀνθρώποις πεμφθέντος παρὰ τοῦ θεοῦ." 91. "Fly for refuge τῷ τὸν ἐσταυρωμένον υἱὸν αὐτοῦ πέμψαντι εἰς τὸν κόσμον." 136. "He that revileth and hateth Christ manifestly revileth and hateth τὸν πέμψαντα." 140. κατὰ τὸ θέλημα τοῦ πέμψαντος αὐτὸν πατρός. The word is a favorite with the author of the Fourth Gospel, and is used by him twenty-five times of the Father "sending" the Son. Elsewhere in the New Testament it is thus applied but once (Rom. viii. 3),

JUSTIN ON THE NEW TESTAMENT. 221

quotes or refers to Zech. xii. 10, as it is quoted in John xix. 37, — "They shall look on Him whom they pierced," — is perhaps a similar indication of his use of the Gospel which ought not to go uncounted.¹ Finally,²

or, at most, twice (see Luke xx. 13). In Ap. i. 63, Justin says Christ is called ἀπόστολος, for he ἀποστέλλεται to reveal, etc.; but the verb was here obviously chosen to correspond to the noun, as in turn the noun was chosen because of the verb in Luke x. 16, which Justin quotes. Abbott (p. 730) admits that Justin's use of πέμψας shows "that he was in sympathy with the later traditions embodied in [the Fourth] Gospel." Why not admit that he was acquainted with that Gospel?

¹ See Ap. i. 52; Dial. 14, 32, 64, 118. Abbott (p. 722) says that ἐκκεντεῖν is actually introduced in the passage of Zechariah by the versions of Aquila, Theodotion, and Symmachus, of which the first was written in the first half of the second century. He refers also to Rev. i. 7, as making it probable that this reading existed before the second century. Probably he would be right in saying that "this passage is useless as a proof that Justin copied the Fourth Gospel," if this item of evidence stood alone; but taken with the other items it may be fairly mentioned.

² The following additional items of evidence for Justin's acquaintance with the Fourth Gospel are worth noting : —

(a) Ap. i. 16 (ὃς γὰρ ἀκούει μου καὶ ποιεῖ ἃ λέγω, ἀκούει τοῦ ἀποστείλαντός με) and Ap. i. 63 (ὁ ἐμοῦ ἀκούων, ἀκούει τοῦ ἀποστείλαντός με) may imply acquaintance with John xiv. 24, besides Matt. vii. 24, x. 40, or Luke vi. 47, x. 16.

(b) Ap. i. 33 ("God revealed beforehand, through the prophetic Spirit, that these things would happen, ἵν' ὅταν γένηται μὴ ἀπιστηθῇ ἀλλ' ἐκ τοῦ προειρῆσθαι πιστευθῇ") is perhaps an echo of John xiv. 29, καὶ νῦν εἴρηκα ὑμῖν πρὶν γενέσθαι, ἵνα ὅταν γένηται πιστεύσητε.

(c) When Justin (Ap. i. 63) quotes Matt. xi. 27, "No one knew the Father save the Son," etc., to show that Jesus charged the Jews with ignorance of God, Keim (Gesch. Jesu v. Naz., i. 139, quoted by Otto) and Ezra Abbot (Authorship of the Fourth Gospel, p. 45) think he had in mind, also, John viii. 19 or xvi. 3.

(d) Justin's explanation (Ap. i. 11) of the kingdom which the Christians expect, as not ἀνθρώπινον, but τὴν μετὰ θεοῦ, reminds of Christ's reply to Pilate (John xviii. 36, "My kingdom is not of this world," etc.); while his whole conception of Christianity as

as Thoma shows, the prologue of the Fourth Gospel was evidently in Justin's mind, and formed the basis of his theologizing, though he reproduces neither its language nor its doctrine accurately. If the Gospel says "In the beginning was the Logos," Justin says that the Logos "was begotten as a Beginning before all creatures." [1] If the Gospel says "the Logos was with God," Justin says "the Logos before the creatures both being with Him and being begotten."[2] If the Gospel says "the Logos was God," Justin also repeatedly calls Him God,[3] yet gives the doctrine a different turn from the Gospel when he says, for example, "Who, being the Logos and first-begotten of God, is also God."[4] So, if we read in

"the truth," and of Christ's mission as one sent to teach (see Ap. i. 6, 13, 23, etc.), is in the spirit of Christ's words in John xviii. 37 ("For this end was I born," etc.).

Thoma (p. 542) insists that because Justin does not, though quoting Zech. xii. 10 according to John xix. 37, mention the soldier's lance-thrust, he shows that he did not regard the Fourth Gospel as reliable history. But in all the five places where Zech. xii. 10 is quoted or referred to, Justin applies it to the second advent, and does not enter on any explanation of its separate clauses.

[1] Dial. 62. ὅτι καὶ ἀρχὴ πρὸ πάντων τῶν ποιημάτων τοῦτ' αὐτὸ καὶ γέννημα ὑπὸ τοῦ θεοῦ ἐγεγέννητο. See also Rev. iii. 14. ἡ ἀρχὴ τῆς κτίσεως τοῦ θεοῦ. But Justin probably departed from John's language under the influence of philosophy.

[2] John i. 1 has ὁ λόγος ἦν πρὸς τὸν θεόν. Justin has (Ap. ii. 6) ὁ λόγος πρὸ τῶν ποιημάτων καὶ συνὼν καὶ γεννώμενος and (Dial. 62) ἀλλὰ τοῦτο τὸ τῷ ὄντι ἀπὸ τοῦ πατρὸς προβληθὲν γέννημα πρὸ πάντων τῶν ποιημάτων συνῆν τῷ πατρὶ καὶ τούτῳ ὁ πατὴρ προσομιλεῖ. Justin's use of σύ ειμι is another indication of the influence of philosophy on him.

[3] Dial. 34, 36, 37, 56, 58, 63, 76, 86, etc.

[4] John i. 1 has θεὸς ἦν ὁ λόγος. Justin (Ap. i. 63), ὃς λόγος καὶ πρωτότοκος ὢν τοῦ θεοῦ καὶ θεὸς ὑπάρχει. Justin's expression tries to explain the ground of the deity of the Logos. It shows, again, a mind under philosophic influences reasoning on the fact stated in the Gospel.

the Gospel "all things were made through Him," Justin declares that God "created and ordered all things through Him."¹ If the Gospel sets forth the Logos as having life which "was the light of men," and as "the true light which lighteth every man that cometh into the world," Justin has the doctrine of the Seminal Logos "of whom every race partakes,"² and calls Christ "that spotless and just Light sent from God to men."³ If the Gospel teaches that "the Logos became flesh," Justin, likewise, not only teaches the real incarnation of the Logos, but emphasizes the idea that this was His voluntary act.⁴ If the Gospel calls Him "the only begotten of the Father," Justin calls Him "the only begotten of the Father of all;"⁵ while the expression in the Gospel, "No one hath seen God at any time; the only begotten Son [or God] who is in the bosom of the Father, He hath revealed Him," is echoed in Justin's

---

¹ John i. 3. πάντα δι' αὐτοῦ ἐγένετο. Ap. ii. 6. ὅτε τὴν ἀρχὴν δι' αὐτοῦ πάντα ἔκτισε καὶ ἐκόσμησε. So. i. 64. τὸν θεὸν διὰ λόγου τὸν κόσμον ποιῆσαι. The fact that in Ap. i. 59 Justin writes, "λόγῳ θεοῦ the world was made," does not destroy the evidence, from his more careful use elsewhere of διὰ λόγου, that the latter expresses his real doctrine, though it may show again (Abbott, p. 566) the influence of Alexandrianism.

² Ap. i. 46; cf. Lect. IV.   ³ Dial. 17.

⁴ Justin, indeed, nowhere says that the Logos σὰρξ ἐγένετο. He writes that He "*became man*" (see Ap. i. 5, 23, γενόμενος ἄνθρωπος; Ap. ii. 6, ἄνθρωπος γέγονε). But he declares that He was σαρκοποιηθείς, and that He σάρκα καὶ αἷμα ἔσχεν (Ap. i. 66), σαρκοποιηθεὶς ἄνθρωπος γέγονεν (Ap. i. 32), σαρκοποιηθεὶς ὑπέμεινεν γεννηθῆναι through the Virgin (Dial. 45), that τὸν πρωτότοκον τῶν πάντων ποιημάτων σαρκοποιηθέντα ἀληθῶς παιδίον γενέσθαι (Dial. 84); and that σαρκοποιηθείς, ἄνθρωπος ὑπέμεινε γενέσθαι. So he teaches that the Logos incarnated Himself in the Virgin (see Ap. i. 5 and, especially, 33. The Power which "overshadowed" Mary was the Logos).

⁵ Dial. 105.

doctrine of the invisibility and transcendence of the Father, and in the place which he assigns to the Logos both in communion with the Father and in the revelation of the Father to the world.[1]

These examples of the evidence for Justin's acquaintance with the Fourth Gospel will suffice. Exception may be taken to this or that item; but taking all together, it would seem impossible to avoid the conclusion that, as Thoma states it, there was a "literary community of goods" between the two writers. Nor, even at this stage of the argument, can we be satisfied with the view that Justin was merely acquainted with the "Ephesian tradition" out of which the Fourth Gospel is alleged to have sprung. The literary coincidences are too many not to imply the Apologist's use of the written Gospel itself. Moreover, as already observed, Justin's divergences of phraseology and of idea, even when in closest contact with the Gospel, are far more easily explained by the assumption that his philosophical theology proceeded from the Fourth Gospel as a basis than that the Fourth Gospel was a later and purified version of the philosophical theology which Justin represents. The latter hypothesis supposes that the philosophical movement in the early Church eradicated from itself the philosophical element, which is wholly incredible. Once assume the non-philosophical Logos-Gospel as an established Christian authority, and the union of philosophy and Christianity which Justin shows as existing in the orthodox Church of the post-apostolic age, and which, as Justin also shows, departed from the ideas of the Fourth Gospel though building on it, becomes perfectly comprehensible; and this is the natural inference to be drawn

Weight of this evidence.

[1] Dial. 61, 62; see Lect. IV.

JUSTIN ON THE NEW TESTAMENT. 225

from the marks of literary relationship between that Gospel and our Apologist. Those marks show on the one hand Justin's use of the Gospel, and on the other hand his attempts to explain it. This is precisely the literary phenomenon which from the relations of the thought of the two writers we should expect to find.

We are prepared, then, for the further question, *How did Justin use the Fourth Gospel?* Assuming that he was acquainted with it and that he more or less faithfully followed its cardinal ideas, we are yet asked if he regarded it as apostolical and authoritative. Thoma, Abbott, and others assert that he never directly quotes it, that he never uses its historical material, that he did not reckon it among the "memoirs," and consequently could not have held it to be the work of the Apostle John.

How did he use the Fourth Gospel?

To this, however, we reply:—

(1) That Justin in a few instances does clearly seem to use the historical narrative of the Fourth Gospel.

(1) He uses its historical narrative.

Thus, he states [1] that men supposed John the Baptist to be Christ, but "he cried to them, *I am not the Christ, but the voice of one crying;* for He that is stronger than me shall come, whose shoes I am not worthy to bear." Now, while Luke iii. 15 states that the people "mused in their hearts of John whether he were the Christ or not," and while all three Synoptists quote the words of Isaiah ("The Voice of one crying in the wilderness," etc.) and apply them to John, the Fourth Gospel alone puts them, as Justin does so far as he quotes them, into John's mouth.[2]

[1] Dial. 88.
[2] See John i. 20, 23. The fact that in this same chapter of the Dialogue Justin inserts traditions as well as facts taken from

Again, Justin states that Christ healed those "who were *from birth* and in body blind and deaf and lame; making one to leap, and another to hear, and another to see," — a statement which, as we have already seen, is not entirely accurate, but which is most easily explained as arising from Justin's remembrance of the fourth Evangelist's account of the man born blind.[1] In the same connection, also, we read that the Jews called Christ " a magician and a deceiver of the people." The latter phrase corresponds most nearly with the charge (John vii. 12), "Nay, but he deceiveth the people," though it may possibly have been suggested by Matt. xxvii. 63, "That deceiver said, when he was yet alive."[2]

Still again, when Justin, expounding the Twenty-second Psalm, declares that the latter part of it describes how Christ before His crucifixion "knew that

the "memoirs" does not (Abbott, p. 716) show that he regarded the Fourth Gospel as on a level with tradition, nor does the question of how the Fourth Gospel came to put these words into John's mouth affect the fact that Justin used its account as historical. Like the Fourth Gospel, also, Justin treats of John's witness to Christ rather than of his preparatory work among the people.

[1] Dial. 69. τοὺς ἐκ γενετῆς καὶ κατὰ τὴν σάρκα πηροὺς καὶ κωφοὺς καὶ χωλοὺς ἰάσατο, τὸν μὲν ἄλλεσθαι, τὸν δὲ καὶ ἀκούειν, τὸν δὲ καὶ ὁρᾶν τῷ λόγῳ αὐτοῦ ποιήσας. Evidently Justin used πηροὺς in the sense of " blind." So Ap. i. 22. ᾧ δὲ λέγομεν χωλοὺς καὶ παραλυτικοὺς καὶ ἐκ γενετῆς πονηροὺς ὑγιεῖς πεποιηκέναι αὐτὸν καὶ νεκροὺς ἀναγεῖραι κ.τ.λ. Here ἐκ γενετῆς qualifies πονηροὺς alone, which Justin probably used in the same sense as πηροὺς in Dial. 69 (if, indeed, the latter should not be substituted for it. See above, p. 185, note 2). John ix. 1: τυφλὸν ἐκ γενετῆς. So Apost. Const. v. 7, referring to the miracle of John ix., speaks of Christ as τὸ λεῖπον μέρος ἐν τῷ ἐκ γενετῆς πηρῷ ἐκ γῆς καὶ σιέλου ἀποδοὺς; and Clem. Hom. xix. 22 has, ὅθεν καὶ διδάσκαλος ἡμῶν περὶ τοῦ ἐκ γενετῆς πηροῦ κ.τ.λ.

[2] Dial. 69. καὶ γὰρ μάγον εἶναι αὐτὸν ἐτόλμων λέγειν καὶ λαοπλάνον. John vii. 12. Οὔ, ἀλλὰ πλανᾷ τὸν ὄχλον. Matt. xxvii. 63. ὁ πλάνος εἶπεν ἔτι ζῶν.

JUSTIN ON THE NEW TESTAMENT. 227

His Father would give all things to Him as He asked, and would raise Him from the dead," we note at least a striking coincidence with the fourth Evangelist's record, that on the night of His betrayal Jesus, "knowing that the Father had given all things into His hands, and that He came from God and went to God," rose from supper and proceeded to wash the disciples' feet;[1] and if the reference be allowed, it certainly implies acceptance of the narrative as well as of the doctrine of the Evangelist.

These are, to be sure, slight indications, but they accumulate evidence for the use of the Fourth Gospel's historical matter. Discourses form so large a part of that Gospel that it should not surprise us to find Justin's narrative taken almost wholly from the other three; and slight indications, such as these which have been given, are as much as under the circumstances we should expect.

(2) Their testimony, however, is confirmed by what we cannot but consider, in spite of all the criticisms tending to a contrary result, a direct quotation from the Fourth Gospel, and that a quotation of such a form as to demonstrate practically not only Justin's use of the Gospel's narrative, but also his acceptance of it as apostolic. *(2) He directly quotes it as an authority for Christ's teaching.*

Speaking of baptism, he writes: "For also Christ said, unless ye be born again [or regenerated], ye shall not

---

[1] Dial. 106. καὶ ὅτι ἠπίστατο τὸν πατέρα αὐτοῦ πάντα παρέχειν αὐτῷ, ὡς ἠξίου, καὶ ἀνεγερεῖν αὐτὸν ἐκ τῶν νεκρῶν . . . τὰ λείποντα τοῦ ψαλμοῦ ἐδήλωσεν. John xiii. 3: εἰδὼς ὅτι πάντα ἔδωκεν αὐτῷ ὁ πατὴρ εἰς τὰς χεῖρας κ.τ.λ. The coincidence consists not merely in the idea, but in the reference of Christ's trust in the Father to the period immediately preceding the passion, and apparently to the last discourse with the disciples, where, also, John records it.

enter into the kingdom of heaven;" and he immediately adds, "And that it is impossible for those once born to enter into the wombs of those who bare them, is evident to all."[1] This, of course, is not an accurate quotation from the Fourth Gospel. It substitutes "unless ye be regenerated" (ἀναγεννηθῆτε) for "unless a man be born again" (or "from above," ἐὰν μή τις γεννηθῇ ἄνωθεν), and "he shall not enter into the kingdom of heaven," for "he cannot see the kingdom of God." The latter change looks like the introduction of a Synoptic phrase, and corresponds exactly with the second clause of Matt. xviii. 3, "Unless ye be converted and become as little children, ye shall not enter into the kingdom of heaven." Moreover, in the Clementine Recognitions and Homilies similar quotations occur with nearly the same differences from the text of the Fourth Gospel that are here found in Justin, but with additional peculiarities of their own. In the Recognitions we read, "Unless *a man* be born again *of water*, he shall not enter into the kingdom of heaven;"[2] and in the Homilies, "Unless ye be born again *with living water in the name of the Father, Son, and Holy Ghost,* ye shall not enter

[1] Ap. i. 61. καὶ γὰρ ὁ χριστὸς εἶπεν· Ἂν μὴ ἀναγεννηθῆτε, οὐ μὴ εἰσέλθητε εἰς τὴν βασιλείαν τῶν οὐρανῶν. Ὅτι δὲ καὶ ἀδύνατον εἰς τὰς μήτρας τῶν τεκουσῶν τοὺς ἅπαξ γενομένους ἐμβῆναι, φανερὸν πᾶσίν ἐστι. See John iii. 3-5. ἀπεκρίθη Ἰησοῦς καὶ εἶπεν αὐτῷ Ἀμὴν ἀμὴν λέγω σοι, ἐὰν μή τις γεννηθῇ ἄνωθεν, οὐ δύναται ἰδεῖν τὴν βασιλείαν τοῦ θεοῦ. λέγει πρὸς αὐτὸν ὁ Νικόδημος Πῶς δύναται ἄνθρωπος γεννηθῆναι γέρων ὤν; μὴ δύναται εἰς τὴν κοιλίαν τῆς μητρὸς αὐτοῦ δεύτερον εἰσελθεῖν καὶ γεννηθῆναι; ἀπεκρίθη ὁ Ἰησοῦς Ἀμὴν ἀμὴν λέγω σοι, ἐὰν μή τις γεννηθῇ ἐξ ὕδατος καὶ πνεύματος, οὐ δύναται εἰσελθεῖν εἰς τὴν βασιλείαν τοῦ θεοῦ.

[2] Recog. vi. 9. Speaking of the advantages of baptism, the writer says: "Sic enim nobis cum sacramento verus Propheta testatus est, dicens: Amen dico nobis, nisi quis denuo renatus fuerit ex aqua, non introibit in regna coelorum."

JUSTIN ON THE NEW TESTAMENT. 229

into the kingdom of heaven."¹ On the ground of its variation from the Fourth Gospel and resemblance to Matthew, this quotation has been assigned by some critics either to the assumed extra-canonical Gospel of which we have already spoken as a convenient receptacle for all difficult quotations found in Justin,² or to an unwritten or variously written tradition which was afterwards stereotyped in the form preserved by the Fourth Gospel.³

But the testimony of this passage cannot, we think, be thus set aside.⁴ That Justin should not quote accurately is, as we have abundantly shown, in accordance with his usual habit. That both he and the Clementines should mingle with a quotation from the Fourth Gospel one from Matthew, and should fall into the phraseology of the Synoptics to the extent of substituting "kingdom of heaven" for "kingdom of God," cannot be considered strange, nor is the resulting variation from the Fourth Gospel of such kind or importance, even if it had become a traditional form, as to demand any other explanation of its origin than the habit of

[1] Hom. xi. 26. οὕτως γὰρ ἡμῖν ὤμοσεν ὁ προφήτης εἰπών· Ἀμὴν ὑμῖν λέγω, ἐὰν μὴ ἀναγεννηθῆτε ὕδατι ζῶντι, εἰς ὄνομα Πατρὸς, Υἱοῦ, ἁγίου Πνεύματος, οὐ μὴ εἰσέλθητε εἰς τὴν βασιλείαν τῶν οὐρανῶν.

[2] So Thoma, p. 508; Volkmar and Scholten, quoted in Otto; and others.

[3] So Abbott, pp. 737, etc.

[4] Abbott (p. 740) argues that the introduction "Christ said" rather implies that Justin was not quoting from a Gospel, but from a tradition; but, according to his own showing, out of ten cases where Justin introduces a saying with the preface "Jesus Christ" or "Christ" or "our Christ" "said," three are exact quotations from the Synoptics, one is a free quotation from Matthew, two are the two uncanonical sayings of Christ, three are general statements of Christ's teaching, and the tenth is the passage before us. Nothing, therefore, can be concluded from the preface either way.

free memoriter quotation of which Justin has already furnished many examples.¹ The substitution of ἀναγεννηθῆτε for γεννηθῇ ἄνωθεν may likewise be explained by two considerations. The first is that it had become a technical term, as Justin himself shows; for in the preceding sentence he wrote, "Then they [i. e. the candidates for baptism] are brought by us to where there is water, and are regenerated (ἀναγεννῶνται) according to the same manner of regeneration (ἀναγεννήσεως) by which we ourselves were regenerated (ἀναγεννήθημεν): for in the name of God the Father and Lord of all and of our Saviour Jesus Christ and of the Holy Spirit they are then washed in the water." To be "regenerated" was therefore to be "baptized," and thus the words of Christ were understood.² Secondly, the words of Christ were ambiguous, since they might mean either "born again" or "born from above." Hence the substitution for them by Justin and by the Clementines of the word which expressed their meaning, and which was itself a technical term in the Church, was not unnatural.³ Furthermore, the differences between Justin and the Clementines show that neither author quoted their common source accurately, but that they modified

[1] "Kingdom of heaven" is also found in the Sinaitic Manuscript, two old Latin manuscripts, and several early writers. See Westcott and Hort's Notes on Select Readings.

[2] This may itself be a sufficient answer to Dr. Abbott's (p. 741) objection that Justin ought to have quoted "born of water and spirit," if he meant to quote John's Gospel as an authority for baptism. To Justin, "regenerate" meant to wash with water in the name of the Trinity. The language of Christ, therefore, which he quotes, was understood to be a command to do this.

[3] The same substitution was made by Irenæus (Fragm. 34), and is evidently implied in Clement of Alexandria (Cohort. 9). Dr. Ezra Abbot also cites for it some later Fathers (Authorship of the Fourth Gospel).

Christ's language in accordance with the motives which acted in each case upon their minds.¹ Finally, the phrase which Justin adds, "It is impossible for those once born to enter again into the wombs of those who bare them," is so striking a coincidence, both in substance and in connection, with the remark of Nicodemus, that to consider it an original reflection of Justin's, or to refer it to the ever-convenient uncanonical Gospel or to a traditional explanation of the doctrine of regeneration, appears a thoroughly arbitrary and wilful refusal to accept the natural testimony of the passage. We believe the only fair conclusion to be that Justin quoted from the Fourth Gospel words of Christ's.

Of course this quotation settles the question in favor of Justin's recognition of the Fourth Gospel as a trustworthy narrative of Christ's life. Though the evidence be small in amount, when compared with that for his use of the Synoptics, it is enough to overthrow the new theory that he used it *only* as a book of doctrine, or was acquainted only with traditions out of which it grew. Justin was not only acquainted with the Fourth Gospel, but considered it true history. The inference is plain, that he also recognized it as an apostolic authority.² *Justin considered the Fourth Gospel true history, and hence of apostolic origin.*

---

¹ Dr. Edward Abbott (p. 753), speaking of the variations found in the quotations of this verse in the Clementines, says: "If, even after the stereotyping of Christian doctrine by the recognition of the Four Gospels, these variations of quotation from documents were possible, and if their tendency is evidently to lay less stress on the inward reality and more on the outward sign of regeneration, how much more easy was it that changes should take place in the development of a still undefined and sometimes obscure tradition!" The principle which he here applies to the Clementine variations is quite sufficient to explain the variations in Justin, if he too used the Fourth Gospel.

² That he does not name John as the author of the Gospel, but

Nevertheless, it is true that Justin does *not use* John's Gospel *in exactly the same way* in which he uses the Synoptics. It is from them, as we have seen, that he takes nearly all his evangelical quotations and nearly all his narrative of Christ's life. Thinking evidently of them, he states that "brief and concise utterances" fell from Christ's lips.[1] Some of his arguments also are drawn from the Synoptic Gospels when the Fourth Gospel would have served his purpose better.[2] There is this much of truth in the theory of which we have been speaking, that

Yet he does not use it as he does the Synoptics.

does introduce him as the author of the Apocalypse (Dial. 81), is no difficulty. In the latter place he is introduced as a prophet, and Justin constantly cites the Old Testament prophets by name. But he never cites the Apostles by name as authors of either memoirs or other writings, with the single exception of the phrase, "his memoirs" (Dial. 106, referring to Peter), where he probably means our Mark.

[1] Ap. i. 14.

[2] See Ap. i. 63, where he quotes Matt. xi. 27 to prove that Christ charged the Jews with ignorance of God, instead of, e. g., John vii. 28. So too Clem. Hom. xvii. 4, though the Homilist certainly recognized the Fourth Gospel. Cf. also Dial. 100, where Justin appeals, for the fact that Christ is Son of God, to Peter's confession, and says, "We have understood ($νενοήκαμεν$) that He proceeded before all creatures from the Father," etc. When, in Dial. 105, he says, "I have already proved that He was the only begotten of the Father of all things, being begotten in a peculiar way from Him as Logos and Power, and afterwards becoming man through the Virgin, as we learned from the memoirs," the last clause may refer only to the birth from the Virgin. If, however, he makes the "memoirs" teach that Christ is only begotten, etc., this would seem to be a reference to John (so Weiss's Einleitung, p. 45); but as his argument in Dial. 100 seems to make Christ's pre-existence an inference from Peter's confession (and Matt. xi. 27), I cannot cite Dial. 105 with confidence as a proof of his use of the Fourth Gospel. So when, in Dial. 48, he speaks of Christ's pre-existent divinity as taught by Himself, the argument in Dial. 100 makes me question the right to appeal to John.

Justin does mainly derive from the Fourth Gospel forms of doctrinal thought and expression.

How, then, are we to explain this fact? It is not enough to say that the object of Justin's writings caused him to pass over the profound spiritual Gospel which was intended for Christians rather than for their opponents;[1] for, as we have seen, he might have found much in its reports both of Christ's sayings and of events of His life which would have harmonized with his purposes. We rather judge from Justin that the Synoptics furnished the evangelical narrative, which, as narrative, was most deeply impressed on the Christian mind. They had already made this impression before John wrote his Gospel. How widely that Gospel was published in the years immediately following its composition we cannot say. Certainly at the great Asian and Egyptian and Roman centres it was known before Justin wrote. But the already established narrative, embodied in and perpetuated by the Synoptics, seems to have continued to form the staple of the Christian recital of Christ's life for even half a century after the Fourth Gospel was added to them.[2] Moreover, while John's Gospel is strictly historical, the doctrinal objects of its narration are far more obvious than are those of the Synoptics. It was natural that it should be valued more for its doctrinal bearings than for its historical statements. Such was doubtless the purpose of its author, and none of its readers would be more inclined so to value it than this early Christian philosopher who found in its language the connecting link between his Christianity and his philosophy.

How this may be explained.

[1] Westcott's Canon of the New Testament, pp. 95, 150.
[2] See Weiss's Einleitung, p. 46.

But while Justin appears to have valued the Fourth Gospel *chiefly* as a book of doctrine, the evidence for his recognition of it as an evangelical authority is conclusive. When to this we add his description of the "memoirs" as composed by the Apostles and those who followed them, — a statement which naturally implies that there was more than one "memoir" composed by Apostles, and more than one composed by their followers, and which consequently seems to compel us to suppose that Justin had another Gospel written by an Apostle beside Matthew's, — it is fair to infer that he not only recognized the Fourth Gospel as an authority, but included it in the "memoirs." Thus explained, his relation to it appears consistent both with its canonicity and apostolic authorship and with his own disposition and circumstances.

<small>He included it in the "memoirs."</small>

It should here be added that these conclusions, which have been drawn from Justin's testimony, have been confirmed by the recent recovery of Tatian's Diatessaron. Tatian was Justin's pupil [1] or hearer,[2] and composed a work which Eusebius described [3] as "a sort of connection and compilation, I know not how, of the Gospels," which work, he adds, Tatian "called the Diatessaron." In spite of the reputation of Tatian in later life for heresy, this work of his on the Gospels was used for nearly two centuries in the churches of the far East, whither Tatian himself retired from Rome. Theodoret, Bishop of Cyrrhus, near the Euphrates, writing in 453 A.D., says that he had found "more than two hundred copies of it held in respect in the churches in our parts." These he collected and put away, replacing them with

<small>Confirmation of these results by Tatian's Diatessaron.</small>

---

[1] Hippol. adv. Hær. viii. 9. [2] Iren. i. 28. 1.
[3] H. E. iv. 29.

the Gospels of the four Evangelists. He states also that the Diatessaron cut out the genealogies of our Lord, but that nevertheless the work was used by orthodox Christians on account of its brevity.

This information is of itself sufficient to justify the conclusion that Tatian's work was a harmony of our Gospels, and that therefore the Church of his day and by inference his master Justin accepted the authority of these and these alone. Though Tatian was a heretic, there is no reason to doubt that the Gospels which he used were the ones accepted by the church to which Justin belonged. There is, however, the additional testimony of Dionysius Bar-Salibi, an Armenian bishop of the twelfth or thirteenth century,[1] in his commentary on Mark, that "Tatian . . . selected and patched together from the four Gospels, and constructed a Gospel which he called the Diatessaron," and that Ephraem Syrus, who died A. D. 373, "wrote an exposition [of it]; and its commencement was ' In the beginning was the Word.'"

Nevertheless, Credner,[2] and after him other critics,[3] have insisted that Tatian's work was not a harmony of our Gospels, but was the uncanonical Gospel said to have been used by Justin or one similar to it. They argued that Eusebius had not seen it, and declared that the later Church assumed it to be a harmony and gave it the name of Diatessaron. They appealed to the fact that Epiphanius[4] states that "it is called by some 'according to the Hebrews,'" and that Victor of Capua called it the "Diapente."[5] But the contention has

[1] Mœsinger dates his death in 1171; Lightfoot in 1207.
[2] Beiträge, p. 444; Gesch. des Kanons, pp. 17, etc.
[3] See Supernatural Religion, ii. 152, etc.
[4] Adv. Hær. xlvi. 1.
[5] See Lightfoot's "Reply to Supernatural Religion," Contemporary Review, May, 1877. He shows that "Diapente" in

now been settled. In 1876 there was published a Latin translation, made by a Venetian monk, of an Armenian translation of Ephraem's Commentary just mentioned.[1] This conclusively proved that Tatian's work was, as had been supposed, a harmony of our Gospels. More recently an Arabic translation of the Diatessaron itself has been recovered by Professor Ciasca, of Rome, which, though differing in a few details from that recovered through Ephraem's Commentary, is still a harmony of our Gospels;[2] while still more recently, on the occasion of the Jubilee of Pope Leo XIII., the same scholar produced yet another manuscript which he had discovered, and which contains an Arabic translation of a Syriac original of the Diatessaron, corresponding precisely to that used by Ephraem and thus giving us at last Tatian's work entire.[3] That Tatian composed a harmony of our four Gospels admits, therefore, no longer of doubt. We have the book itself. In it he welded the Gospels together with considerable boldness, and omitted from them the genealogies. But he used our Gospels alone, with occasionally a variation from them due to either textual corruption in his sources or to oral tradition.[4] He thus acted quite in the manner of his teacher, Justin. Professor Zahn holds [5] that the Diatessaron was written in Syriac, and thinks that thus the remark of Epiphanius that "it was called by some 'according to

Victor is probably a clerical error, as Victor's own language implies "Diatessaron."

[1] See Zahn's Tatian's Diatessaron, and articles by Henry Wace in the Expositor, vols. ii. and iv.

[2] See Encycl. Britan., xxii. 864, note 17 (Amer. ed.).

[3] This manuscript is announced as in preparation for publication, and an English translation is being published by Prof. A. L. Frothingham, Jr.

[4] See Zahn's Tatian's Diatessaron, pp. 240, etc.

[5] Ibid., pp. 18, 220.

the Hebrews'" may be accounted for.¹ The same fact may explain why so little was known of the Diatessaron in the early Western Church. But, however these questions of detail may be settled, the fact that Justin's pupil composed a harmony of our Gospels adds the strongest confirmation to the conclusion which we have reached that Justin and the Church of his age received these four Gospels alone as established evangelical authorities.

III. It now only remains to exhibit briefly the way in which Justin regarded apostolic literature in general, the degree of authority which he attributed to it, and the amount of testimony which he bears to the existence of a collection of apostolic writings. *III. Justin and the New Testament Canon.*

Besides the facts pertaining to his use of the Gospels which have been already presented, Justin's use of the New Testament may be described in a few words. He does not mention nor quote from any other New Testament book except the Apocalypse. Of it he speaks ² as the work of "a certain man among us ³ whose name was John, one of the Apostles of Christ, who prophesied, by a revelation that was made to him, that those who believed in our Christ would dwell a thousand years in Jerusalem, and that afterward the universal and in short eternal resurrection and judgment of all men together would forthwith take place." At the same time, however, the knowledge and use of many of the other New Testament books may be inferred from Justin's language, in a way often similar to that in which we have found in his writings traces of the Fourth Gos- *His use of other New Testament books than the Gospels.*

¹ Lightfoot thinks that Epiphanius simply blundered.
² Dial. 81.   ³ παρ' ἡμῖν.

pel. Satisfactory evidence may thus be adduced for his acquaintance with the Acts,[1] the Epistle to the Romans,[2]

[1] See, e. g., Ap. i. 49, where the sentence Ἰουδαῖοι γὰρ, ἔχοντες τὰς προφητείας καὶ ἀεὶ προσδοκήσαντες τὸν χριστόν, παραγενόμενον ἠγνόησαν κ.τ.λ. seems clearly to have been moulded by Acts xiii. 27, 28, 48; Ap. i. 50, where the description of the ascension and the outpouring of Divine Power on the Apostles (καὶ εἰς οὐρανὸν ἀνερχόμενον ἰδόντες καὶ πιστεύσαντες καὶ δύναμιν ἐκεῖθεν αὐτοῖς πεμφθεῖσαν παρ' αὐτοῦ λαβόντες) is not explained by Luke xxiv. 49, as Overbeck (Zeitschr. für wissensch. Theol., 1872, p. 313) maintains, but is a distinct reference to historical facts, which occurred before the Apostles went forth on their mission, as given in Acts i. 8, 9, and ii. 33; Dial. 16, where ἀπεκτείνατε γὰρ τὸν δίκαιον καὶ πρὸ αὐτοῦ τοὺς προφήτας αὐτοῦ is a reminiscence of Acts vii. 52 (see also Acts iii. 14); Dial. 20, where we read, "But if we distinguish between green herbs, not eating all, it is not because they are common or unclean (κοινὰ ἢ ἀκάθαρτα)," after Acts x. 14. Compare also Ap. i. 40 (τὴν γεγενημένην Ἡρώδου τοῦ βασιλέως Ἰουδαίων καὶ αὐτῶν Ἰουδαίων καὶ Πιλάτου τοῦ ὑμετέρου παρ' αὐτοῖς γενομένου ἐπιτρόπου σὺν τοῖς αὐτοῦ στρατιώταις κατὰ τοῦ χριστοῦ συνέλευσιν) with Acts iv. 27; Ap. ii. 10 (Socrates exhorted the Greeks πρὸς θεοῦ δὲ τοῦ ἀγνώστου αὐτοῖς διὰ λόγου ζητήσεως ἐπίγνωσιν) with Acts xvii. 23; Dial. 39 (οὐ μέμηνα οὐδὲ παραφρονῶ) with Acts xxvi. 25; Dial. 68 (where Trypho quotes 2 Kings vii. 12–16 (Ps. cxxxi. 11) changing κοιλίας to ὀσφύος) with Acts ii. 30, though the text of the LXX. may have varied; Dial. 120 (the reference to Simon Magus) with Acts viii. 10.

[2] In Dial. 23, Justin's argument about Abraham's circumcision is clearly an echo of Rom. iv. 10, 11. Note ἐν ἀκροβυστίᾳ ὢν in connection with the quotation of Gen. xv. 16 and εἰς σημεῖον. True, Justin did not grasp Paul's thought. He makes Abraham justified διὰ τὴν πίστιν, and circumcision a σημεῖον, not a σφραγῖδα; but he clearly had Paul's teaching in mind. So in Dial. 11 (Ἰσραηλιτικὸν γὰρ τὸ ἀληθινόν, πνευματικόν καὶ Ἰούδα γένος καὶ Ἰακὼβ καὶ Ἰσαὰκ καὶ Ἀβραάμ, τοῦ ἐν ἀκροβυστίᾳ κ.τ.λ.) we have a reminiscence of Rom. iv. 10, 17, and in Dial. 92 (περιτομὴν ἔχοντες... τῆς καρδίας, with the context), of Rom. iv. and ii. 29. In Dial. 32, 55, 64, the description of "the remnant" (Isa. i. 9; x. 22), as left κατὰ χάριν, implies remembrance of Rom. ix. 29 with xi. 5; while Dial. 44 (καὶ ἐξαπατᾶτε ἑαυτούς κ.τ.λ.) seems to be a reminiscence of Rom. ix. 7, not only in its general thought, but in the intro-

JUSTIN ON THE NEW TESTAMENT. 239

the First Epistle to the Corinthians,[1] the Second Epistle to the Thessalonians,[2] and the Epistles to the Gala-

duction of τὰ κατηγγελμένα ... ἀγαθά from the αἱ ἐπαγγελίαι of Rom. ix. 4, and τὰ τέκνα τῆς ἐπαγγελίας of verse 9. In Ap. i. 40 and Dial. 42, Justin interprets Ps. xix. as prophetic of the preaching of the Apostles. Rom. x. 18 uses the language of the Psalm to describe the same, though without calling it a prediction. Dial. 39, like Rom. xi. 2–4, quotes Elijah's complaint as applicable to the later Israel (observe ἐντυγχάνων); and in Ap. i. 5 we read, πᾶσα γλῶσσα ἐξομολογήσεται αὐτῷ, like Rom. iv. 11 (Isa. xlv. 23 (LXX.) has ὀμεῖται). Note that the parts of Romans with which Justin shows acquaintance are those which treat of the relation of the Jews to the Church; namely, the discussion of circumcision and Abraham's faith, and of the rejection of Israel with the exception of a "remnant." So we would expect from the subject of the Dialogue in which the above references are mainly found. Yet he does not reproduce Paul's argument, but only his practical position towards Judaism.

[1] See Ap. i. 19, the growth of a seed used as illustrative of resurrection. Note, especially, παρατάξει θεοῦ and ἀφθαρσίαν ἐνδύσασθαι. Comp. 1 Cor. xv. 38 and 53. So Ap. i. 52: ἐνδύσει ἀφθαρσίαν. Dial. 14 — " For this is the symbolism of the unleavened bread, that ye do not the old deeds of the wicked leaven (ἵνα μὴ τὰ παλαιὰ τῆς κακῆς ζύμης ἔργα πράττητε) " — is at least a striking coincidence with 1 Cor. v. 8; while in Dial. 111 the statement ἦν γὰρ τὸ πάσχα ὁ χριστός, ὁ τυθεὶς ὕστερον doubtless came from the first clause of the same verse of 1 Corinthians. In Dial. 35 (see also Dial. 51), the words attributed to Christ, ἔσονται σχίσματα καὶ αἱρέσεις, probably arose from a confusion of 1 Cor. xi. 18, 19, with Christ's predictions in Matt. xxv. In Ap. i. 66; Dial. 41, 70, the words παρέδωκαν (or παρέδωκε) and εἰς ἀνάμνησιν (Luke's account was probably early modified by Paul's) evidence the knowledge of 1 Cor. xi. 23, 24; while in Dial. 39 the description of the spiritual gifts bestowed by Christ on believers, while perhaps influenced by Isa. xi. 2, appears to have been founded on 1 Cor. xii. 7–10; and in Dial. 42 the use of the physical body to illustrate the unity of the Church recalls 1 Cor. xii. 12. Compare also Ap. i. 60 (ὡς συνεῖναι οὐ σοφίᾳ ἀνθρωπείᾳ ταῦτα γεγονέναι ἀλλὰ δυνάμει θεοῦ λέγεσθαι) with 1 Cor. ii. 4, and Dial. 38 (οἶδα ὅτι, ὡς ὁ τοῦ θεοῦ λόγος ἔφη (i. e., Isa. xxix. 14), κέκρυπται ἀφ' ὑμῶν ἡ σοφία κ.τ.λ.) with 1 Cor. i. 19, 24; ii. 7, 8.

[2] See Dial. 32, where, after saying that Antichrist would be

tians,[1] Philippians,[2] Colossians,[3] and Hebrews,[4] as well destroyed at Christ's coming, but would continue "a time, times, and half a time," he concludes that at least τὸν τῆς ἀνομίας ἄνθρωπον τριακόσια πεντήκοντα ἔτη βασιλεῦσαι δεῖ. So in Dial. 110, ὁ τῆς ἀποστασίας ἄνθρωπος ... ἄνομα τολμήσῃ εἰς ἡμᾶς, and in Dial. 116, ὁ διάβολος ἐφέστηκεν ἀεὶ ἀντικείμενος. Compare 2 Thess. ii. 3, 4, 8.

[1] Dial. 44 (καὶ ἐξαπατᾶτε ἑαυτοὺς κ.τ.λ.) seems clearly an echo of Gal. iii., as well as of Rom. ix. 7, though Paul's argument is not Justin's. So Dial. 119 : "We shall inherit the Holy Land with Abraham, receiving forever the inheritance, τέκνα τοῦ Ἀβραὰμ διὰ τὴν ὁμοίαν πίστιν ὄντες." In Dial. 95, 96, Justin quotes, "Cursed is every one who continueth not in all things written in the book of the law to do them," to show man's universal guilt, and therefore the reason why Christ died for all men. Christ ought, therefore, to be reverenced; but the Jews curse Him and His, thus fulfilling the other prophecy, "Cursed is every one who hangeth on a tree." The latter, Justin says, did not mean that Christ would be cursed by God, but by the Jews. The collocation of the two quotations from Deuteronomy shows clearly acquaintance with Gal. iii. 10–13, though Justin misunderstood verse 13. He was governed in his understanding of it, as is shown by Trypho's remarks in Dial. 32, 89, by the desire to retort on the Jews their declaration that the passage proved Jesus to have been disapproved by God. Here, as with Romans, we notice Justin's inability to grasp Paul's thought, though supposing that he was following the Apostle. Compare also Dial. 116 ("We who through the name of Jesus believed as one man in God") with Gal. iii. 28.

[2] See Dial. 33 (ὅτι ταπεινὸς ἔσται πρῶτον ἄνθρωπος εἶτα ὑψωθήσεται) and Dial. 134 (ἐδούλευσε καὶ τὴν μέχρι σταυροῦ δουλείαν ὁ χριστός), where Justin had clearly in mind Phil. ii. 7–9.

[3] See Ap. i. 23, 46, 63 (πρωτότοκος τοῦ θεοῦ), 33, 53 (πρωτότ. τῷ θεῷ); Dial. 84 (πρωτότ. τῶν πάντων ποιημάτων), 85 (πρωτότ. πάσης κτίσεως), 100 (πρωτότ. τοῦ θεοῦ καὶ πρὸ πάντων τῶν κτισμάτων), 125 (τέκνον πρωτότοκον τῶν ὅλων κτισμάτων), 138 (πρωτότ. πάσης κτίσεως ὤν). In Ap. i. 58, Justin has τοῦ πρωτογόνου αὐτοῦ, which is Philonian (cf. Dr. E. A. Abbott, Modern Review, July, 1882); but his usual phrase is apostolic, and evidently taken from Col. i. 15. Compare also Dial. 43 ("We receive circumcision through baptism") with Col. ii. 11, 12, and Dial. 28 ("If there be any Scythian or Persian," etc.) with Col. iii. 9–11.

[4] See Ap. i. 12, 63, where Christ is called ἀπόστολος. So Heb.

as with the First Epistle of John.¹ Reminiscences of Second Corinthians,² Ephesians,³ First Timothy,⁴ Titus,⁵

iii. 1, only in the New Testament. Cf. also Dial. 11 and following chapters, where Christianity is called διαθήκην καινὴν, and Jer. xxxi. 31 is quoted. So Heb. viii. 7–9. Cf. especially Dial. 13 (τοῖς ... μηκέτι αἵμασι τράγων καὶ προβάτων ἢ σποδῷ δαμάλεως ἢ σεμιδάλεως προσφοραῖς καθαριζομένοις ἀλλὰ πίστει διὰ τοῦ αἵματος τοῦ χριστοῦ) with Heb. ix. 13, 14 ; Dial. 67 (the new covenant, unlike the old, was not established μετὰ φόβου καὶ τρόμου) with Heb. xii. 18, 19 ; Ap. i. 45 (David predicted that the Father would exalt Christ to heaven καὶ κατέχειν ἕως ἂν πατάξῃ τοὺς ἐχθραίνοντας αὐτῷ δαίμονας) with Heb. x. 13.

¹ See especially Dial. 123, καὶ θεοῦ τέκνα ἀληθινὰ καλούμεθα καί ἐσμεν οἱ τὰς ἐντολὰς τοῦ χριστοῦ φυλάσσοντες. Compare 1 John iii. 1–3. Compare also Dial. 32 (Believers are a robe ἐν οἷς οἰκεῖ τὸ παρὰ τοῦ θεοῦ σπέρμα, ὁ λόγος) with 1 John iii. 9, and Dial. 45 (Christ was made flesh ἵνα διὰ τῆς οἰκονομίας ταύτης ὁ πονηρευσάμενος τὴν ἀρχὴν ὄφις καὶ οἱ ἐξομοιωθέντες αὐτῷ ἄγγελοι καταλυθῶσι) with 1 John iii. 8.

² See Dial. 35, where "many false Christs and ψευδαπόστολοι shall arise" are quoted as Christ's words. The previous quotation, "There shall be schisms and heresies," was, as already observed, probably due to a confusion of 1 Cor. xi. 18, 19, with Matt. xxv. ; and as ψευδαπόστολοι only occurs in the New Testament in 2 Cor. xi. 13, the latter place may have originated the expression used by Justin. See, however, Rev. ii. 2 ; and the word would be easily suggested to follow "false Christs."

³ Compare Dial. 47 (ἡ γὰρ χρηστότης καὶ ἡ φιλανθρωπία τοῦ θεοῦ καὶ τὸ ἄμετρον τοῦ πλούτου αὐτοῦ) with Eph. ii. 2, iii. 8 ; Dial. 120 (The Simonians said that Simon was God ὑπεράνω πάσης ἀρχῆς καὶ ἐξουσίας καὶ δυνάμεως) with Eph. i. 21 ; Dial. 114 ("Circumcised by the words of the apostles of the Chief Corner-stone") with Eph. ii. 20 ; Dial. 137 (Christ called τοῦ ἠγαπημένου) with Eph. i. 6 (here only in the New Testament).

⁴ Compare Ap. i. 6 ("the host of the other good angels") with 1 Tim. v. 21, and Dial. 7 (τὰ τῆς πλάνης πνεύματα καὶ δαιμόνια), 35 ("the doctrines ἀπὸ τῶν τῆς πλάνης πνευμάτων") with the πνεύμασι πλάνοις of 1 Tim. iv. 1.

⁵ See Dial. 47. ἡ γὰρ χρηστότης καὶ φιλανθρωπία τοῦ θεοῦ. Compare Tit. iii. 4.

James,[1] and First Peter[2] may also with more or less probability be pointed out. This is far more testimony to the Epistles than we should have reason to expect in books addressed to pagans and to Jews.

How did he regard apostolic literature? But the question is, How did Justin regard apostolic literature? We observe in answer:—

(1) That he strongly declares the authority of the Apostles as teachers of Christianity. "By the power of God they proclaimed to every race of men that they were sent by Christ to teach to all the word of God."[3] "They preached Christ's teaching."[4] Going out from Jerusalem, "they preached the mighty word."[5] After Christ's ascension they "received power, sent to them from Him from heaven, and coming to every race of men they taught these things and were called Apostles."[6] Speaking of baptism, Justin says, "and this reason for this we learned from the Apostles;"[7] so that the latter were not only held to have repeated Christ's teaching, but to

(1) He recognized the authority of the Apostles as teachers,

---

[1] In Ap. i. 16, Matt. v. 34, 37, appears to have been modified by Jas. v. 12. See above, on Justin's quotations from the Synoptics.

[2] Compare Dial. 139 (εἰς φιλίαν καὶ εὐλογίαν ... καλῶν) with 1 Pet. iii. 9. Possibly the pseudo-quotation from Jeremiah, "The Holy Lord God of Israel remembered His dead, who slept in the grave, and descended to them to preach His salvation," which Justin (Dial. 72) says the Jews had cut out, may indicate an early interpretation of 1 Pet. iii. 19; iv. 6. But Justin says nothing elsewhere of preaching to the dead.

[3] Ap. i. 39.

[4] Ap. i. 40. περὶ τῶν κηρυξάντων τὴν διδαχὴν αὐτοῦ.

[5] Ap. i. 45. [6] Ap. i. 50.

[7] Ap. i. 61. The fact that the reason given by Justin for baptism is not apostolic, at least in the form in which he states it, does not lessen the significance of his reference to apostolic instruction as that to which the faith of the Church appealed.

have explained it with authority. He declares, further, that "as twelve bells were attached to the robe of the high-priest, so the twelve Apostles depended on the power of the eternal priest, Christ, and through their voice the whole earth was filled with the glory and grace of God and His Christ."[1] The Gentiles believed "when they heard the word preached by His Apostles and when they learned it through them."[2] Christians have learned the true worship of God "from the law and the word which came forth from Jerusalem through the Apostles of Jesus."[3] "The words [which came] through the Apostles of the Chief Corner-stone" have spiritually circumcised us; that is, have brought us into newness of life.[4] "We have not been misled by those who taught us such doctrines."[5] "We have believed *the voice of God which was again spoken through the Apostles of Christ*, and which was preached to us through the prophets."[6] Manifestly, Justin regarded the Apostles as infallible witnesses to Christ's life and teaching, and as authoritative expounders of Christianity. He does not apply to them the term "inspired;" but he declares them to have been endowed with power from on high, so that their teaching was the teaching of Christ and their word the voice of God. From them the Church had learned Christianity. Only through their preaching could the revelation through Christ be known.

(2) Hence the written "memoirs of the Apostles," or Gospels, are spoken of by Justin as authoritative sources

[1] Dial. 42. [2] Dial. 109.
[3] Dial. 110. ἀπὸ τοῦ νόμου καὶ τοῦ λόγου τοῦ ἐξελθόντος ἀπὸ Ἱερουσαλὴμ διὰ τῶν τοῦ Ἰησοῦ ἀποστόλων τὴν θεοσέβειαν ἐπιγνόντες.
[4] Dial. 114. [5] Dial. 118.
[6] Dial. 119. Credner naturally concluded that these words are spurious. See Otto's note.

for Christian faith. They were authoritative to him because they were apostolic. "Those who recorded all the things concerning our Saviour Jesus Christ taught" His miraculous birth.[1] To the "memoirs" he appeals for proof that Christ is Son of God.[2] In the "memoirs" the Apostles handed down the account of the institution of the Eucharist.[3] He tells us that in public service on the Lord's Day "the memoirs of the Apostles or the writings of the prophets are read as long as time permit,"[4] and that an exhortation by the president followed, based on the passages which had just been read. The Apostles, therefore, to the Church of Justin's time were not only infallible witnesses and teachers of Christianity, but their *written* testimony, so far at least as the Gospels were concerned, was the source and guide of Christian faith and practice. To them Christians appealed both for facts and for doctrines. If any other facts concerning Christ were accepted on tradition, the statements of the Gospels were nevertheless the authority to which appeal was made, and the witness of tradition was incomparably less in amount and in importance than theirs. They were read in the assembly interchangeably with, and, it would seem from the order of Justin's language, oftener than, the writings of the prophets.

(2) and their memoirs as authoritative sources for faith.

(3) Furthermore, Justin at least six times introduces a quotation from or a reference to the Gospels with the sacred formula "It is written;"[5] and in one place remarks that "with us the prince of the demons is called Serpent and

(3) Quotes the Gospels as "Scripture."

---

[1] Ap. i. 33.   [2] Dial. 100.
[3] Ap. i. 66.   [4] Ap. i. 67.
[5] γέγραπται. Dial. 49, 100, 101, 106, 107, 111. In 103, also, Otto conjectures it with reference to Luke xxii. 44.

Satan and Devil, as also ye can learn by inquiring of our writings,"[1] — a sentence in which we may not only see another reference to the Apocalypse,[2] but also a reference to a distinct Christian literature which, while nothing definite is said of its authority in the Church, was evidently regulative of the Church's faith.

If to these facts we add the many instances in which Justin followed, or at least thought he was following, the teaching of the New Testament epistles, we have a considerable amount of evidence tending to show that apostolic writings were regarded as the authoritative exponents of Christianity.

On the other hand, certain facts seem to point to a different conclusion: —

(1) Justin uses the Old Testament as inspired Scripture, calling it constantly "the Scripture" or "the Word," in marked contrast to the indefinite way in which he speaks of Christian literature other than the Gospels. It would seem, at first sight, as if he ranked only the Gospels on a level with "the prophets."

(2) He makes, as we have observed, no direct appeal to any apostolic writing besides the Gospels, except to the Apocalypse; and this latter he introduces almost incidentally, after he had already sought to prove his point from the Old Testament.

(3) He makes no mention of public ecclesiastical use of any apostolic writings except the "memoirs."

(4) He speaks of believing the testimony of the Apostles because it agreed with the Old Testament,[3]

---

[1] Ap. i. 28. ὡς καὶ ἐκ τῶν ἡμετέρων συγγραμμάτων ἐρευνήσαντες μαθεῖν δύνασθε.
[2] Rev. xx.   [3] Ap. i. 33.

thus seeming to place them in a subordinate position; while the various points in which he deviated from the teaching of the New Testament, and the freedom with which he explained the Gospel by philosophy often seem inconsistent with a recognition of the divine authority of the apostolic writings.

But in estimating the weight of these items of negative evidence several considerations should be borne in mind: —

(1) For one thing, Justin's apologetic purpose necessarily prevented him from appealing to purely Christian teachers as authorities. He appealed to the prophets because they were recognized by Trypho, and would, he thought, be convincing even to pagan readers because of their antiquity and the remarkable fulfilment of their predictions. But neither Jew nor pagan would have been moved by the citation of apostolic teaching. The teaching of Christ is presented mainly to exhibit its moral and reasonable character or its fulfilment of prophecy. To the Jew the prophets, and to the pagans philosophy, were the only authorities that Justin could quote. Had his work against heresies been preserved, his attitude toward the epistles of the Apostles might appear very different from what it now does. Tertullian, whose acceptance of the Canon is certain, does not once appeal to any New Testament passage in his Apology.

But (1) his apologetic purpose prevented appeal to apostles as authoritative teachers.

The same apologetic motive may explain, also, why Justin bases his belief in the Apostles on their agreement with the prophets. To give a reason for faith is one thing. Thereafter to accept truth upon authority is another. Justin was convinced of the credibility of the Apostles, as he was of the credibility of Christ, chiefly because they and Christianity in general fulfilled the prophetic predictions; but this was not inconsistent with taking his Christianity from the apostolic teaching and testimony, which, as we have seen, he did.

(2) But, furthermore, Justin's prevailing thought of the personal Logos led him to represent Christianity as the teaching of Christ, rather than to distinguish between His statements and those of His messengers. Even the Old Testament is represented as given by the Logos,[1] though the prophets are cited by name. But the incarnation of the Logos was to Justin the central fact both of Christianity and of human history. The person of Christ was, in his view, the substance and foundation of the Church's faith. So far, therefore, as the original Christian teaching was presented at all by him, it was naturally cited in the very words of the Logos, rather than in those of even His chosen emissaries. *(2) His doctrine of the Logos led him to appeal to Christ's words.*

(3) The single statement that in public worship "the memoirs of the Apostles or the writings of the prophets" were read, may not be pressed so as to exclude from public reading all other apostolic works than the "memoirs," since we have frequent testimony from other ancient writers that even non-apostolic epistles were often thus used. *(3) His language should not be pressed too far.*

(4) Finally, Justin's deviations from New Testament teaching were evidently unconsciously made. He believed himself to be repeating the doctrines of the Apostles and to be defending the original faith of the Church; and if he did not see that he was in reality departing *(4) His deviations from apostolic teaching unconsciously made.*

[1] Ap. i. 36.

from that faith and those doctrines, he did only what many have since done, whose acceptance of the New Testament as inspired is unquestioned.

After balancing these considerations, certain points appear sufficiently distinct. It is impossible, we think, to affirm fairly, as rationalistic critics have often done, that Justin did not have the idea of an authoritative New Testament Scripture. It is likewise impossible to affirm categorically that he did have it in the complete form in which it was expressed by the next generation. But the probabilities of the case accumulate decidedly in favor of the latter rather than of the former view. It is clear that he appealed to apostolic writings rather than to oral tradition as authority for his representation of Christianity. It is clear that at least the Gospels had been formed into a sacred collection, called "the Gospel,"[1] which ranked on an equality with the Old Testament, and that other apostolic books were used to regulate the faith of the Church. It is perfectly fair to infer that these other books were held in precisely the same estimate as the Gospels; for the authority of the Apostles as teachers was fully confessed and their doctrines echoed by Justin even when he misunderstood them. True, oral tradition was still followed when believed to be pure and well-attested. Distance and heresy had not yet sufficiently increased to compel exclusive reliance on written records, though they were fast leading to that result. No doubt, also, not all of the New Testament books were as yet known and accepted in all parts of the Church. But when we remember the apologetic object and the philosophizing spirit of Justin's writings, we ought to acknowledge that

Conclusion.

[1] Dial. 10, 100.

he gives as much testimony to the Canon as we should expect to obtain from him. His positive testimony, so far as it goes, distinctly proves at least a Gospel canon, and renders a larger canon not improbable. His negative testimony is largely counterbalanced by his object and his spirit. He, moreover, is but a single witness, and the acceptance by the Church of the New Testament as "Scripture" may be proved by others. The testimony of Irenæus is in reality that of the Asian churches of the first half of the second century. The "Muratori Fragment" speaks for the Roman Church at but a little later date than Justin. Even in the apostolic age itself Paul called the Gospel of Luke "Scripture;"[1] and in Second Peter, which we hold to be genuine, the epistles of Paul are similarly termed;[2] while Ignatius, in the first decade of the second century, not only repeatedly declares the authority of the Apostles as teachers,[3] but evidently had a collection of apostolic writings besides the Gospels which formed with the Gospels his Christian Scriptures.[4] This combined testimony Justin does not oppose, though his own is more limited in extent. So far as his testimony does go, when read in the light of the purpose of his writings and the characteristics of his mind, it confirms the conviction that the Church of the post-apostolic age possessed in more or less completeness, in different localities, our New Testament and regarded it in

[1] 1 Tim. v. 18.   [2] 2 Pet. iii. 16.
[3] See, e. g., ad Rom. 4. "I do not, as Peter and Paul, issue commandments unto you. They were Apostles; I am but a condemned man."
[4] Ad Phil. 5. "While I flee to the Gospel as to the flesh of Jesus, and to the Apostles as to the Presbytery of the Church." How could he flee to the Apostles except by turning to their writings?

substantially the same way that Irenæus did, as forming with the Old Testament the Christian Scriptures, an authoritative rule of faith and practice. These books, also, in Justin's time had practically supplanted oral tradition as trustworthy witnesses to the inspired apostolic message.

LECTURE VI.

THE TESTIMONY OF JUSTIN TO THE ORGANIZATION AND BELIEF OF THE POST-APOSTOLIC CHURCH.

WE are now, finally, to examine Justin's testimony to the Church itself, — to look through him at those early Christian communities of which we have already learned much from his writings, but whose internal conditions and ruling beliefs we may more directly observe.

In a previous lecture we examined the external relations of the Church of the second century, and the popular and legal objections then *Review.* made to Christianity; and in doing so we found the Church to consist of locally organized societies, scattered widely throughout the Empire, everywhere the object of popular distrust, and liable under the law at any moment to suffer persecution. We have learned, further, that the Church of Justin's age was distinctly and consciously a Gentile society, which looked back indeed to a Hebrew parentage and contained a minority who united Jewish rites with Christian faith, but which felt itself to be as a body emancipated from Jewish limitations. Gentiles were regarded as its natural adherents. The Church rejoiced to believe in a Redeemer of whose kingdom every race was to be equally a partaker, and was even disposed to look beyond its Hebrew parentage, and to declare itself the child of the universal conscience and reason of mankind. Hence we found Christianity at this period influenced by the ideas which heathen culture had previously originated, affected by the more spiritual philosophy of paganism, grappling with the problems which its exclusive claims suggested to the heathen world, as it had already grappled with those suggested to the Jewish race, and endeavoring either to reconcile reason and revelation or to prove the rights of revelation against the established dominion of reason. Then in the last lecture we found from Justin that the Church of his age was in possession of a sacred literature besides that which it had inherited from the Hebrews, which it regarded of apostolic origin and to the statements of which it appealed as giving the rule of faith and conduct. It claimed to rest its beliefs on apostolic authority, and with the progress of time was depending less and less on tradition and was becoming more and more a religion of a book. It remains, then, to ask what glimpses we may obtain from our Apologist of the internal constitution and doctrinal tenets of the Church itself. We know, from the testimony of the following age, that changes of form and elaboration of belief had taken place since the days of the Apostles. What information does Justin give concerning these changes, and what light does he consequently throw on the character of the Church, both in his own and in the preceding age?

Justin's testimony to the constitution and faith of the Church.

To appreciate, however, the value of this part of Justin's testimony, it is necessary first to observe that he openly claimed and manifestly thought himself to be the fair representative of the great body of Christians, and that with them his Christianity had been received from the generation before him. We have several times remarked this, but now it should be particularly proved. Justin did not

He claimed to represent the Church.

defend a sect of Christians, but the beliefs and usages followed by the great majority of the Christian community. He insists on his orthodoxy, as we may fairly term it, — on his fidelity to the faith handed down from the Apostles; and though, as we have seen, his philosophy did in reality seriously modify that faith, he was himself evidently unconscious of any departure from it. Thus Justin not only presented his Apology in the name of all true Christians, but he specially makes the point that these should not be confounded with Christians falsely so called.[1] Of the real moral character of these false Christians he professes to know nothing, and had, it would seem, no dealings with them.[2] The doctrine which he represented was, on the other hand, the traditional belief of the churches. "We have *received by tradition*,"[3] he says, "how God is to be worshipped." " We *have been taught*,[4] and have been persuaded and believe, that He only accepts those who imitate His excellences." By these expressions he meant that they had been persuaded by Christ's teaching delivered to them through the Apostles.[5] So likewise had the rite of baptism and the reason for its observance been, according to our author, received from the Apostles;[6] and the purpose of Justin and the Church to adhere to the apostolic commands appears when he says of the Eucharist that the Apostles in the " memoirs " thus *delivered* what was enjoined on them.[7] In opposition, therefore, to false Christians, he classes himself with those " who are *disciples of the true and pure doctrine* of Jesus Christ."[8]

[1] Ap. i. 4.
[2] Ap. i. 26.
[3] Ap. i. 10. παρειλήφαμεν.
[4] Ibid. δεδιδάγμεθα.
[5] Ap. i. 53.
[6] Ap. i. 61.
[7] Ap. i. 66. παρέδωκαν.
[8] Dial. 35. ἡμεῖς οἱ τῆς ἀληθινῆς Ἰησοῦ Χριστοῦ καὶ καθαρᾶς διδασκαλίας μαθηταί.

Speaking of Chiliasm, he admits that "many who are *of the pure and pious faith*"[1] reject it. He chooses not, like the false Christians, to follow men or men's doctrines, but God and the doctrines which are from Him,[2] and speaks of himself and those who agree with him as thus being "in all respects right-minded Christians,"[3] or, in other words, "orthodox." It is evident from these expressions that to Justin Christianity was a body of definite beliefs which he had received, and which the vast majority of Christians accepted as having been handed down from the Apostles. Justin's philosophy had not made his Christianity, though he found the two harmonious, and though he understood the latter by the aid of the former. He was positive that the Christianity which he professed was that which had been delivered to the Church at the beginning.

Furthermore, Justin's declared attitude toward heresy testifies in the same direction. Most keenly was he aware of the existence of heresies. Most positively did he declare them to be novelties, introduced by the demons to destroy the work of Christ. Most anxious was he not to be identified with heretics, and most vigorously did he repudiate their teaching. Thus in the Apology he declares that Simon Magus and Menander and Marcion had been put forward by the devils to deceive men.[4] The two former he speaks of as magicians; but Marcion he specifies as a heretic proper, who was at that time alive and causing many of every nation to utter blasphemies

His opposition to heresy.

---

[1] Dial. 80. πολλοὺς δ' αὖ καὶ τῶν τῆς καθαρᾶς καὶ εὐσεβοῦς ὄντων Χριστιανῶν γνώμης.
[2] Ibid. τοῖς παρ' ἐκείνου διδάγμασιν.
[3] Ibid. ὀρθογνώμονες κατὰ πάντα Χριστιανοί.
[4] Ap. i. 26, 56, 58.

against the Creator of the universe. He insinuates, unfairly no doubt so far as the Marcionites were concerned, that the slanderous tales circulated about the Christians might be true of these heretics,[1] and speaks of them all and of Marcion in particular with no little bitterness, declaring of the latter that "many have believed him as if he alone knew the truth, and laugh at us, though they have no proof of what they say, but are carried away irrationally as lambs by a wolf, and become the prey of atheistical doctrines and of devils."[2] So also he declares that the appearance of heretics in the Church only makes the true disciples more firm in the faith, since Christ had predicted the coming of such false teachers.[3] He shrewdly points out, also,[4] that the heretical doctrines bear the names of their founders; the sects being called Marcionites,[5] or Valentinians, or Basilidæans, or Saturnilians, after the individuals who originated them. They were thus stamped as novelties, unlike the original apostolic doctrine. Against all these Gnostic heretics Justin speaks with the utmost indignation. "They blaspheme," he says, "the Creator and Christ."[6] "We have nothing in common with them, since we know them to be atheists, impious, unrighteous, and sinful, and confessors of Jesus in name only, instead of worshippers of Him."[7] "Many have taught godless, blasphemous, and unholy doctrines, forging them in Christ's name;"[8] that is, imputing them falsely to Christ. All these

[1] Ap. i. 26.   [2] Ap. i. 58.
[3] Dial. 35, 51, 82.   [4] Dial. 35.
[5] Μαρκιανοί, either a corruption from Μαρκιανισταί or else formed from the Latin *Marcius*. See Otto's note.
[6] Dial. 35.   [7] Ibid. See also 80.
[8] Dial. 82. ἐν ὀνόματι αὐτοῦ παραχαράσσοντες. May not this refer to the falsification of apostolic writings, such as Marcion's

heretical sects were popularly called Christians, but Justin repudiates them as recent perverters of Christianity. Some of them ate meat which had been offered to idols;[1] some denied the resurrection of the dead;[2] all blasphemed the Creator, and misrepresented Christ, and stood, in fact, outside of the pale of the true, apostolic Church.

The significance of these statements of our Apologist is very great. It is true that these heretics against whom he inveighed so bitterly were Gnostics, and that he spoke in a much gentler way even of the extreme sect of Jewish Christians.[3] But it is not to be inferred from this that he represents a fusion of Jewish Christianity with a portion of the Gentile Christians who reacted against Gnosticism. How firmly he stood on Gentile ground, and how plainly he speaks of even moderate Jewish Christianity as a weakness, we have already learned; and his apparent gentleness in speaking of some who denied the divinity of Christ did not prevent him from branding their belief as a mere " human doctrine."[4] But his description of the heretics clearly shows that the Church of his day esteemed their doctrines as *novelties*. As Justin says, these sects bore the names of their founders. The Church, however, *bore no man's name.* Such is clearly Justin's implication. As the absence from his writings of any direct appeal to the apostolic epistles is of itself a proof that in the Church stress was not laid on the teaching of indi-

Marginal note: Significance of his testimony for the unity and apostolicity of the orthodox churches.

mutilation of Luke, and perhaps the Valentinian " Gospel of Truth " (Iren. iii. 11. 9)?

[1] Dial. 35. He does not say that all the sects mentioned were guilty of this. Both the Marcionites and the Saturnilians were vegetarians.

[2] Dial. 80.   [3] See Lect. III.   [4] Dial. 48.

JUSTIN ON THE POST-APOSTOLIC CHURCH. 257

vidual apostles, but on their united proclamation of Christ, so the man-named sects stood in contrast to the great body of believers, their teaching being stamped as an innovation on the apostolic faith. Justin testifies, therefore, to the complete separation of the orthodox Christians from the pseudo-Christian sects or schools of thought which had already arisen. He and the Church held to the apostolic teaching. Such, at least, was the position which they tried to occupy. His Christianity betrays no consciousness of having arisen from the fusion of, or compromise between, previously antagonistic parties; and the differences which existed between it and apostolic Christianity may, as we have seen,[1] be explained in another way. It was a Christianity which knew Gnosticism to be a novelty, and considered Jewish Christianity, if not carried too far, a pardonable weakness, but which itself stood on the foundation which it was assured, both by tradition and by written records, had been laid by the Apostles of Christ.

Nor is there any reason to believe that Justin misrepresented the essential features of Christianity for the purpose of commending it to the unbelievers for whom he wrote. That he would be influenced by this purpose in the selection of arguments and in modes of expression, would be almost inevitable; and the fact may be perceived especially in the Apology. The resemblances which he adduces between the facts of Christ's life and the tales of mythology are to be referred to this motive. His desire to secure belief in Christ as sent from God, even if His divinity be denied,[2] betrays no doubt the same apologetic spirit. It is not improbable, also, that he felt that his doctrine of the Logos would commend itself to the better

His testimony trustworthy.

[1] Lect. IV.   [2] Ap. i. 22; Dial. 48.

17

class of pagans, and would make Christianity appear to them, as it did to him, the perfection of philosophy. In his descriptions, likewise, of the Christian ceremonies, he evidently sought to represent them as being as simple as possible; and the stress which he laid on the Christian requirement of obedience to and imitation of God may have seemed to him likely to find favor with at least the two purest and greatest of the Antonines. But while Justin was an Apologist, there is nothing to show that he consciously misrepresented facts. His character was too rugged and bold for such dishonesty. His sneers at the worship of the emperors and at the deification of Antinous are certainly not the language of a sycophant. His bold arraignment of the treatment of the Christians as unjust and irrational shows him a man who would speak the truth; while the willingness to suffer and die rather than deny their Lord is of itself a sufficient proof that Justin and his fellow-Christians were not the men knowingly to misstate facts. Moreover, his teaching in the Apology and in the Dialogue is essentially the same, though the persons addressed were very different. We may positively conclude that when Justin speaks from his own knowledge, we may trust him absolutely. His testimony, therefore, to the condition of the Church is that of one who honestly represented, so far as his purpose called for it, and so far as his peculiarities of thought allowed, the real Christian Church of the post-apostolic age. He defended no party but the Church itself, and he did so as honestly and as earnestly as he could.

I. So far as church organization is concerned, Justin gives us but little information. It did not lie within his purpose to describe the internal organization of the Christian societies at all. He throws light on the subject only when describing the public worship of the Christians, the celebration of their two great rites, and the distribution of their alms. Moreover, his effort manifestly was to exhibit the simplicity and harmlessness of these few ceremonies; so that we could not expect from him a careful description of the relations sustained by the officers of the Church to one another and to the whole body.

I. Organization of the churches.

What little he does say, however, is worth examination. He describes, first, the rite of baptism.[1] The candidates, he says, are instructed to pray God with fasting for the remission of past sins, the Church praying and fasting with them. They are then taken where there is water, and are "regenerated,"[2] as the others had been; "for in the name of God the Father and Lord of the universe, and of our Saviour Jesus Christ, and of the Holy Spirit, they then receive the washing with water.[3] . . . This washing is also called illumination,[4] since they who learn these things are illuminated in their understandings." The new member is then brought, writes Justin,[5] to where "the brethren" are assembled, where "we offer prayers in common for ourselves, and for the one who has been illuminated, and for all others in every place, that we may be counted worthy, now that we have learned the truth, by our works to be found good citizens and keepers of the commandments. . . . After the prayers, we salute one another with a kiss.

Baptism.

Prayers.

The kiss.

---

[1] Ap. i. 61.
[2] ἀναγεννῶνται. On the doctrine of baptism, see below.
[3] τὸ ἐν τῷ ὕδατι τότε λουτρὸν ποιοῦνται.
[4] φωτισμός.   [5] Ap. i. 65.

Then there is brought to the president of the brethren [1] bread and a cup of water and wine, and he having received them renders praise and glory to the Father of all, through the name of the Son and of the Holy Spirit, and offers at length thanksgiving [2] for being counted worthy of these things from Him." When he has concluded the prayers and thanksgiving, all the people present give assent by saying Amen. Then they whom we call deacons give to those present to partake of the bread and wine and water, and carry it away to the absent. Afterwards, Justin adds,[3] " we continually remind one another of these things. The wealthy among us help the needy, and we are always together. . . . And on the day which is called the day of the Sun, there is an assembly of all who live in cities or country to one place, and the memoirs of the Apostles and the writings of the prophets are read as long as time permits. Then, when the reader has ceased, the president gives verbal [4] instruction and invitation [5] to the imitation of these good things. Then we all rise together and pray." The Eucharist is celebrated, and afterward " they who are well to do and are willing give, each according to his own free choice, what he wills; and what is collected is deposited with the president for the relief of the needy."

The Eucharist.

Charity.

Public worship on the first day of the week.

Now, so far as the organization of the Christian societies is concerned, these passages contain only the following items of importance:—

---

[1] Or, to the presiding brother. προσφέρεται τῷ προεστῶτι τῶν ἀδελφῶν.

[2] εὐχαριστίαν . . . ἐπὶ πολὺ ποιεῖται.

[3] Ap. i. 67.   [4] διὰ λόγου.

[5] πρόκλησιν. Some editions read, παράκλησιν, exhortation.

We infer from them that there was but one society or "church" in each community. Such seems to be the fair inference from the expression "there is an assembly of all those in cities and country to one place." There was but one congregation in each locality. *One church in each locality.* If this be thought incredible in for example so large a place as Rome, where the Christians must have been too numerous to meet all together, the reply may be made that Justin none the less regarded the local church as a unit, and that if several meeting-places be assumed, they must have been considered as but parts of one assembly.

We infer, further, from his language that the local society had a permanent president. This follows not so much from the expression, "the president of the brethren," for that might be translated *A permanent president.* "the brother who is presiding," but from the statement that the alms of the society were deposited with the president, who was therefore the permanent agent of the society for the distribution of its charity. He also presided at the public assembly, preached and administered the Eucharist. The deacons were his assistants, and he appears to have come to control the duties which the deacons were originally ordained to discharge.[1] *Deacons.*

But why did Justin designate the chief officer as "the president"? Was it simply from the wish to avoid technical terms? Yet he mentions the "deacons," and in his account of baptism[2] he uses the technical term "regeneration" with marked emphasis. Moreover, "bishop" and "presbyter" would not have been unfamiliar terms *Why the title of "the president" not given.*

---

[1] Acts vi.   [2] Ap. i. 61.

to the pagans.[1] The same term used by Justin, or one similar to it, is also found in Hermas,[2] though there applied, expressly in one instance, and probably in others, to "the presbyters." It was the natural phrase for our Apologist to use, if for any reason he preferred not to give the title of the officer in question. May we not conjecture that his avoidance of both "bishop" and "presbyter" was due to the fact that their use varied in different churches, and even in the same church ? It is a significant fact that the term "bishop" is not applied in extant writings to *the chief officer* of the Roman Church until a period later than Justin. Forty years earlier it had come to be used in the churches of Asia, as the genuine epistles of Ignatius show,[3] for the particular title of the presiding presbyter. About Justin's period Hegesippus applies the term to Symeon of Jerusalem,[4] as Polycrates also does[5] to Polycarp, Thraseas, and other pastors of Asia Minor. But not only does Clement of Rome, at the close of the first century, use "bishop" and "presbyter" convertibly, and with the implication that there was a plurality of such officers at the head of the local church;[6] but Ignatius himself is significantly silent in his epistle to the Romans, as to any presiding officer in that place, as is also Polycarp in his letter to the Philippians. The testimony of Hermas concern-

[1] See Hatch's Organization of the Early Christian Churches, Lect. II.

[2] Vis. ii. 4. σὺ δ' ἀναγνώσεις εἰς ταύτην τὴν πόλιν μετὰ τῶν πρεσβυτέρων τῶν προϊσταμένων τῆς ἐκκλησίας. Vis. ii. 2; iii. 9. τοῖς προηγουμένοις τῆς ἐκκλησίας.

[3] See not only Ad Polyc. 1, but Ad Eph. 1, 2, 4, 5, 6 ; Ad Mag. 2, 3, 6, 7 ; Ad Tral. 1, 2, 3, etc.

[4] Eus. H. E. iv. 22.   [5] Ibid., v. 24.

[6] See Ad Cor. 21, 42, 44, etc.

JUSTIN ON THE POST-APOSTOLIC CHURCH. 263

ing the organization of the Roman Church is obscure.[1] His language seems to associate the episcopate with the executive work of the church, and the presbyterate with the work of teaching and ruling;[2] but no such separation of titles as to prove distinct offices can be discerned in his pages. Hegesippus also states[3] that on his arrival at Rome he "drew up a list of the succession down to Anicetus, whose deacon was Eleutherus," —

[1] See Lightfoot's Commentary on Philippians; Essay on the Christian Ministry.

[2] See Vis. ii. 2: "Tell those who rule (τοῖς προηγουμένοις) the Church to direct their ways in righteousness." Vis. ii. 4: "You will write therefore two books [or copies, βιβλιδάρια], and send one to Clement and one to Grapte. Clement will then send (his) to the foreign cities, for to him has this duty been intrusted (ἐκείνῳ γὰρ ἐπιτέτραπται); and Grapte will admonish the widows and orphans; and thou shalt read it to this city along with the presbyters who preside over the church (τῶν πρεσβυτέρων τῶν προϊσταμένων τῆς ἐκκλησίας)." Observe here not only presbyters as controlling the worship of the church, but Clement singled out as the church organ of communication with other churches. There is nothing to show whether Clement was but one of the presbyters, or whether he was regarded as having a distinct office; but the impression is made by the language that he was the church's executive and probably its presiding presbyter. Vis. iii. 5, "apostles, bishops, teachers, and deacons" named as the officers of the church. Probably "teachers" represents "presbyters," and "bishops," the chief presbyters, as executive officers; but, as Lightfoot admits, the terms may designate "the one presbyteral office in its twofold aspect." Vis. iii. 9: "I say to you who preside (προηγουμένοις) over the church and hold the first seats (τοῖς πρωτοκαθεδρίταις)," etc. Sim. ix. 25: "Apostles and teachers who preached to the whole world," etc. If this refer to others besides the founders of Christianity, it describes only the teaching work of church officers without discriminating their offices. Sim. ix. 27: "Bishops given to hospitality . . . never failed to protect the widows . . . and maintained a holy conversation." Here the administrative and executive work of the "bishop" appears; but whether the word is applied to ordinary presbyters, or only to the chief, is uncertain.

[3] Eus. H. E. iv. 22.

thus, while evidently testifying to the existence of a single chief ruler in the Roman Church at and before his time, not giving his title. At a little later date indeed than Justin, Dionysius of Corinth wrote to the Roman Church, and spoke of "your blessed bishop Soter;"[1] but Irenæus, who was familiar with the usages of both Asia and Rome, calls Polycarp in one place[2] a "bishop," and in another[3] a "presbyter," and in his letter to Victor of Rome,[4] speaks of "the *presbyters* preceding Soter in the government of the church which thou dost now rule." Furthermore, none of the extant epitaphs of the Roman bishops give the title "Episcopus" during the second century, nor even later.[5] It would thus seem that the title applied to the presiding officer of the Christian societies still varied in Justin's time in different localities, and perhaps in the same localities as well. Such a state of things would at least harmonize with Justin's failure to mention the official title of the president. We may suppose that, not wishing to enter into more particulars than were necessary, nor to explain the different usages and perhaps the different opinions which existed in the churches, he used a term which would apply to all the modifications of government which might be found in all the Christian societies of the Empire.

But however this may have been, the president was but one of "the brethren," merely the leader of their devotions and the agent of their charity. No sacerdotal ideas were as yet attached to him.[6]

No sacerdotalism.

[1] Eus. H. E. iv. 23. [2] Adv. Hær. iii. 3, 4.
[3] Eus. H. E. v. 20. [4] Eus. H. E. v. 24.
[5] De Rossi, Bulletina di Archeologia Christiana, Ann. II. 1864, p. 50, quoted by Hatch, "Organization," etc., p. 88.
[6] See also Dial. 116, where Justin teaches the priesthood of all believers.

Justin makes no mention, however, — if we suppose the president to have been the "bishop," — of any officers corresponding to the "presbyters." No doubt this may be in part attributed to the fact that he was describing the public worship of the church, and not its discipline, nor in detail its methods of instructing its members; yet the omission confirms the impression already made that in his time the chief officer had gone far towards monopolizing not only the original functions of the deacons, but also those of the presbyters.

Slight as this evidence is, it accords with what we elsewhere learn of the progress of local church organization during the second century. From the beginning there was but one society established in each locality. This was originally governed by a body of equal presbyters or bishops.[1] Their office, however, was at first chiefly disciplinary and executive, for the supernatural gifts of the apostolic Christians regulated to a large degree the conduct of the service. But toward the close of the apostolic age itself, the teaching function, which had always pertained in idea to the presbyter, was called into greater prominence,[2] though an itinerant ministry of prophets and other supernaturally gifted teachers continued to exist with it.[3] But early in the

Justin's description accords with the known facts of church organization in the second century.

---

[1] I cannot accept Hatch's theory of the origin of the episcopate. See his "Organization," etc., Lect. II. The use of the term in the apostolic churches as synonymous with "presbyter" is clearly proved by Acts xx. 17, 28, as well as Tit. i. 5-7; and the term itself could as easily have been obtained by the Jewish Christian churches from the LXX. as by the Gentile Christians from the clubs. See Dr. Sanday's article in the Expositor, Feb., 1887, "Origin of the Christian Ministry, II., Criticism of Recent Theories."

[2] See the Pastoral Epistles and Heb. xiii. 7, 8; 1 Pet. v. 1-3.

[3] See "The Teaching of the Apostles," 11, 12, 13.

second century we find in the Asian churches, at the head of the local or congregational presbytery, a permanent president or pastor, called the bishop, who was the centre of both the administrative and liturgical and disciplinary service of the society. With him appear the presbyters as counsellors, but they are already sinking into a subordinate rank. The bishop is the permanent pastor of the flock; and in this centralization, which is thus shown to have taken place, the Church found her safeguard against the disorganizing influence of heresy. As the second century passed on, the importance and power of the local bishop naturally increased. The services of the assembly and the management of the society's affairs fell more and more into his hands. The deacons became his assistants in the administration of the finances and of the benevolent work of the Church. The latter especially, as Justin intimates, occupied a large part of his attention, and must have aided to augment the power of his office. The presbyters, while remaining the bishop's council and assisting him in teaching and discipline, fell into the background, or became pastors of the subordinate chapels, as we would call them, which with the growth of the society became necessary. Such was in outline the movement in local church government which the second century witnessed. By the end of the century the elevation of the episcopate over the presbyterate had been so firmly established in nearly all the churches of the Empire,[1] that it was commonly supposed to have been the arrangement from the beginning. The slight glimpse which Justin gives of the services of the Chris-

[1] In Alexandria the process seems to have been slower than elsewhere. See Lightfoot's Commentary on Philippians; Essay on the Christian Ministry, p. 225.

tian assemblies reveals, so far as it goes, the same picture.¹

But was there any external bond uniting these local societies together? We reply that Justin gives no hint of such a thing. His expressions concerning the unity of Christendom are the following. Expounding the Forty-fifth Psalm, he writes,² that those who believe in Christ are one soul and one synagogue and one church, even as the Word speaks, — "Hearken, O *daughter*, and behold and incline thine ear."³ Again,⁴ Christ " hath made us *a house* of prayer

Unity of the churches purely spiritual.

---

[1] It should be noted that I have used the term "presbytery" for the governing body of a local church or single society. So it is used in the New Testament. It was, since there was but one society in each locality, in one aspect equivalent to the modern "session," in another equivalent to the modern "presbytery," as the terms are used in the American Presbyterian Church. Nor must the "bishop" of the early part of the second century be identified with the diocesan bishop of later times. He was the pastor of a single society. Had the "bishop" of the Ignatian epistles been associated with other bishops of the same province or of several adjacent localities in the government of the churches under them, or had he and his presbyters divided on terms of equality the members of their church, as it grew, into several societies, each organized after the original pattern, and governed by the joint council, the result would have been what is now understood as government by presbytery. But in fact the importance of the chief pastor increased. The presbyters were given subordinate positions under him. The local church remained an organic unit, and the way was paved for the later diocesan episcopate. Both presbyterianism and episcopacy therefore concur in the first change which passed over the apostolic churches; namely, the rise of the local bishop. From that point they diverge: the former preserving the idea of local self-government after the original model, and securing the unity of all by a series of ascending courts; the latter continuing the development of the central personal power.

[2] Dial. 63.   [3] Cf. Eph. v. 23-27.
[4] Dial. 86.

and worship."[1] Christians are "the vine planted by God and Christ the Saviour,"[2] and are "the robe of Christ," because in them the Seed of God, the Logos, dwells.[3] They have believed "as one man" in God, and "being inflamed by the word of His calling, are the true high-priestly race."[4] They are the true Israel.[5] Still more particularly, he states[6] that the prophet[7] predicted that the wicked shall become subject to Christ, "and that all shall become *as one child*. Such a thing," he adds, "as you may witness in the body; although the members are enumerated as many, all together are called one, and are a body.[8] For indeed a commonwealth[9] and an assembly,[10] though many individuals numerically, yet, because they are one in fact,[11] are called and addressed by the one appellation." The unity of Christendom was therefore to Justin a most real, but at the same time a purely spiritual fact. There is nothing, either in the charges made against the Christians or in the Apologist's defence, which indicates that a formal organization of the separate Christian societies into one external framework had arisen. Their unity was one of life and faith; and it is evident that Paul's figures of a temple and a body were still controlling Justin's language. This spiritual bond certainly united the churches closely together. We early learn of letters of inquiry or counsel sent from church to church,[12] or written by distinguished

---

[1] Cf. Eph. ii. 21, 22; 1 Tim. iii. 15; 1 Pet. ii. 5.
[2] Dial. 110.
[3] Ap. i. 32. Cf. Dial. 54, 87. [4] Dial. 116.
[5] Cf. Dial. 119, 125, 130, 135. [6] Dial. 42.
[7] Isa. liii. 2, according to the LXX.
[8] Cf. 1 Cor. xiv. 12, etc. [9] δῆμος.
[10] ἐκκλησία.
[11] ὡς ἓν ὄντες πρᾶγμα; as being one object.
[12] Cf. Clem. Rom. ad Cor.

pastors to other churches than their own.[1] With the growth of heresy and the planting of new churches, the original societies, because the depositaries of apostolic traditions, rose in influence. Important churches and bishops attained commanding positions in the entire brotherhood. But all the evidence goes to show that the local churches were in the second century independent. Christian unity lay in the consciousness of a common faith and life and hope. It divided the orthodox from the heretics. It made believers seem to themselves, though scattered over the Empire, one body, one race, one church. No church or bishop held any official primacy; yet the sense of spiritual oneness among the brethen and attachment to an established apostolic faith was so strong that it was not difficult in time to embody the Church's unity in an external form.[2] Not yet, however, had that form been created. The Catholic Church of the post-apostolic age was simply the total number of those who professed the apostolic faith. In Justin we find the same spiritual conception of the Church that we find in Paul. He betrays no conception of the Church as a whole more advanced than that of his predecessors. While we know that the forces were already beginning to work which produced a world-wide external organization with which the Church was identified, Justin stands on the older ground, and thus testifies to the falsity of the ecclesiastical claims of modern Rome, as we have found

[1] Compare the Epistles of Ignatius, Polycarp, Dionysius of Corinth.
[2] The first external expression of the Church's unity was in the form of councils, consisting of the representatives of the churches of a certain district. They appear to have been held irregularly, and had no binding authority. See Hatch's Organization of the Early Christian Churches, Lect. VII.

him to do to the claims of some modern critics that in his age Catholic Christianity first began.

II. What, then, was the faith by which these early Christians were united, and which they claimed to have received from the Apostles? To this question we are naturally led as the conclusion of all our inquiries.

<small>II. The faith of the Church.</small>

In seeking a reply to this question from Justin, we have only to abstract from his statements of doctrine that philosophical element which we have found he introduced into his Christianity. By his philosophy he endeavored to understand and explain Christianity; and the effects of this upon his theology were so great as to modify nearly every statement by him of the Christian belief. And yet, as was remarked in a previous lecture,[1] the two elements, the philosophical and the Christian, are equally evident in his expressions. He believed much which his philosophy could not appropriate or could only rationalize away. His philosophy was clearly superimposed upon his Christianity. Not only technical terms, taken from the language of the Church, but also beliefs which his philosophy never would have created, and which therefore must have come from his adopted religion, are found on his pages. Finally, his close connection with the body of orthodox believers, his confessed reliance on apostolic teaching, and his horror of heresy make it certain that while his views were modified by philosophical influences, he is, if allowance for these modifications be made, a competent witness to the faith of the early Church.

<small>How obtained from Justin.</small>

<small>(1) The person of Christ.</small>

(1) The first point to be noticed in the faith of the Church as witnessed by Justin,

[1] Lect. IV.

is that the divine-human person of Christ was its central article.

On the one hand, the reality of Christ's humanity, and the facts of His birth, life, death, resurrection, and ascension formed the historical foundation on which the Church's faith rested. His birth from the Virgin is defended by Justin as the common belief.[1] His gradual and natural growth into manhood is mentioned.[2] Stress is laid on the reality of His humanity[3] in general, as well as of His sufferings in particular.[4] He was held to be sinless,[5] holy,[6] and righteous.[7] He rose from the dead, and ascended to heaven, where He waits in glory the day of His final triumph.[8] These facts, accepted on apostolic testimony in just that version which is recorded in our Gospels, were not only received as historical, but were the foundation, unquestioned by any save by those who by questioning them were stamped as heretical, upon which the very existence of Christianity was held to repose. *Humanity of Christ.*

But, on the other hand, the divinity of Christ is even more emphatically mentioned by Justin as a fundamental belief of the Christians. He was worshipped and adored.[9] "We reasonably worship Him, having learned that He is the Son of the true God, holding Him in the second place;" and on this very account was Christianity esteemed madness by its enemies.[10] "Son of God" was, in fact, the term commonly applied to Christ by the Christians;[11] and while *Divinity of Christ.*

[1] Ap. i. 33; Dial. 43, 54, 99, etc.
[2] Dial. 88.
[3] Dial. 84, 98.
[4] Dial. 98, 99, 103.
[5] Dial. 23, 110.
[6] Dial. 98, 119.
[7] Dial. 119.
[8] Ap. i. 45, 51, 52; Dial. 32, 34, 36, 85, etc.
[9] Ap. i. 6.
[10] Ap. i. 13.
[11] See Ap. i. 22.

the term itself might be understood in a sense in which it could be applied to other men, it was not so understood by the Church when applied to Christ. It referred to His relation to the Father before the creation of the world;[1] and in this particular was the Church, according to Justin, separated from the extreme sect of Jewish Christians.[2] Christ's birth, therefore, was a divine incarnation.[3] This was not merely Justin's own doctrine. Of that we have already spoken. This was, according to his testimony, the faith of the Church. His explanation of the way in which Christ was divine is one thing. His testimony to the Church's non-philosophical belief in Christ's divinity is another thing, and quite distinguishable from the former. The latter was unquestioned except by heretics. Ebionism, or at least the belief of those who considered Christ a mere man, is distinctly declared[4] by Justin not to be the opinion of the Church, but a "human doctrine," or the teaching of man, in opposition to the teaching of the prophets and of Christ Himself. Moderate Jewish Christianity stood, as would appear from Justin's language, in full accord with the rest of the Church in this belief.[5] Marcion, on the contrary, is declared to be impious for denying that Christ is the Son of the Creator,[6] as well as for denying that the Creator is the Supreme God. Thus Christ was to the Christians the God-Man; Son of God from before the foundation of the world; the divine Logos who became man for the salvation of men.[7] Justin's doctrine of the Logos presupposes, as

---

[1] Ap. i. 23.
[2] Dial. 48.
[3] See Ap. i. 5, 23, 63, etc.
[4] Dial. 48.
[5] Dial. 47, 48.
[6] Ap. i. 58.
[7] In Ap. ii. 10, Justin says, διὰ τὸ λογικὸν τὸ ὅλον τὸν φανέντα δι' ἡμᾶς χριστὸν γεγονέναι, καὶ σῶμα καὶ λόγον καὶ ψυχήν. This is,

we have previously observed, the doctrine of John as the accepted faith of the Church. He does not write as one establishing a new belief, but as one defending and explaining an admitted belief. Dean Mansel has well remarked that the earliest heresies found it easier to deny the humanity than the divinity of Christ, and thus testify to the universal belief of the Christians in the latter.[1] In like manner, in Justin's time was the divinity of Christ a fundamental article of Christianity. As such it was defended and explained. We repeat that the attempt, apparent in Justin, to reason out the

perhaps, the most difficult passage to interpret in Justin's books. I believe, however, that he wished to oppose the views of those who, like Marcion, divided Christ. The whole Logos appeared in Christ; and the whole Christ, physical and rational, was the appearing of the Logos. The body of Christ was produced in the womb of the Virgin by the Logos (Ap. i. 33); the Logos Himself dwelt in this body. And then Justin adds, to make the enumeration complete, that the ψυχήν (human soul; see Dial. 105) of Christ contained also the manifestation of the Logos. Certainly Justin recognized in Christ three parts, — body and logos and soul. But the order of the words shows that Justin did not mean by these terms to enumerate the parts of Christ's humanity, for then he would surely have said, body and soul and logos (or reason). By logos he therefore meant Christ's divinity, and, besides it, attributed to Him a real body and a human soul. There is nothing to show how he defined the relation of the Logos to the soul in Christ, just as he does not define the relation of the Logos to the human reason generally (see Lect. IV.). Though his language here looks Apollinarian, the probability is that he did not anticipate that heresy. So Otto (*sub loco*), Weizsäcker (Jahrb. für deutsche Theol., 1867, p. 96, note), and Von Engelhardt (Das Christenthum Justins, p. 121, where the various views of the passage are given). See also Dorner's History of the Doctrine of the Person of Christ (Eng. trans.), div. i. vol. i. p. 277. Dial. 105, in which Justin shows that by ψυχή he understood the immortal spirit and not the mere animal life of man, seems to have been overlooked by those who make him a trichotomist.

[1] Gnostic Heresies, Lect. VIII.

relation of the Son to the Father was one thing; the belief in Christ's pre-existent, divine Sonship with the worship of Him as God manifest in the flesh was another thing. The belief occasioned the philosophical efforts to explain the mystery; philosophy did not create the belief. This is the manifest order as the matter lies in the testimony of Justin.

(2) Necessarily connected with belief in Christ's divinity was the Church's substantial faith in the Trinity.

<small>(2) The Trinity.</small>

Justin's testimony to this is the more significant from the fact that his philosophy tended to modify the doctrine which we believe was taught by the Apostles, and would certainly at least never have led him to it. When describing his theology we spoke of the way in which, under the influence of philosophy, he emphasized the divine transcendence. At the same time, indeed, we found that his doctrine of God contained many elements of another type, so that two conceptions of Deity seemed to be contending in his mind, — the one derived from his philosophy; the other from a living sense of God's moral character and affectionate interest in men, and due doubtless to his Christianity. Still Justin thought of God as above and beyond the world, and of the Logos as a divine being produced by the Father's will out of Himself, and through whom alone God's relation to the world is mediated. So, as to the relation of the Son to the Father, we found Justin describing the Logos as not personally eternal, and yet as neither a creation of nor an emanation from God. While numerically distinct from the Father, He is yet represented as one with Him in such a way as to imply that the distinction between them referred to their personalities, but not to their nature. At the same time He is sub-

JUSTIN ON THE POST-APOSTOLIC CHURCH. 275

ordinate to the Father, not only in office but in being, since He was produced as a distinct subsistence by the Father's will. But to the Logos pertains, according to Justin's thought, the whole work of mediation between God and the world. His affinity with human reason is very close, and His activity in human history has been constant. So much stress was thus laid on the idea of the Logos that little place was left for the work of the Spirit. Though continually using the phrase "prophetic spirit," Justin represents the Logos as the real author of prophecy.[1] Quoting the words spoken to the Virgin by the angel, "Behold, thou shalt conceive of the Holy Spirit," Justin says that it is wrong to understand here the "Spirit" as anything else than the Logos, who Himself caused the Virgin to conceive and became incarnate in her.[2] Significant variations of phrase from that of the New Testament indicate the same habit of thought. Instead of Saint John's "worship in spirit and in truth," Justin has, "We worship, honoring in reason and truth."[3] Believers are those "in whom dwells the Seed from God, the Logos,"[4] rather than those in whom God or Christ dwells by the Spirit. The doctrine of "the Seminal Logos, of whom all men partake,"[5] while not inconsistent necessarily with the doctrine of the Spirit, manifestly takes its place in Justin's mind. These examples will suffice to show that the Apologist's own thought strongly *tended away from the doctrine of a Trinity.* It tended to a sort of dytheism, although it held to the consubstantiality of the Logos and the Father of all.

What means, then, the fact that in spite of all this

[1] See Ap. i. 36; ii. 10.
[2] Ap. i. 33.
[3] Ap. i. 6. λόγῳ καὶ ἀληθείᾳ.
[4] Ap. i. 32.
[5] See Lect. IV.

Justin testifies to the worship of three divine persons by the Christians? Such worship was involved in the already established formula of baptism, "in the name of God the Father and Lord of all, and of our Saviour Jesus Christ, and of the Holy Spirit;"[1] or, as Justin adds in the same connection, "in the name of God the Father and Lord of all," and "of Jesus Christ who was crucified under Pontius Pilate," and "of the Holy Spirit, which predicted through the prophets all things concerning Jesus." So he elsewhere explicitly declares "we worship the Son, holding him in the second place and the prophetic Spirit in the third order."[2] That he

[1] Ap. i. 61.
[2] Ap. i. 13. υἱὸν ... ἐν δευτέρᾳ χώρᾳ ἔχοντες πνεῦμά τε προφητικὸν ἐν τρίτῃ τάξει, ... τιμῶμεν. See Ap. i. 6, 65, 66. In Ap. i. 6, he mentions the objects of Christian worship as follows: "The most true God and Father of righteousness and temperance and other virtues (who is) free from wickedness, and the Son who came from Him and taught us these things, and the *host of other good angels who follow and are like Him* and the prophetic Spirit." This mention of angels is to be explained by Justin's desire to set over against the bad angels and demons whom pagans worshipped the whole number of good celestial beings as objects of Christian veneration, thus showing that universally the Christians adore what is good. His object was to prove that Christians are not atheists. So far from this, he says, they have as objects of reverence a great number of heavenly beings, but all of them good. Certainly Justin's language was misleading; for that he did not really mean that Christians in the strict sense worshipped angels is proved by the fact that in Ap. i. 13, 61, 65, 66, he names only the Father, Son, and Spirit as objects of worship. His language in Ap. i. 6 shows, however, that the subordination of the Son and Spirit to the Father was so strongly impressed on his thought that it was not difficult for him thus to include angels as, in a general way, objects of veneration. He did not have a Jew's jealousy of whatever might seem to infringe on monotheism, but was more concerned for the worship of *the good* than of *the One*. This was another result of the course by which Justin approached Christianity; and the isolated expression before us betrays his

ascribed divinity to the Logos, even to the extent of making Him of the same substance with the Father, we have already stated; but his testimony concerning the Spirit is more remarkable. *The Spirit.* For though his own theology had really no place for the Spirit, yet Justin speaks of the Spirit as not only an object of worship, but as the power of Christian life. Not only is the Spirit repeatedly represented as having spoken through the prophets,[1] but certain prophecies are distinguished from those uttered in the name of the Father and from those uttered in the name of Christ as being specially prophetic of future things, with the evident implication that they were spoken in the name of the Spirit.[2] The province of the Spirit lay, according to Justin, in the domain of Christian life. The prophecies just referred to as having been spoken in the name of the Spirit were those which predicted the progress and victory of the Christian religion. The

---

own peculiar cast of mind, but not the belief of the Church. See Von Engelhardt's Das Christenthum Justins, p. 146, and his quotation from Nitsch, that "to the Gentile Christians, as long as they did not scientifically reflect, there was not the same need of a strict monotheism as to the Jewish Christians," which was because, Von Engelhardt adds, "in rising from polytheism to the truth of divine unity, the conception of God became abstract and easily consistent with the thought of subordinate beings who manifested the powers of Deity." The view that Justin classed angels with the Spirit and regarded the Spirit as an angel is an unnatural construction of his language, and opposed to his general representation of the Spirit. So the rendering, "The Son who taught us and the host of other good angels these things," is a mere effort to escape difficulties. Dr. E. A. Abbott (Modern Review, July, 1882, p. 568) regards this passage "as a remnant of the undeveloped Philonian doctrine, whereby the Logos is but the elder and foremost of a number of Logoi, Angels, or Powers."

[1] Ap. i. 31, 32, 35, 40, etc.; Dial. 7, 25, 32, 34, etc.
[2] Ap. i. 39.

aged believer who led Justin to Christ is represented as maintaining that the mind of man cannot see God unless instructed by the Holy Spirit.[1] Justin declares to Trypho that Christians have not believed fables, but words filled with the Spirit of God.[2] "What need have I," he cries, "of that other baptism, who have been baptized with the Holy Ghost?"[3] The special "gifts" which Christian men and women possessed are said to have been received from the Spirit of God.[4] It would appear from these expressions that he conceived of the Spirit as the agent employed by the Father and the Logos in operating upon men's minds. Thus alone can we understand him, when he writes of the Spirit as speaking through the prophets, and yet of the divine Logos as the author of prophecy. So likewise he declares that Joshua received strength from the Spirit of Jesus;[5] and in one particularly notable passage[6] he uses this language: "Though the devil is ever at hand to resist us, and anxious to seduce all to himself, yet the Angel of God, that is the Power of God sent to us through Jesus Christ, rebukes him, and he departs from us." This latter passage manifestly refers to the Holy Spirit.[7] It is true, indeed, that Justin's idea of the Spirit was vague. In no

---

[1] Dial. 4.   [2] Dial. 9.
[3] Dial. 29.
[4] Dial. 88. χαρίσματα ἀπὸ τοῦ πνεύματος τοῦ θεοῦ ἔχοντας.
[5] Dial. 113.   [6] Dial. 116.
[7] See Neander's Church History, Eng. trans., i. 609; also Otto's note in his edition of Justin. The fact that Justin also called the Logos an angel shows that his use of the word here does not necessarily imply that he considered the Spirit a creature. The phrase, "The Power of God," etc., may be understood personally or not. The Spirit was, at any rate, to Justin a distinct being sent to men from God through Christ, whom Justin represents as a person (angel), though in his own thought he may have regarded him as impersonal.

case does he clearly declare the personality of the Spirit, though he often seems on the verge of doing so. Nevertheless the Spirit was to him a distinct object of worship, and the immediate power of a Christian's life; and this although his own theology felt no need of the Spirit in order to explain the philosophy of Christianity.

Thus Justin in spite of himself testifies to the threefold object of Christian worship. He even finds[1] in Plato an adumbration of the first, second, and third powers in the universe, though in doing so he misunderstands and misrepresents that philosopher. Justin's own conception is vague, or, when not vague, unscriptural in certain important points. He unduly subordinates the Son to the Father, and the Spirit to both. He hovers between the ideas of the Spirit as divine Influence and as a divine Person. But he declares these three to be the divine objects of Christian worship. He describes the functions of each in the economy of salvation in nearly[2] the same way in which they are described in the New Testament. He thus most effectively testifies to the traditional faith of the Church in the Father, Son, and Spirit as the threefold object of Christian worship, and the threefold source of Christian life.

(3) Furthermore, according to Justin, the Church believed in a redemption wrought out by the Son of God through His incarnation, death, and resurrection. *(3) Redemption.*

Here, again, we must allow for the influence of Justin's philosophy upon his statements. The main facts

---

[1] Ap. i. 60.

[2] The most marked exception is his failure to bring out the Spirit's work in regeneration (Ap. i. 61); but this was due to the stress which he laid on human freedom and activity in moral affairs.

of his testimony concerning the work of Christ were exhibited when we discussed his theology.[1] To him Christianity was supremely the full revelation of truth, because Christ was the incarnation of the divine Logos. In accordance with his exaltation of reason, he attributed the evil of life to the subjection of man's rational powers to the demons of ignorance and sin, and believed that if men be shown the truth, they have the power to recognize it and the ability to choose and obey it. Hence his favorite representation of Christ is as the Teacher. Christianity is the new law, and man's great duty is obedience to Christ's commands.

What mean then, we again ask, the expressions which are scattered through his writings and which represent Christ as saving men by His death and resurrection? He is said to have brought us healing by becoming partaker of our sufferings.[2] By His blood He cleanses believers.[3] He endured all for our sakes and on account of our sins.[4] By dying and rising He conquered death.[5] "He became the beginning of another race, who have been born again by Him *through water and faith and wood, which* contains the mystery of the Cross."[6] In baptism believers receive remission of sins[7] by the blood of Christ.[8] "His Father caused Him to suffer in behalf of the human race."[9] The Jews did not know, when they inflicted the suffering upon Him, that He was "the eternal Priest and King and Christ."[10] The fifty-third chapter of Isaiah is not only

---

[1] Lect. IV.　　　[2] Ap. ii. 13; Dial. 86, 137.
[3] Ap. i. 32; Dial. 13, 40, 54.
[4] Ap. i. 56, 70, 103; Dial. 63.
[5] Ap. i. 63.　　　[6] Dial. 138.
[7] Dial. 54.　　　[8] Dial. 111.
[9] Dial. 95.　　　[10] Dial. 96.

JUSTIN ON THE POST-APOSTOLIC CHURCH. 281

in whole or in part repeatedly applied to Christ, but is quoted with such unusual accuracy as to seem to show that it was a specially familiar passage to the Christians, and that every clause of it was literally applied to Him. Christ is the Passover, whose blood will deliver from death those who have believed.[1] Christ served for men even unto the cross, and acquired[2] them through its blood and mystery.[3] With great emphasis also does Justin represent Christ's death and resurrection as a triumph over the demons.[4] Of this victory the Cross was the sign.[5] Death has come to the Serpent through Him who has been crucified, by coming to whom men also may be saved.[6] The demons are now subject to His name and to the dispensation of His suffering.[7] They are frequently exorcised in His name, so that His power over them is proved.[8] Christ is now sitting at the right hand of the Father, waiting till He make His enemies His footstool.[9]

It would seem impossible to mistake the significance of these expressions. Justin could only have received them from the faith of the Church. He had no thought of modifying that faith. In it he practically shared. Therefore he freely expressed it, although it had little in this case to do with the philosophical ideas which were controlling his intellectual apprehension of Christianity. It is true that neither in his representation of Christianity as the new law nor in the stress which he laid on obedience as a condition of salvation, did Justin introduce a novelty. We have already remarked that the

[1] Dial. 111. [2] κτησάμενος.
[3] Dial. 134.
[4] Ap. i. 46 ; ii. 6; Dial. 91, 131, etc.
[5] Ap. i. 55 ; Dial. 90, 91.
[6] Dial. 91. [7] Dial. 30.
[8] Dial. 76. [9] Dial. 26.

tendency to a Christian legalism was characteristic of his time. We have suggested as causes of it precisely these philosophical ideas operating in union with the felt necessity of laying stress on Christian conduct and of upholding Christian character in the face of paganism. But none the less does it appear that the Church's faith rested not merely in the word of truth which Christ had spoken, but also in the redemption which Christ had wrought out by His death and resurrection. The power of Christ lay not only in His character and teaching, but in what He was believed to have done for men upon the cross. In that sign the Church was conquering. In His blood she was trusting. And though, in the confusion which was caused by the contact of Christian faith with the great world of pagan thought, by the awakening of speculation, by the stern practical necessities of the hour, the doctrine of redemption was conceived in crude and fragmentary ways, yet the faith in redemption by the death of Jesus was fundamental and catholic, and is thus attested as the faith which had been received from the Apostles.

(4) The privileges and prospects of the Christian.

(4) Finally, Justin testifies to the faith of the post-apostolic church concerning the spiritual privileges and future prospects of the Christian.

(*a*) Christianity was the actual enjoyment of a new life in and from Christ. It is true, again, that this is not the phase of Christianity upon which Justin lays most stress; but his testimony to it is all the stronger for being incidental.

(*a*) Christianity a new life.

Most obviously was it a new life in being a new morality. Justin dwells upon the contrast between pagan vices and Christian virtues, and points his Imperial readers to the astounding moral change which had passed

JUSTIN ON THE POST-APOSTOLIC CHURCH. 283

over the lives of their persecuted Christian subjects.[1] This new morality was based upon a new standard of living, which had been derived from the knowledge of the holy and loving character of the true God, whom the Christians strove to imitate. The change of life had been caused by a new discovery of God through Jesus Christ. "We have been taught," writes the Apologist, "and have been persuaded, and do believe that He accepts those only who imitate the excellences which reside in Him, — temperance and justice and philanthropy, and as many virtues as are peculiar to a God who is called by no proper name."[2] A new world had already formed itself in the Christian mind around the manifestation of God in Christ; and that divine revelation, as the Christians believed it to be, was the motive-power of the new morality which had made its appearance in them.

A new morality.

As to the origin of this life in individuals, Justin expresses himself for the most part after almost a Pelagian manner.[3] Insisting on man's full ability to repent and change his life, and seeing in Christianity the perfection of that rational living of which heathen as well as Hebrew antiquity afforded examples, he could even speak of a man's undertaking to be able to live according to Christ's commands, and therefore choosing to be born again.[4] We obtain in baptism the forgiveness of past sins; but Justin writes as if, after baptism, a Christian's salvation depended on his own obedience.[5] Of an immediate and unchangeable justification he says nothing.[6]

[1] Ap. i. 14, 25, 27; Dial. 110.   [2] Ap. i. 10.
[3] See Lect. IV.   [4] Ap. i. 61.
[5] Ap. i. 65; Dial. 44.
[6] In Dial. 116 we read, "We who believed have been stripped of the filthy garments, i. e., of our sins;" but, just before, Justin speaks of the "prepared garments" as to be put on us in the

Nevertheless, we discover in him the consciousness of God's special favor to the believer, of a mystical relationship to Christ, and of supernatural grace received in the sacraments, which proves that, with all his Pelagianism, he believed that Christian life was a communion with, and a gift from God through Jesus Christ. "Pray," said the aged Christian to the young Platonist, "that the gates of light may be opened to you; for these things cannot be perceived or understood at all, but only by the man to whom God and His Christ have imparted wisdom."[1] Christians, therefore, are a holy people, whom God has chosen.[2] To them it has been granted to hear and understand and be saved by this Christ, and to recognize all the things revealed by the Father.[3] They are the true Israel, begotten of faith and the Spirit.[4] So also is Christ represented as always present among them by His power,[5] even as in them the Seed from God, namely, the Logos, dwells;[6] and Christ, possessing the fulness of the Spirit, imparts grace to believers according as he deems each one worthy.[7] Particularly in his idea of the sacraments does Justin combine rationalistic modes of expression with evident belief in their mys-

Conversion.

Christ's presence.

The sacraments.

future kingdom, so that he evidently confined the stripping off of the old garments to forgiveness of past sins in baptism.

[1] Dial. 7. So see Dial. 30: "Have received grace to know;" 32: "A remnant left by the grace of the Lord of Sabaoth;" 55: God has withheld from the Jews the ability (τὸ δύνασθαι) to discern the wisdom of the Scriptures (compare also 58, 119); 116: the Power of God sent to us (i. e., the Spirit) through Jesus Christ. Compare also Ap. i. 10; Dial. 110, 131, 136, though these passages may be understood in a rationalistic sense.

[2] Dial. 119. [3] Dial. 121.
[4] Dial. 135. [5] Dial. 54. δυνάμει.
[6] Ap. i. 32. [7] Dial. 57.

tical efficiency. Thus baptism[1] was, on the one hand, the rite of initiation into the Church, and was administered to those who had been persuaded that what Christ taught was true, and undertook to be able to live accordingly. By it they "dedicated themselves to God" when they had been "made new through Christ," — a phrase, however, by which Justin, as the following sentences show, merely meant, when they had been taught by Christ's word and had accepted it. But, on the other hand, there was received in baptism the forgiveness of past sins; and the rite itself was commonly called "regeneration." The rite, therefore, was identified with that which it represented, — was regarded as the appointed means of entrance, not only into the church, but into divine favor,[2] — was in consequence of Christ's work the beginning of a new life;[3] which, indeed, Justin says, a man assumed of himself, but from which the burden of past sins was removed, and through which the mind was "illuminated" so as faithfully to wait and work for the full salvation. In like manner the Eucharist was not common food; "but as, through the Word of God,[4] Jesus Christ our Saviour, having been made flesh, took both flesh and blood for our salvation, so also were we taught that the food over which thanks has been rendered through the prayer of the word which is from Him,[5]

Baptism.

The Eucharist.

[1] Ap. i. 61.   [2] Ap. i. 61; Dial. 138.

[3] Dial. 43: a spiritual circumcision; 86: a purification of the soul (ἡμᾶs βεβαπτισμένους ταῖς βαρυτάταις ἁμαρτίαις ἃς ἐπράξαμεν, διὰ τοῦ σταυρωθῆναι ἐπὶ τοῦ ξύλου καὶ δι' ὕδατος ἁγνίσαι ὁ χριστὸς ἡμῶν ἐλυτρώσατο).

[4] διὰ λόγου θεοῦ; i. e. (see Ap. i. 33), through the incarnation of the Logos.

[5] δι' εὐχῆς λόγου τοῦ παρ' αὐτοῦ εὐχαριστηθεῖσαν; i. e., through the repetition of the words of institution which Christ used, and of

and by[1] which our blood and flesh through transmutation[2] are nourished, is the flesh and blood of that Jesus who was made flesh."[3] Justin speaks of the Eucharist as a *memorial* of God's goodness both in creation[4] and redemption,[5] and as *the pure sacrifice of thanksgiving* which the Christians offered everywhere to God.[6] He cannot fairly be accused of the later doctrine of transubstantiation; but he nevertheless declares, like Ignatius[7] before him and Irenæus[8] after him, that the consecrated bread and wine became the flesh and blood of Christ, and that by partaking of it even the bodies of believers were spiritually nourished. He attributed actual power to the Eucharist, as he did to baptism, and saw in both of them channels by which grace flowed from Christ to His people. He thus curiously combined with his rationalism a tendency toward a mechanical and mystical view of the sacraments; so

---

which Justin in the next sentence gives an account. See Otto (*sub loco*), for various views of this disputed sentence.

[1] ἐξ.

[2] κατὰ μεταβολήν; i. e., not in the common way, but as the result of a change produced in the bread and wine. The Eucharistic elements nourished the bodies of believers, but after a heavenly manner (see Iren. iv. 18. 5), because, as the body of Jesus was the body of the incarnate Logos, so had the elements become the flesh and blood of Christ. Justin's conception of the incarnation is the key to his conception of the Eucharist. Christ had a real body; yet the whole Christ, physical and spiritual, was the revelation of the Logos (Ap. ii. 10). The elements of the Eucharist were real bread and wine; yet the Logos had made them His flesh and blood, the manifestation of His being and power. See Weizsäcker's "Die Theologie des Märtyrers Justinus," Jahrb. für deutsche Theol., 1867, pp. 96-99.

[3] Ap. i. 66. [4] Dial. 41.
[5] Ap. i. 66; Dial. 41, 70, 117. [6] Dial. 28, 41.
[7] Ad Eph. 20; Ad Rom. 7; Ad Phil. 41.
[8] Adv. Hær. iv. 18. 5.

that, in spite of the way in which his philosophy led him to minimize the supernatural character of individual Christian life, he testifies to the Church's faith in that life as a gift from God, and sustaining a constant relation of dependence upon the work and power of the once crucified but now victorious Redeemer. So strong was that faith that, as we have just seen, it was already disposed to find in the two Christian sacraments a constantly repeated miracle.

(b) But Christianity was still more emphatically to Justin and the Church a new and joyful hope. The tendency of his own thought was to conceive of salvation as future, and to direct its gaze on the glorious reward which the Master would bestow at the second advent on His faithful servants. Such was a natural attitude, also, in an age of persecution; and therefore in describing Christian hope Justin uttered, in most particulars, the common mind of the Church. *(b) Christianity a new hope.*

It is true that Christianity in its promises and expectations gave definite expression to convictions of the human soul, which were already widely spread, and which pagan religion and culture had uttered in divers parts and manners. Plato had reasoned of immortality. Future retribution was not only taught by the popular religions and described by the poets, but, with immortality, had been taught by philosophers. A future conflagration of the world was also a doctrine of the Stoics. Justin, however, did not hold these doctrines as they were taught by philosophy, but in the totally distinct form in which they were taught by Christianity; and to them he added other doctrines which, as the resurrection, were scorned by philosophy, and could only have en- *It uttered in its own way the hopes of mankind.*

tered his system from the faith of the Church. That he was sensible, indeed, of the agreements between Christian hope and certain types of pagan thought is evident enough, since he expressly points them out.[1] Not only so, but in his descriptions in the Apology of future blessedness, he uses phrases[2] which agree strikingly with the Platonic conception of divine reward, and which have seemed to some[3] inconsistent with the doctrine of a bodily resurrection. The inconsistency, however, is only apparent; and from the Dialogue we learn of Justin's strong belief, not only in a literal resurrection, but also in a visible reign of Christ with His risen people upon earth. Moreover, he plainly points out the differences between pagan and Christian hopes, and witnesses to the latter, not as these were influenced by paganism, but as they were taught by the facts and founders of original Christianity.

We thus learn that the Christians were comforted in their trials and encouraged in their confession by the expectation of Christ's visible return. In this sense was the prophecy understood, "He shall be the desire of all nations."[4] This hope was held alike by those who expected and by those who denied that at the advent Christ would establish for a thousand years a visible kingdom at Jerusalem. Of Chiliasm we have spoken in a previous lecture.[5] It was a widely spread but by no means universal belief of the post-apostolic Church, as Justin expressly states.[6] But all shared in the belief in a visible and

The second advent.

Chiliasm.

---

[1] Ap. i. 18, 20. [2] ἀφθάρτους. ἀπαθεῖς.
[3] So Aubé's Saint Justin, Philosophe et Martyr, part iii. ch. iv. and v.
[4] Ap. i. 32. [5] Lect. III.
[6] Dial. 80.

JUSTIN ON THE POST-APOSTOLIC CHURCH. 289

literal second advent. Then will Christ both finally conquer His enemies[1] and judge the world.[2] Chiliasm only gave a particular and more definite form to the universal expectation of the future and public victory of Christ. In this expectation all Christians shared, and by it they were consoled amid the existing hatred of the world. With the advent, moreover, the resurrection of the dead was expected to occur; and upon this non-philosophical doctrine Justin is particularly explicit.[3] In the Apology, in which Chiliasm does not appear, the advent and the resurrection and the judgment are all spoken of as if contemporaneous. In the Dialogue Justin brings out his Chiliastic views. The advent, he says, will be preceded by the coming of Elijah,[4] and will secure the conquest of Christ's enemies,[5] and particularly of the "man of sin," whose previous appearance will bring the climax of the Church's sufferings.[6] He distinguishes also two resurrections,[7] after the second of which the general judgment will ensue.[8] Christ, at His coming, will gather the Church to Jerusalem, and give her rest. Justin does not teach the restoration of the Jews nor of the Jewish ritual. He regards the manifestation of the "man of sin" as impending,[9] but expresses no opinion as to how near the advent may be, though apparently thinking it not very far off.[10] With it was connected the judgment of the whole world by Christ,[11]

The resurrection.

The judgment.

[1] Dial. 110, 121. [2] Ap. i. 28, 52; Dial. 35.
[3] Ap. i. 8, 18, 19, 52 · Dial. 69, 80, 81, 113, 117.
[4] Dial. 49. [5] Dial. 121.
[6] Dial. 32, 110. [7] Dial. 81, 113.
[8] Dial. 81, 117. [9] Dial. 32.
[10] Dial. 28. "So short a time is left you in which to become proselytes," i. e., Christians.
[11] Ap. i. 8, 53, 68; Dial. 35, 38, 58, 81, 118, 132.

after which it was believed that the righteous will enter upon incorruption, and freedom from suffering, and everlasting fellowship with God, and will reign with Him in immortality and glory,[1] while the wicked will be cast with the demons into the eternal fire of hell.[2] Of the state of the dead before the resurrection Justin says little. He only intimates that the final reward of the righteous will not be received till after the resurrection.[3] When the judgment has been concluded, the world will be destroyed by fire.[4]

The final reward of the righteous.
Hell.
World to be destroyed by fire.

Such was the outlook of these early Christians into the future. Amid the hatred and distrust of the world, in

[1] Ap. i. 10, 13, 18, 21, 42, 52, 57; Dial. 46, 69, 116, 117.
[2] Ap. i. 28, 44, 45, 52, 117.
[3] In Dial. 80, he blames heretics for maintaining that at death their souls go immediately to heaven. He referred, doubtless, to the Gnostic idea of immediate participation through γνῶσις in divine blessedness (cf. Iren. v. 31. 1), an idea which was united with denial of the resurrection. In Dial. 99, he says that the Jews fancied that Christ, *like a common mortal*, would remain in Hades. Yet by death Christians enter on the heavenly kingdom (Ap. i. 11). He thus seems to have distinctly identified heaven with the post-resurrection state, but to have expected blessedness also immediately after death. The pseudo-quotation from Jeremiah (Dial. 72), "The Lord remembered His dead, who slept in the grave, and descended to them to preach His salvation," may indicate belief in Christ's *descensus ad inferos* and the then preaching to the Old Testament saints; but Justin does no more than quote the passage. In Dial. 119, he says, "Along with Abraham we [Christians] shall inherit the Holy Land." Abraham therefore was regarded as, with the other pious dead, still waiting for the full reward.
[4] Ap. i. 20. Aubé (Saint Justin, p. 182) is wrong in saying that Justin confounded the fire which is to destroy the world with the fire of hell. He keeps them distinct. Of the future conflagration, however, he only states that it will not be, like the Stoic ἐκπύρωσις, a natural process, but a divine judgment.

the face of the constant liability to be called to suffer for their faith, and the probable increase of persecution with the diffusion of their doctrines, these hopes sustained them; and as the night grew darker, these stars gleamed the more brightly in their sky. And their hopes were manifestly summed up in the hope of Christ. They were founded on belief in Christ's divine Sonship, His resurrection from the dead, and His appointment by the Father as universal King and Judge. Only the historical reality of His life and death and resurrection, and the apostolic teaching concerning His person and His work, will account for the form and the strength of Christian hope in the post-apostolic age. The tenacity with which belief in a future literal resurrection of the body was held by all except heretics, can be explained only by the universal belief in Christ's resurrection, even as this latter belief in turn can be only explained by the fact of His resurrection itself. The universal expectation of Christ's return rested on faith in both His divinity and resurrection, and harmonized His divinity with the lowliness of His recorded life. It was a hope in Christ and of Christ to which Justin testifies as the joyful power of Christian life; and if it encouraged the early believers by its promises, it sprang from their unquestioning faith in the facts, attested by Apostles, of Christ's divine Sonship, and His accomplished victory over sin and death.

"Christ our hope."

As, then, we bring to a close our examination of Justin's testimony to early Christianity, we can better judge the man and his Church.

Conclusion.

It is impossible, we think, in the light of his testimony, to believe that post-apostolic Christianity was caused by any fusion of previously hostile Pauline and Jewish parties; for it avowedly regarded Jewish Christianity as a weakness and an imperfect type, it denied any peculiar privileges in the Church to the Jew, it was entirely unconscious of any division having existed among the Apostles but considered their united mission to have been to all nations, and it accepted our four Gospels as the apostolic and authoritative record of Christ's life. To suppose that this testimony of the post-apostolic Church was mistaken, and that in the course of two or three generations the Christians had rewritten the history of their origin, and had persuaded themselves that their own fictions were divine truths on which salvation depended and for which they cheerfully died, is, apart from the many historical and critical facts which disprove the supposition, to argue by a method which is capable of making any evidence appear worthless.

Post apostolic Christianity not the result of the fusion of Paulinism with Jewish views.

Nor can we believe, in the light of Justin's testimony, that post-apostolic Christianity was caused, so far as its essential character was concerned, by the union of Pauline or apostolic teaching with Hellenic culture; for while we have found Hellenic elements entering largely into combination with Christianity, we have also found that it was with a Christianity already established before its contact with paganism began.

Nor created by the union of apostolic Christianity with Hellenism.

On the contrary, the Christianity of Justin presupposed, both positively and negatively, just that foundation which is described in the New Testament.

It was apostolic Christianity continued, though modified.

But at the same time Justin reveals the direction from which the influences proceeded which principally modified the Christianity of the Apostles in the age immediately following them. The new faith, launched on the broad sea of pagan society, was exposed to new winds and currents, and the men who succeeded the Apostles as pilots and captains were far from being able perfectly to grasp and carry on the ideas of their great predecessors. *The modifications came chiefly from paganism and pagan surroundings.* Minds which had not been trained in Hebrew conceptions were likely either to neglect or misuse them. The necessity of devoting attention to practical matters of Christian life and ecclesiastical arrangement, and the stress laid on moral duties by the glaring contrast between the Christian ideal and the manners of heathen society, naturally hindered the immediate and complete realization of doctrine. On the other hand, the rise of heresy confined doctrinal controversy, so far as this existed at all, to the particular subjects disputed by Doketics and Gnostics, and left other topics undeveloped. Truth is apprehended in its integrity only after it has been doubted and denied. Otherwise it is likely to lie, even in the minds of its adherents, in a chaotic and fragmentary state. It is not strange, therefore, that we discover in the post-apostolic Church a manifest fall in several particulars, and notably in the doctrine of justification, from the teaching of the Apostles. Nor is it strange that Justin combined ideas which were really antagonistic. It is not wonderful that his mind, trained in pagan culture and naturally inquisitive, sought to conform the religion whose power he experienced to the forms of thought in which he had been reared, or that, when testifying to the confessed belief of the Church, he taught doctrines which, when trying to explain them by philosophy, he mutilated and distorted. In this very fall of post-apostolic doctrine below the completeness of apostolic teaching may we rather perceive a fresh testimony to the supernatural construction of the latter. It is easy to understand that an age of inspiration might be followed by an age which very imperfectly comprehended the ideas of its predecessor. But it is very difficult to understand how the later age could impute to its predecessor ideas, and even records, which convey the impression of a completeness of thought which the later age did not itself possess.

Justin, therefore, was the fair representative of the Church, of the faith which it had received from the Apostles, and of the influences which were here developing and there corrupting it. Whether, however, it was development or corruption, the process, as disclosed by him, implies the already fixed establishment of the faith in the minds of its followers as apostolic and fundamental. The marvellous spectacle of Christian morality arising in the depraved society of paganism, like the sun out of a dense mist, and of Christian brotherhood and charity shedding the bright, warm rays of love upon a world which was divided into distrustful and envious classes and worshipped in the temple of brute Force, is a convincing proof that a new moral power had been awakened in human life. The reliance of the Christians of the second century on apostolic teaching is further proof that from the apostolic age and circle had the new power come. It was not generated by the friction of ecclesiastical parties. It did not spring from the union of Hellenism and Judaism. Justin testifies not only to the belief, but, by fair inference, to the fact that it had sprung from the Christ whom all the Apostles had

Justin the fair representative of his Church.

The inferences to be drawn from his testimony.

unitedly proclaimed. And faith in Christ as God manifest in the flesh, thus revealing at once the divine Father and a new ideal of human life; faith in His teaching as the new and true law of man's present righteousness and future salvation; faith in His death and resurrection, as God's victory for man over sin and death; the consciousness of a new life, full of peace and satisfaction, derived from this faith in the Redeemer; the confident expectation of glory to come on earth and after death, — these were the ideas which, like the light that streamed over chaos at the first creation, were the sign and the beginning of the new creation which by the Word of the Lord was appearing out of the chaos of the ancient world. That it was indeed a divine creation, wrought by the divine Word, is the sum and substance of Justin's testimony to early Christianity.

INDEX.

ABBOT, Ezra, 221, 230.
Abbott, E. A., 153, 214–223, 225, 226, 229–231.
Acts of the Apostles, authenticity of the, 114.
    Justin's acquaintance with the, 238.
    rationalistic theory of the, 112–114.
Advent, Second, 120, 288.
Alexandrianism, influence on Christian thought of, 9, 89, 96, 98, 127, 153, 158, 165.
    not a Judaizing influence, 166.
Angels, worship of, 276.
Anthropology, Justin's, 156–160.
Antoninus: policy toward the Christians, 68, 69.
Apocalypse, quoted by Justin, 117, 237.
Apologetic motives: influence on Justin's statements, 246, 257.
Apologies, Justin's:
    argument of the first of, 33, 35, 73–82.
    contents of, 30–38.
    date of, 28.
    mutual relation of, 27.
Apologists, early Christian, 2, 130.
Apostles: their authority as teachers, 242, 243.
    Justin's description of the, 116.
    mentioned by name, 117.
Aristotle, influence on Justin of, 13, 137, 146.
Athenagoras, 2, 25, 124.
Aubé, Barth., 13, 18, 19, 21, 28, 29, 66, 121, 135, 139, 150, 158, 160.
Aurelius, Marcus: policy toward Christians, 56, 70.

BAPTISM, 164, 259, 283, 285.
Barnabas, Epistle of, 112, 121, 124, 130, 165, 177, 210.
Basilideans, 255.
Basilides, quotation of John by, 177.
Baur, F. C., 48, 88, 106, 113, 173.
Bindemann, 172.
Bithynian persecution, 63.
Bleek on Justin's use of Gospels, 173.

CABALISM, 9.
Canon of the New Testament, formation of the, 5, 87, 170, 171.
    Justin's testimony to the, 178, 237–250.
    other testimony to the, 249.
Ceremonies, simplicity of Christian, 79.
Charges popularly made against Christians, 31, 36, 37, 54, 55, 57.
Charity, early Christian, 260.
Christ, doctrine of the person of, 270–274.
    humanity of, 271.
    divinity of, 149–154, 271–274.
Christ's coming, object of, 161–163.
Christ's life, Justin's account of, 179–182.
Church a Gentile society, 102, 126.
    faith of the early, 270–291.
    government of the, 265–267.
    Justin a fair representative of the, 252.
    parties in the, 105–107.
    in each locality a single, 261.
    organization of the early, 258–267.
    unity of the early, 267–270.
Ciasca, Professor, 236.

INDEX.

Clementine Homilies and Recognitions, 112, 115, 119, 127, 159.
Clementine quotations compared with Justin's, 202–205, 228–230.
Clement of Rome, 68, 125, 177, 262, 268.
Colossians, Epistle to, Justin's acquaintance with the, 240.
Commodus: policy toward Christians, 70.
Corinthians, First Epistle to, Justin's acquaintance with, 239.
  Second Epistle to, Justin's acquaintance with, 241.
Creation, doctrine of, 139.
Credner, K. A., 47, 48, 172, 174, 178, 235, 243.
Crescens, 14.
Critical theories of early Christianity, 3, 86–91, 111–113.

DEACONS, 7, 8, 261, 266.
Dead, state of the, 159, 160, 290.
Defence of Christianity, Justin's, 73–82.
Demonology, 158–160.
Descent of Christ to Hades, 160, 290.
Destruction of world by fire, 290.
De Rossi, 65, 264.
Dialogue with Trypho:
  how far historical, 18, 39.
  date of the, 28.
  contents of the, 38–44.
Diffusion of Christianity in second century, 51.
Dio Chrysostom, 58.
Diognetus, Epistle to, 3, 57, 130, 177.
Dion Cassius, 58, 68.
Dionysius of Corinth, 72, 264, 269.
Dorner, J. A., 48, 121, 122, 151, 273.

EBIONITES, 23, 106, 109, 126.
  Gospel of the, 184, 185.
Eclecticism, philosophic, 132–134.
Eichhorn, J. G., 47, 172.
Emperors, worship of the, 66, 78.
Empire, the Church and the, 57–59.
Engelhardt, Moritz von, 15, 18, 22, 27–29, 48, 49, 91, 139, 147, 150, 174, 176, 202, 208, 273, 277.

Ephesians, Epistle to, Justin's acquaintance with, 241.
Ephraem Syrus, 235, 236.
Epiphanius's account of Justin's death, 12.
Episcopate, the early, 8, 261–267.
Eternal rewards and punishments, 290.
Eucharist, the, 260, 285, 286.
Eusebius's account of Justin, 12, 13, 19, 20, 24, 27, 47.
Exorcism of demons, 159.

FISHER, G. P., 179.

GALATIANS, Epistle to, Justin's acquaintance with, 240.
Gibbon, 66.
Gieseler, 67, 69, 70.
Gildersleeve, B. L., 27, 138.
Gnostics, 9, 130, 255, 256.
God, Justin's conception of, 141–147.
"Gospel": early use of the term, 177.
"Gospels": application of the term to evangelical narratives, 176.
Government, attitude toward Christianity of the Roman, 60–73.

HABITS of the early Christians, 53, 59.
Hadrian: letter to Fundanus, 62, 63, 67.
  letter to Servianus, 69.
  policy toward Christians, 67–69.
Harmony of the Gospels, whether used by Justin, 206–211.
Harnack, A., 15, 19–21, 25, 26, 28, 29, 47.
Harris, Prof. Rendel, 209.
Hatch, Dr. E., 7, 265.
Hebrew economy, Justin's view of the, 97–100.
Hebrews, Epistle to, Justin's acquaintance with, 240.
Hegesippus, 3, 262, 263.
Heresy, a novelty, 254–256.
  of demoniacal origin, 159, 254.
  repudiated, 254–256.

INDEX.

Heretics not recognized by "orthodox," 53, 253.
Hermas, 2, 177, 262, 263.
Hilgenfeld, A., 48, 88, 90, 147, 173.
Hippolytus, 15, 47, 177.
Holtzmann, H., 89, 112.
Hope, Christianity a new, 287-291.
Hostility of Roman world to Christians explained, 59, 60.

"IDOL-MEAT," abstinence from, 111-115.
Ignatius, 8, 71, 89, 177, 191, 249, 262, 269.
Immortality, doctrine of, 140.
Impatience of pagan society with Christians, 56-58.
Incarnation, doctrine of the, 83, 84, 161.
Inspiration of the Scriptures, 93, 94, 242-246.
Interpretation, Justin's method of Scriptural, 95, 96.
Irenæus, 1, 5, 7, 14, 22, 23, 42, 46, 121, 125, 191, 264.

JAMES, Protevangelium of, 204.
  Epistle of, Justin's acquaintance with, 242.
Jewish Christianity: attitude of the Church toward, 104, 105, 107-110.
  a diminishing element in the Church, 126, 292.
Jewish Christians: Justin's opinion of, 104, 256.
  two classes of, 105.
John the Apostle: author of the Apocalypse, 117.
  his doctrine of the Logos, 149.
John's Gospel: used by Justin, 213-225.
  how used by Justin, 225-234.
  not a book of doctrine merely, 231.
  one of the "memoirs," 234.
  early diffusion of, 233.
John, First Epistle of, Justin's acquaintance with, 241.
Jowett, Professor, 141.

Judaism, rejected by post-apostolic Church, 100, 104, 110.
  not appreciated, 101.
Judgment, the last, 289.
Justin Martyr:
  his life, 12-24.
  date of birth, 12.
  studies in philosophy, 13, 132.
  conversion, 16-18.
  activity and influence, 14.
  arrival at Rome, 21.
  death, 15.
  chronology of his life, 19-21.
  his writings, 24-27.
  importance of his testimony, 45, 46.
  honesty of his testimony, 50, 257, 258.
  ancient and moderate estimates of, 46-49.
  his defence of Christianity, 73-82.
  his theology, 141-164.

KAYE, Bishop, 93, 172.
Kiss, the, 259.

LACTANTIUS, 42.
Legalism in Justin, 122-124.
  in post-apostolic Church, 113, 122-126.
  not necessarily due to Judaism, 125, 167.
Life, Christianity a new, 282-287.
Lightfoot, J. B., 51, 58, 61-63, 65, 66, 68-72, 187, 235, 263, 266.
Literature, Christian, of the second century, 1-3.
Logos, Christianity explained by the incarnation of the, 83, 84.
  Justin's and John's doctrines of the, 146, 149, 153, 216.
  Justin's doctrine of the, 94, 148-156.
  Justin's use of New Testament influenced by his doctrine of the, 247.
  the Seminal, 136, 155, 156, 275.
Lucian, 56, 71.
Luke's Gospel, Justin's use of, 118, 181, 200.

"Man of Sin," 289.
Mansel, Dean, 273.
Marcion, 21, 23, 33, 107, 127, 254, 255, 272.
Mark's Gospel, Justin's use of, 178, 201.
Marsh, Bishop, 172.
Martyrology of Justin, 15, 20.
Matthew's Gospel, Justin's use of, 181, 200.
Melito, 2, 70.
"Memoirs of the Apostles":
  description of the, 175, 178, 179.
  public ecclesiastical documents, 179, 244.
  sources of evangelical knowledge, 179, 243, 244.
  quotations by Justin from the, 197–201, 244.
  their relation to our Gospels, 171–174, 178, 191.
Menander, 33.
Ministry, origin of the Christian, 7, 261, 264–266.
Mommsen, Th., 65.
Morality, argument from Christian, 78–82.
  Christianity a new, 282, 283.

Neander, 48, 69, 70, 90, 278.
New Testament, Justin's use of the, 170–250.

Old Testament: a Christian book, 96.
  corruptions by Jews alleged, 42.
  highly esteemed, 92–94.
  quotations from the, 194–196.
  said to have been known to pagans, 94.
Oral tradition, 190, 248.
  supplanted by the New Testament, 244, 250.
Orthodoxy, early, 11, 253–257.
Otto's edition of Justin, 15, 17, 20, 26, 30, 39, 42, 44, 47, 48, 51, 119, 137, 184, 273, 278.
Overbeck, Fr., 91, 238.

Paganism, Christianity realized aspirations of, 168, 287.
  explains the modifications of Christianity in post-apostolic age, 166–168, 292–294.
  demoniacal origin of, 159.
  vices of, 81.
Papias, 121, 176, 177.
Paul, Justin and, 100, 101, 103, 104, 108, 110, 112, 116–120, 123.
Pauline Epistles, Justin's use of, 118, 162, 190, 238–240.
Paulus, H. E. G., 172, 174.
Persecution, no formal, 61, 68.
  frequent outrages, 62, 72.
  less than at later period, 71, 72.
Peter, First Epistle of, Justin's acquaintance with, 242.
Pfleiderer, Otto, 89.
Philippians, Epistle to, Justin's acquaintance with, 240.
Philo, 133, 150, 153, 158, 216.
Philosophy and Christianity, 9, 10, 128, 130, 131.
Philosophy a preparation for Christianity, 135, 287.
  Christianity presupposed by Justin's, 166.
  Christianity represented as, 74–77.
  relation of the New Testament to, 9, 128, 129.
Platonism, Justin's relation to, 13, 18, 35, 47, 135, 139–141, 145, 146.
Pliny, the younger, 58, 63–67.
Plutarch, 58, 133.
Polycarp, 72, 262, 269.
Prayer, public, 259.
Presbyters, 7, 8, 262–267.
Prophecy, argument for Christianity from, 33, 75.
Prophets, Christian, 265.
Prophets, Hebrew, inspiration of the, 94, 154, 155.
Pythagoreans, Justin's relation to, 137.

Quotation from John's Gospel, 227–231.
  Justin's habit of, 192, 196.

INDEX. 301

Quotations from classics in Justin, 193.
   from Old Testament, 194-196.
   from "Memoirs," 197-201, 244.

RATIONALISM, Justin's, 162, 284.
Redemption, doctrine of, 161, 279-282.
Regeneration, 283-285.
Resurrection, the, 120, 288, 289, 291.
Reuss on the Canon, 5, 170, 201.
Ritschl's theory of post-apostolic Christianity, 48, 90, 91.
Roman Church at middle of second century, 11, 23.
   title of president of the, 261-264.
Romans, Epistle to, Justin's acquaintance with, 238.
Rusticus, Junius, 15, 20.

SACERDOTALISM, not in early church, 264.
Sacraments, the, 79, 164, 259, 260, 283-286.
Sanday, W., 173, 174, 183, 184, 188, 200, 202, 265.
Saturnilians, 255.
Schürer, 26.
Schwegler, 48, 173.
Second century: importance of its study, 1-11.
Semisch, 48, 150, 172.
Semler, J. S., 47.
Septuagint, use of the, 92, 93, 194, 196.
Simon Magus, 33, 254.
Societies, the Christian, 52, 53, 78.
   independent, 52, 269.
   illegal, 61, 65.
   unity of the, 269.
Societies, laws against unauthorized, 65.
Soteriology, Justin's, 163-165.
Spirit, doctrine of the Holy, 275-279.
Stählin, Ad., 48, 147.
Stoicism, 13, 133.
   Justin's relation to, 136, 138, 139.
Suetonius, 57, 58.

Sunday, observance of, 260.
Synoptic Gospels used by Justin, 175-205.
   furnished the staple of evangelical narrative in early Church, 233.

TACITUS, 57, 68.
Tatian, 2, 15, 46, 77, 176, 234.
Tatian's Diatessaron, 210, 234-237.
Taylor, Dr. Chas., 209.
"Teaching of the Apostles," 2, 121, 177, 209, 210, 265.
Tertullian, 14, 22, 43, 46, 55, 77, 121, 125, 246.
Textual corruption of MSS., 189.
   proves antiquity of Gospels, 212, 213.
Textual differences between Justin's quotations from "Memoirs" and our Gospels, 192-201.
Theological aim of eclectic philosophy, 134.
"The Twelve," 117, 119.
Thessalonians, Second Epistle to, Justin's acquaintance with, 239.
Thoma, Albrecht, 118, 162, 214, 215, 222, 224, 225, 229.
Timothy, First Epistle to, Justin's acquaintance with, 241.
Titus, Epistle to, Justin's acquaintance with, 241.
Trajan, correspondence of Pliny and, 63-66.
   policy toward the Christians, 66-69.
Trinity, doctrine of the, 274-279.
Tübingen School, theory of the, 48, 86-88, 108, 173, 291, 292.
   modifications of the, 88-90, 111.

ÜBERWEG, 135, 140, 156.
Uncanonical Gospels, Justin's alleged use of, 184, 185, 189, 190, 204.
Uncanonical words of Christ, 187, 188, 190.
Unity of the early Church, 10, 52, 267-270.
Urbicus, Q. Lollius, 28, 61, 62.

VALENTINIANS, 255.
Variations in Gospel texts in early writers, 204.
Völter, Dan., 26.

WARFIELD, B. B., 2, 177.
Weiss, B., 89, 153, 232, 233.
Weizsäcker, 21, 38, 48, 91, 137, 146, 147, 150, 153, 286.

Westcott and Hort: Notes on Select Readings, 186, 212, 230.
Westcott, B. F., 170, 174, 179, 183, 199, 207, 233.
Wieseler, 70.
Worship of the Christians, public, 244, 247, 260.

ZAHN, 210, 236.
Zeller, E., 75, 96, 135, 139, 156.

Printed by BoD™in Norderstedt, Germany